# MULTICULTURAL EDUCATI(

## James A. Banks, *Series Editor*

*(continued)*

# Reaching and Teaching Students in Poverty

## Strategies for Erasing the Opportunity Gap

## Paul C. Gorski

TEACHERS COLLEGE PRESS

**TEACHERS COLLEGE** | COLUMBIA UNIVERSITY

NEW YORK AND LONDON

Published by Teachers College Press, 1234 Amsterdam Avenue, New York, NY 10027

*Library of Congress Cataloging-in-Publication Data*

Gorski, Paul C.
  Reaching and teaching students in poverty : strategies for erasing the opportunity gap / Paul C. Gorski.
    pages cm. — (Multicultural education series)
  Includes bibliographical references and index.
  ISBN 978-0-8077-5457-3 (pbk. : alk. paper)
  ISBN 978-0-8077-5458-0 (hardcover : alk. paper)
    1. Children with social disabilities—Education—United States. 2. Poor chil-
dren—Education—United States. 3. Educational equalization—United States. 4.
Poverty—United States. I. Title.
  LC4091.G595  2013
  371.826'94—dc23                                                    2013020733

ISBN 978-0-8077-5457-3 (paper)
ISBN 978-0-8077-5458-0 (hardcover)


Printed on acid-free paper
Manufactured in the United States of America

20  19  18  17  16  15              8  7  6  5

## Dedication

For Grandma Wilma

# Contents

# Series Foreword

This engaging, compassionate, and informative book has several salient characteristics that make it a unique, original, and significant contribution to the scholarly literature that focuses on educating students who are born and grow up in low-income communities. In the 1960s most books that dealt with educating poor students described their cultural deficits and the ways in which their family and community values and behaviors caused their low academic achievement (Bereiter & Engelman, 1965; Bloom, Davis, & Hess, 1965; Riessman, 1962). A number of books in contemporary times also describe the deficits and problems of the cultures of low-income students (Payne, 2001; Thernstrom & Thernstrom, 2003). Paul Gorski's book is refreshing, empowering, and timely because it emphasizes the resilience of low-income students and families and explains why educators need to identify and examine their attitudes, beliefs, and behaviors toward low-income students in order to change their perceptions of poor students and create equitable classrooms and schools in which these students can learn and flourish.

Gorski describes how difficult it is for teachers and other educators to change their beliefs, attitudes, and behaviors toward low-income students and their families and become "equity literate educators." This is an ongoing and difficult process because of the stereotypes and misconceptions of poor people that are institutionalized and perpetuated in the mainstream media and in the national culture writ large. Gorski describes movingly and compellingly how he internalized and had to "unlearn" many of the popular stereotypes and misconceptions about poor people even though he grew up in a home with a father from an urban working-class family and a mother from a poor Appalachian family. He uses this telling and powerful personal example to underscore how deeply embedded stereotypes, misconceptions, and negative attitudes toward poor people are within American society and how hard they are to overcome. Gorski reports research which indicates that most Americans believe that poor people are poor because of their "own deficiencies" and that the problems they experience result from their own behaviors because "America is a land of opportunity for all."

Paul Gorski believes that schools can make a difference in the lives of students and that teachers can become transformative educators if they examine and change their attitudes and beliefs about poor students and families and replace their deficit conception of them with a "resilient" conception. A resilient conception of poor students and communities reveals and portrays the ways in which they survive harsh conditions and environments, show tremendous compassion toward other people, give generously to charity, and cooperate and share with the people in their communities. Gorski thinks that these characteristics of low-income people can help to humanize us all.

Gorski draws upon several decades of research to deconstruct numerous myths, misconceptions, and popular educational practices that undercut rather than enhance the educational achievement of low-income students. He describes how popular educational "lists" that describe the cultural characteristics of poor students—such as the widely disseminated and popular list authored by Ruby Payne (2001)—are detrimental because they essentialize low-income students and conceal the tremendous cultural differences among low-income population groups. Gorski compellingly describes the differences that exist among population groups that are victimized by poverty and insightfully illustrates how "class is experienced in multiple lens."

There are a number of excellent books that describe the wide social-class gap between the rich and the poor in the United States and the structural and economic factors that cause this growing and alarming gap (Anyon, 1997; Kozol, 1991; Stiglitz, 2012; Weis, 2008). Gorski's book is unique because although he describes the structural factors that perpetuate inequality in U.S. society, he primarily focuses on what teachers and other educators can do in schools now to create more equitable learning environments for low-income students. He derived his recommendations by reviewing research that had been conducted over several decades. Consequently, his book has a strong empirical foundation, which greatly enriches it. He points out, for example, that many schools are implementing strategies that are designed to improve the academic achievement of low-income students but have the opposite effect. Examples include eliminating art, music, and physical education programs, while research indicates that these programs improve student academic achievement, especially among low-income students. Another example is the widespread practice of teaching low-level math and literacy skills in schools with a high incidence of poverty, while research indicates that students in high poverty schools learn best when they are taught high-level conceptual and reasoning skills.

This book will encourage teachers and other educational practitioners to rethink their attitudes, values, and beliefs about poor students and families and to critically examine many of the practices designed to increase the academic achievement of low-income students that have the opposite effect. Reconceputalizing and rethinking the ways in which low-income students are educated and implementing thoughtful ways to create classrooms and schools in which they will experience educational equity will greatly benefit the increasing population of students from diverse groups who are now enrolling in the nation's school. Students of color and immigrant students are disproportionately poor and most of them attend schools in low-income and racially segregated communities.

American classrooms are experiencing the largest influx of immigrant students since the beginning of the 20th century. Almost 14 million new immigrants—documented and undocumented—settled in the United States from 2000 to 2010. Less than 10% came from nations in Europe. Most came from Mexico, nations in Asia, and nations in Latin America, the Caribbean, and Central America (Comarota, 2011). A large but undetermined number of undocumented immigrants enter the United States each year. The U.S. Department of Homeland Security (2010) estimated that in January 2010 10.8 million undocumented immigrants were living in the United States, which was a decrease from the estimated 11.8 million that resided in the United States in January 2007. In 2007, approximately 3.2 million children and young adults were among the 11.8 million undocumented immigrants in the United States, most of whom grew up in the this country (Perez, 2011). The influence of an increasingly ethnically diverse population on U.S. schools, colleges, and universities is and will continue to be enormous.

Schools in the United States are more diverse today than they have been since the early 1900s when a multitude of immigrants entered the United States from Southern, Central, and Eastern Europe. In the 20-year period between 1989 and 2009, the percentage of students of color in U.S. public schools increased from 32% to 45% (Aud, Hussar, Kena, Blanco, Frohlich, Kemp, & Tahan, 2011). If current trends continue, students of color will equal or exceed the percentage of White students in U.S. public schools within one or two decades. In 2010–2011, students of color exceeded the number of White students in the District of Columbia and in 13 states (listed in descending order of the percentage of ethnic minority students therein): Hawaii, California, New Mexico, Texas, Nevada, Arizona, Florida, Maryland, Mississippi, Georgia, Louisiana, Delaware, and New York (Aud, Hussar, Johnson, Kena, Roth, Manning, Wang, & Zhang, 2012). In 2009, children of undocumented immigrants made up 6.8% of students in Kindergarten through the 12th grade (Perez, 2011).

Language and religious diversity is also increasing in the United States' student population. The American Community Survey indicates that approximately 19.8% of the school-age population spoke a language at home other than English in 2010 (U.S. Census Bureau, 2010). The Progressive Policy Institute (2008) estimated that 50 million Americans (out of 300 million) spoke a language at home other than English in 2008. Harvard professor Diana L. Eck (2001) calls the United States the "most religiously diverse nation on earth" (p. 4). Islam is now the fastest-growing religion in the United States, as well as in several European nations such as France, the United Kingdom, and The Netherlands (Banks, 2009; Cesari, 2004). Most teachers now in the classroom and in teacher education programs are likely to have students from diverse ethnic, racial, linguistic, and religious groups in their classrooms during their careers. This is true for both inner city and suburban teachers in the United States, as well as in many other Western nations such as Canada, Australia, and the United Kingdom (Banks, 2009).

The major purpose of the Multicultural Education Series (MES) is to provide preservice educators, practicing educators, graduate students, scholars, and policymakers with an interrelated and comprehensive set of books that summarizes and analyzes important research, theory, and practice related to the education of ethnic, racial, cultural, and linguistic groups in the United States and the education of mainstream students about diversity. The dimensions of multicultural education, developed by Banks (2004) and described in the Handbook of Research on Multicultural Education and in the Encyclopedia of Diversity in Education (Banks, 2012), provide the conceptual framework for the development of the publications in the Series. They are content integration, the knowledge construction process, prejudice reduction, an equity pedagogy, and an empowering institutional culture and social structure.

The books in the MES provide research, theoretical, and practical knowledge about the behaviors and learning characteristics of students of color, language minority students, and low-income students. They also provide knowledge about ways to improve academic achievement and race relations in educational settings. Multicultural education is consequently as important for middle-class White suburban students as it is for students of color who live in the inner city. Multicultural education fosters the public good and the overarching goals of the commonwealth.

This creative, caring, and incisive book can help teachers and other school practitioners to rethink their attitudes, beliefs, and behaviors toward poor students and families as well as to deconstruct popular and detrimental stereotypes and misconceptions about them. It provides educators with the conceptual arguments and empirical information needed to reject some of the harmful educational recommendations that are being made for teaching low-income students and to identify effective ones that are grounded in research. This book is a powerful, informed, and elegant treatise for the right of all children, including our nation's most neglected and marginalized group of students, to be educated, respected, valued, and affirmed.

—James A. Banks

## REFERENCES

Anyon, J. (1997). *Ghetto schooling: A political economy of urban educational reform.* New York: Teachers College Press.

Aud, S., Hussar, W., Johnson, F., Kena, G., Roth, E., Manning, E., Wang, X., & Zhang, J. (2012). The condition of education 2012 (NCES 2012-045). Washington, DC: U.S. Department of Education, National Center for Education Statistics. Available at http://nces.ed.gov/pubsearch

Aud, S., Hussar, W., Kena, G., Bianco, K., Frohlich, L., Kemp, J., & Tahan, K. (2011). The condition of education 2011 (NCES 2011-033). U.S. Department of Education, National Center for Education Statistics. Washington, DC: U.S. Department of Education, National Center for Education Statistics. Available at http://nces.ed.gov/programs/coe/pdf/coe_1er.pdf

Banks, J. A. (2004). Multicultural education: Historical development, dimensions, and practice. In J. A. Banks & C. A. M. Banks (Eds.), *Handbook of research on multicultural education* (2nd ed., pp. 3–29). San Francisco: Jossey-Bass.

Banks, J. A. (Ed.). (2009). *The Routledge international companion to multicultural education.* New York: Routledge.

Banks, J. A. (2012). Multicultural education: Dimensions of. In J. A. Banks (Ed). *Encyclopedia of diversity in education* (vol. 3, pp. 1538–1547). Thousand Oaks, CA: Sage Publications.

Bereiter, C. & Engelmann, S. (1966). *Teaching disadvantaged children in the preschool.* Englewood Cliffs, NJ: Prentice-Hall.

Bloom, B. S., Davis, A., & Hess, R. (1965). *Contemporary education for cultural deprivation.* New York: Holt.

Camarota, S. A. (2011, October). A record-setting decade of immigration: 2000 to 2010. Washington, DC: Center for Immigration Studies. Retrieved from http://cis.org/2000-2010-record-setting-decade-of-immigration

Cesari, J. (2004). *When Islam and democracy meet: Muslims in Europe and the United States.* New York: Palgrave Macmillan.

Cremin, L. A. (1965). The genius of American education. New York: Vintage Books.

Eck, D. L. (2001). *A new religious America: How a "Christian country" has become the world's most religiously diverse nation.* New York: HarperSanFrancisco.

Kozol, J. (1991). *Savage inequalities: Children in America's schools.* New York: Crown Publishers.

Lightfoot, S. L. (1983). *The good high school: Portraits of character and culture.* New York: Basic Books.

Payne, R. K. (2001). *A framework for understanding poverty.* Highlands, TX: aha! Process.

Perez, W. (2011). *Americans by heart: Undocumented Latino students and the promise of higher education.* New York: Teachers College Press.

Progressive Policy Institute. (2008). 50 million Americans speak languages other than English at home. Available at http://www.ppionline.org/ppi_ci.cfm?knlgA realD=108&subsecID=900003&contentID=254619

Riessman, F. (1962). *The culturally deprived child.* New York: Harper & Row.

Roberts, S. (2008, August 14). A generation away, minorities may become the majority in U. S. *New York Times*, vol. CLVII [175] (no. 54,402), pp. A1 & A18.

Stiglitz, J. E. (2012). *The price of inequality: How today's divided society endangers our future.* New York: W.W. Norton.

Thernstrom, A. & Thernstrom, S. (2003). *No excuses: Closing the racial gap in learning.* New York: Simon & Schuster.

U.S. Census Bureau. (2008, August 14). Statistical abstract of the United States. Available at http://www.census.gov/prod/2006pubs/07statab/pop.pdf

U.S. Census Bureau. (2010). 2010 American community survey. Available at http://factfinder2.census.gov/faces/tableservices/jsf/pages/productview. xhtml?pid=ACS_10_1YR_S1603&prodType=table

U.S. Department of Homeland Security. (2010, February). Estimates of the unauthorized immigrant population residing in the United States: January 2010. Available at http://www.dhs.gov/files/statistics/immigration.shtm

Weis, L. (Ed.). (2008). *The way class works: Readings on school, family, and the economy.* New York: Routledge.

# CHAPTER 1

# Introduction

*Education is the great equalizer.* That's what I heard growing up, the son of a mother from poor Appalachian stock and a father from middle class Detroit. *If you work hard, do well in school, and follow the rules, you can be anything you want to be.* It's a fantastic idea. How remarkable it would be if only it were true.

I've been working with and around educators for the better part of 20 years now, and this I know for certain: A vast majority of us *want* it to be true. We desire an education system that works for every student—not only one that gives everybody a fair shake, but also one that helps make up for the challenges faced by some of our most vulnerable students. Many of us celebrate the Horatio Alger education stories: the low-income young woman who becomes valedictorian, the homeless student who wins a scholarship to college, the janitor who works his way through Harvard. We want to believe that schools, of all places, give all people an equal shot, even when the odds are stacked against them.

Unfortunately, schools as they are constituted today are not the equalizers they are cracked up to be. Not for most students, at least (Neuman, 2009). This, too, I know for certain: Students from poor families continue to be subject, on average, to what Jonathan Kozol (1992) has called the *savage inequalities* of schooling. The examples of these inequalities are numerous. Poor students are assigned disproportionately to the most inadequately funded schools (Strange, 2011) with the largest class sizes (Barton, 2004) and lowest paid teachers (Palardy, 2008). They are more likely than their wealthier peers to be bullied (von Rueden, Gosch, Rajmil, Bisegger, & Ravens-Sieberer, 2006) and to attend school in poorly maintained buildings (National Commission on Teaching & America's Future [NCTAF], 2004). They are denied access to the sorts of school resources and opportunities other children take for granted, such as dedicated school nurses (Berliner, 2009), well-stocked school libraries (Constantino, 2005), and engaging pedagogies (Tivnan & Hemphill, 2005). In fact, by these and almost every other possible measure, students from poor families, the ones most desperate to find truth in the "great equalizer" promise, appear to pay a great price for their poverty, even at school. Of course, these conditions are not the fault of teachers, who often are blamed unjustly for their effects. In fact, teachers who teach at high-poverty schools, as well as an increasing number of their colleagues at *all* public schools, too often are themselves denied access to adequate resources.

Complicating matters, students in poverty, in Sue Books's (2004) words, "bear the brunt of almost every imaginable social ill" (p. 34), many of which have direct or indirect effects on their abilities to do well in school. Starting at birth, poor youth have less access than their wealthier peers to quality preschool (Freeman, 2010), preventive medical attention (Pampel, Krueger, & Denney, 2010), healthy food (Cutler & Lleras-Muney, 2010), and living spaces that are safe from environmental hazards (Evans, 2004). As I was gathering materials for this book, what stood out most to me about these inequalities was that none of them, *not a single one*, has anything to do with students' intellectual capabilities or their desires to learn. These conditions do not reflect or result from low-income families' "cultures" or attitudes about education. If anything, they reflect just the opposite: the level of society's commitment—*our* commitment—to fulfill the promise of equal educational opportunity.

If you are a teacher or school administrator you might be thinking, "That's awfully sad, but it's a little outside my purview. It is not my job to ensure that every student has healthcare and high-quality preschool."

Fair enough. In fact, in today's world of hyperaccountability in education, where high-stakes testing is used to assess not only student learning, but also teacher and administrator performance, teachers often are held accountable for not doing what is more or less impossible to do: making up for all of the inequalities poor youth begin to experience at birth, or even prior to birth if we consider who has access to prenatal care. As schools decrease children's access to nurses, to art and music education, to recess and physical education, and to all manner of other resources and opportunities that improve school performance (particularly for low-income youth, who are most likely not to have access to them outside of school), they also limit teachers' abilities to do their jobs in the most effective and rewarding ways.

This, I believe, is a bit of a setup and a dangerous shift of attention. The testing regimens and test score obsession have shifted our attention away from the savage inequalities of schooling as well as bigger societal disparities that affect student learning. And they have shifted that attention onto teachers and their unions, administrators, and other educators. Imagine, for instance, how patterns of family involvement might change if every parent or guardian had access to a job that paid a living wage, or how patterns of student attendance and engagement might change if every student had access to preventive healthcare.

I initially intended to write a book about that very problem: about how we ultimately cannot eliminate educational outcome disparities, such as graduation rates, without addressing these larger societal and socioeconomic disparities. *However*—and this is a big fat "however"—all of us, whether we are teachers, school counselors, school social workers, administrators, or anybody who plays any role at all in the educational lives of students, do have a substantial amount of power to mitigate these inequalities. We have the power and, of course, the responsibility to ensure that we are not reproducing inequitable conditions in our own classrooms and schools.

In the end, I decided to write a book about *that* responsibility, about how best to prepare ourselves, as people working in schools and school systems, to create and sustain equitable learning environments for poor and working class students. But I decided to do so by making a connection that I find sorely lacking in most conversations about poverty and schooling today: I simply cannot understand the experiences of economically disadvantaged students and their families, or how they relate to school, or how best to engage them, if I do not consider what it means to be poor in contemporary society and its schools. I made this decision for two reasons. First, many of the best minds in education recently have written books and essays that detail with impressive precision the relationships between larger economic inequalities and educational disparities. I find John Marsh's (2011) book, *Class Dismissed*, and David Berliner's (2006) essay, "Our Impoverished View of Education Reform," particularly helpful in this regard. The limitation of these exposés, as poignant as they are, is that they never quite manage to describe how on-the-ground educators can help create the change for which the authors advocate. Yes, of course, all youth ought to have access to healthcare. Yes, of course, we should confront economic inequality. I have spent much of my own scholarly and activist energies on these issues. But what shall teachers and principals and counselors and others who walk into classrooms and schools full of students every day do in the meantime?

The other reason I chose to write a book about teaching for class equity in schools and school systems is that among the many recent books that do introduce practical blueprints for teachers and school leaders (such as Jensen, 2009; Payne, 2005; Templeton, 2011), few even acknowledge the larger inequalities described by John Marsh, David Berliner, and others. Absent this acknowledgment, so much of the literature on which educators have leaned in order to develop deeper understandings of poverty have tended, even if implicitly, to interpret educational outcome disparities almost exclusively as reflections of what they deem to be the deficient or diminished cultures, values, intellectual capabilities, and attitudes of poor families. If we want to fix educational outcome disparities, this argument goes, we must begin by fixing poor students and families rather than by fixing the inequities experienced by poor students and families. The result, unfortunately, tends to be lists of ubersimplistic practical solutions to super complex and misunderstood problems—solutions based more on stereotypes than reality.

So I decided to write a book from a practitioner point of view, but one that takes an "open systems" or "relational" approach. This approach nudges us to see what happens in school at least partially in the context of conditions that exist outside school walls (Flessa, 2007). After all, these external conditions—experience with class bias, for example, or experience with economic inequality—influence teachers' and students' perceptions of school, of teaching and learning, and of one another (Knapp, 1995; Weiner, 2003).

Consider the example of family involvement, often assumed by educators and policy wonks alike to be the panacea for school success among poor and working class students (Hill & Craft, 2003). It is all too common for those of us who have not experienced sustained poverty to assume that, if parents or guardians do not participate in on-site opportunities for school involvement, they simply do not care about their children's education. How often have you heard those sentiments in a faculty meeting or teachers' lounge? How often have you thought them yourself? "*Those* parents never show up for anything. No wonder kids are failing when their parents don't care about their education." Unfortunately, many educators seem to have bought into this stereotype—this false stereotype, as it turns out (Lee & Bowen, 2006). (More on this in a moment.) Given a limited understanding, though, it can be easy to interpret lower rates of on-site school involvement among poor and working class parents as indicative of a "culture of poverty" that devalues education. We might respond, as many schools do, by offering parenting workshops or by circulating memos about the importance of family involvement.

How might our perspective change, though, if we step back for a moment and attempt to understand on-site family involvement patterns in relation to the social conditions described by Marsh (2011) and Berliner (2006)? What if we loosen our grip on the deficit lens so that a fuller picture can come into focus, even if there are parts of that picture we don't feel empowered to change? What if we take into account the fact that low-income parents and guardians are more likely than their wealthier peers to work multiple jobs and to work evening jobs? They are less likely to have paid leave from work and, as stands to reason, less likely to be able to afford to take unpaid leave. Finding and affording childcare is more difficult for economically disadvantaged parents than for wealthier parents, and they are less likely to have convenient transportation options (Gorski, 2008a; Li, 2010; Newman & Chin, 2003; Votruba-Drzal, 2003). And, of course, parents in low-income families are more likely than wealthier parents to have experienced school as unwelcoming or even hostile when they were students (Lee & Bowen, 2006).

Then there is this: Several studies from the past 5 years have shown that parents of economically disadvantaged families are as involved, or even *more* involved, in their children's educational lives when compared with their wealthier peers when we take into account not just on-site involvement, but also at-home involvement (Cooper, Crosnoe, Suizzo, & Pituch, 2010; Li, 2010). Similarly, decades of research has shown that, in fact, poor families and communities of all races and ethnicities, whether they are from rural or urban regions, care deeply about their children's education—that they have the exact same attitudes about the value of schooling as their more economically solvent counterparts (Compton-Lilly, 2000; Jennings, 2004; Moll, Amanti, Neff, & Gonzalez, 1992; West-Olantunji, Sanders, Mehta, & Behar-Horenstein, 2010). The issue, these studies suggest, is not that low-income families don't care about education, but that without understanding a fuller picture of inequality and the challenges faced by poor families, it can be easy for teachers to *assume* a lack of interest on the parts of parents and other caretakers. If I consider, for instance, how family involvement patterns might be different if every working adult had access to a living wage job—even if I don't feel that I have the power to make that level of societal change—I might, at the very least, understand what families in poverty are up against rather than relying on stereotypes to make sense out of unfortunate circumstances.

I wrote this book, in part, to nudge educators, including myself, past those assumptions and toward a deeper, more empathetic, and more holistic understanding of the effects of poverty and class bias on the school experiences of poor and working class students. I wrote it to nudge us past the simplifications and stereotypes that I believe hamper our abilities to be the teachers and leaders we want to be for all of our students.

I wrote it, too, because I believe in the transformative power of teachers, perhaps not in the fight to end global poverty (at least not on their own), but in the commitment to walk into classrooms and schools full of students, dedicated, despite all the challenges, to do right by each of them. I believe that we want a more complex conversation about poverty and that we're capable of digging deeper into questions about what we can do to better facilitate educational opportunity for every family. I believe we can, and that we must, begin by dropping the deficit views and stereotypes and ideas about fixing low-income kids and by equipping ourselves with a broader, more detailed view of what it means to be a poor or working class student in today's schools. We begin there and then, with that view, start gathering tools and strategies based on what works. That, in a nutshell, is what this book is about.

In pursuit of these goals I use in this book an approach, co-developed by my super genius colleague, Katy Swalwell (2011), called *Equity Literacy*. I dedicate all of Chapter 2 to describing the Equity Literacy Approach and how it builds upon and differs from other popular frameworks for discussing poverty and schooling, from cultural proficiency to funds of knowledge. The gist, for now, is this: Equity Literacy is comprised of the skills and dispositions that enable us to recognize, respond to, and redress conditions that deny some students access to the educational opportunities enjoyed by their peers (Gorski, in press). Whereas many of the existing approaches ask us to focus on culture—the *culture* of poverty, *cultural* competence, *culturally* relevant pedagogy—Equity Literacy asks us to focus on *equity*, on how to create and sustain equitable learning environments free of even the subtlest biases. This requires different, although in some ways complementary, kinds of knowledge and skills. After all, simply knowing something about a student's culture, or having the skills to interact cross-culturally, is not the same as knowing how to spot subtle class biases in learning materials or school policies.

Parts of the picture I paint are uplifting and full of hope, partially due to the amazing resiliency of low-income communities and partially because of the equally inspirational capacities of teachers to advocate for their students. Other parts are, admittedly, bleak. The odds are stacked, and heavily so, against the poorest students and families, despite all of the skills and gifts and determination they bring to the table. But there is something we can do about it, and we all have a role in that something, whether we are classroom teachers or community activists or building- or district-level administrators or parents or students or just concerned citizens.

## DEFINITIONS AND DISTINCTIONS

Let's start at the beginning, with terminology. Already I've been using words like "poverty" and "low-income" and "working class" and, admittedly, it can be difficult to find two people willing to agree on what any one of these words means. My intention here is not to provide economics-textbook definitions for these terms or to debate the widely variable semantic arguments for this or that definition. Rather, my intention is to describe how I use terminology related to class and poverty, both in this book and more broadly. I acknowledge, of course, that there is no "correct" definition for any of these terms. However, our understandings of poverty and class can be influenced by the ways we've been taught to imagine what they mean.

### Socioeconomic Status

When I ask people what it means to live in poverty, they usually mention the financial component first. "Poverty," they might say, "means not having adequate financial resources." Almost inevitably, though, they turn quickly to other sorts of resources: everything from *life attitudes* to *family strength* to *association with religion*. Certainly students' life circumstances are affected by more than their families' access to money. Support networks, whether through extended family, religious organizations, or community organizations, can be critically important for low-income families, as they can be for *all* families.

I worry, however, that such a broad conception of socioeconomic status clouds an important distinction. In the end, in a capitalistic society, the only commodities that *guarantee* somebody consistent access to basic human necessities like food, clothing, lodging, and healthcare are *financial* commodities. Sure, associating with a mosque or synagogue or church or some other religious organization may provide a person in poverty with a network of people willing to lend a helping hand. It might even help her feel spiritually fulfilled. In other words, it might help a poor person feel a little more comfortable or secure or happy *within a state of poverty*. But without greater access to financial resources, she is still in poverty and, as a result, without guaranteed access to the most basic life resources.

This is why, when I talk about socioeconomic status, I am referring explicitly to students' or families' access to financial resources. I am referring to resources they can exchange for food, clothing, lodging, and healthcare. In my view, and in this book, socioeconomic status refers to an individual's or family's financial condition relative to other individuals and families. More wealth means more choices, more opportunity, more access (Hout, 2008). This, to me, is the essence of socioeconomic status.

I describe below the somewhat imperfect terms I use to describe people and families who occupy various points along the continuum of socioeconomic status. That word, *continuum*, is important here in the sense that there is tremendous diversity, or what Katherine Turpin (2009) describes as "plentiful variation," within each of these groups. I use these terms as approximations and reject the notion, popularized by all the talk in education circles about what turns out (as I'll explain in more detail later) to be a fictitious idea called the "culture of poverty," that I or anyone else can attribute a shared set of values, beliefs, dispositions, or behaviors to any of these groups. In fact, as I learned growing up among my Appalachian grandma's relatively poor people, there is as much diversity of values and dispositions among poor people as there is between poor and wealthy people.

This is why many people, including me, who write about class and poverty struggle with the limitations of class categories. Any system of categorizing humans is, in some ways, arbitrary. Consider, for instance, how conversations about racial categories tend to render multiracial people invisible.

Despite these reservations, I chose in this book to use a five-category model (poverty, working class, middle class, managerial class, owning class) for distinguishing socioeconomic groups. Like every other model, it's imprecise. However, despite their imperfections, these categories, described in detail below, are intended to help us understand relative differences in material realities among people who have more or less access to financial resources and, as a result, to equitable school experiences.

## Poverty

In many countries, governments assign a dollar figure to the financial condition of poverty, commonly called the "poverty line." For example, according to the U.S. government, a family of four earning less than $22,400 per year is in poverty (Kaufmann, 2011). What most people don't realize is that in the U.S. this poverty line is calculated primarily through a process developed in 1965 to estimate the annual cost of a humble but adequate household diet (Eberstadt, 2006). In many ways that figure, $22,400, like any estimate of a complex condition, is as arbitrary as class categories. It's an imperfect estimate that probably results in an underestimation of the number or percentage of families who are in poverty (Eberstadt, 2006), a reality I discuss in greater detail in Chapter 3. This is why I don't limit my understanding or use of the term *poverty* to a specific dollar figure.

Instead, extending my understanding of socioeconomic status, I use the term *poverty* to describe a financial condition in which an individual or family cannot afford the basic human necessities described earlier, including food, clothing, housing, healthcare, childcare, and education (Children's Defense Fund [CDF], 2008). I use the term *poor* to describe people who live in poverty. I use *low-income* for the same purpose, although it, like much of the language related to socioeconomic status, is imprecise. Somebody can be wealthy, after all, and earn a low income. However, my stylistic sensibility requires me to vary my language, and *low-income* is a common enough term that it appears to be my best alternative. On occasion I also use *economically disadvantaged* to describe people and families without adequate financial resources to meet their basic needs.

The term *generational poverty* is often used to distinguish long-term, sustained poverty that spans generations from situational poverty, which is more temporary. This is an important distinction, and can help clarify some of the contextual messiness of socioeconomic status. For example, individuals who have spent most of their lives in the working or middle class, but who, after losing a job or struggling to manage the financial hardships of a health crisis, find themselves unable to pay for basic necessities, are much more likely to have attained a greater level of education than their counterparts in generational poverty, making their prospects for finding new living wage work somewhat brighter. Similarly, they are much more likely than people in generational poverty to have friends or family members who are able to provide substantial enough financial support that their experience of poverty can be fairly short. On the other hand, whether poverty is temporary or generational, it poses many of the same challenges to people experiencing it; in either case it constrains access to healthcare, housing, schooling opportunities and options, and myriad other services. So, generally speaking, I use *poverty* to cover both situational and generational poverty, and specify *generational poverty* when I am referring to it in particular.

## Working Class

It can be easy, with all the talk about *students in poverty*, to forget that working class families also are denied many of the options and opportunities that wealthier families enjoy. This is why I often refer to poor *and* working class students or families, both of which face tremendous barriers in and out of school.

Working class people generally are able to afford their most basic necessities, but only at a subsistence level. They make just enough money to get by and, as a result, are unable to save money or accumulate wealth. This leaves working class people and families in a precarious position, balancing on the brink of poverty. If an adult in a working class family is out of work for just a couple of weeks or experiences unforeseen car trouble, or if a child in a working class family is faced with an unexpected medical condition, the family can find itself suddenly in debt, trying to decide whether to see a doctor or pay the electric bill.

Many people who think of themselves as middle class actually are working class. Imagine, for a moment, what would happen if you lost your job. If that would put you in more or less immediate danger of falling behind on rent, being unable to pay your power bill, or struggling to afford groceries, you probably are in the working class.

## Middle Class

If, on the other hand, your family has adequate financial resources to survive for a few months with no income without accruing debt, you probably are in the middle class. As a middle class person or family you have accumulated enough wealth, like savings or, perhaps, annuity in a home, that you can meet your basic human needs with enough resources left over to create and sustain a safety net. This allows you to cover unexpected expenses or enjoy some of the luxuries to which working class and poor people do not have access. However, those unexpected expenses could create a temporary hardship or force you to forego luxuries; if a working adult from a middle class family were out of work for more than a couple of months, the family probably would be on its way to at least temporary poverty.

Interestingly, in the United States, most people want to believe they are middle class even if they are better described as wealthy, working class, or even poor. As Dante Chinni (2005) explained in a *Christian Science Monitor* article,

> Who *is* the middle class? . . . Well *you* are, of course. And me, while we're at it. . . . Everyone wants to believe they are middle class. For people at the bottom and the top of the wage scale the phrase connotes a certain Regular Joe cachet. But the eagerness to be part of that group has led the definition to be stretched like a bungee cord . . . (pp. 4–5)

He later speaks to the arbitrariness of trying to define socioeconomic status by income ranges. Ridiculing the Drum Major Institute, which defines the middle class as people who make between $25,000 and $100,000, Chinni quips, "Ah yes, *there's* a group of people bound to run into each other while house-hunting" (p. 9).

## Managerial (or "Upper Middle") Class

If you are in what I call the managerial class, you likely have an advanced academic degree and a six-figure family income. Many people in the managerial class have highly esteemed occupations. They are doctors, lawyers, diplomats, and engineers. But the managerial class gets its name from its members who manage or run the businesses owned by the uber-wealthy owning class (which we will meet momentarily). According to Paul Kivel (2004), other members of the managerial class may include small- to midsize business owners, directors of big nonprofit corporations, and upper-level administrators in national, state, or local offices.

A considerable majority of, but not all, families in the managerial class are White. They tend to live in exclusively or almost exclusively White neighborhoods where their children attend predominantly White schools—often, but not always, private schools (Kivel, 2004). Their access to great amounts of financial resources means that they have a lot more educational options than middle class and poorer families. They can afford to pick up and move to neighborhoods that have strong public school systems if they are unhappy with their neighborhood public schools, for example, or pay for expensive tutors and preparatory classes for college entrance exams.

## Owning Class

I use the term *owning class* to describe people who make adequate income off of investments alone to support a wealthy lifestyle without actually being employed. Of course, this doesn't mean that people in owning class families don't have jobs; often they do, or at least did at some point, but they have so much wealth that they can live lavishly on the interest and dividends accrued by their assets.

Owning class people own the means of mass production, including access to natural resources such as oil, and control the most powerful corporations in the world. Just as importantly, they own the means of *perception*, including the mass media, and comprise a majority of high-ranking political leaders, too (Dye, 2002). As you might guess, they include the CEOs of the wealthiest corporations, presidents of financial institutions such as banks, and high-ranking politicians and bureaucrats (Rosenthal, 2007). What may come as a surprise, though, is that they also include the highest-ranking military officers (Dye, 2002).

Despite what we might assume based on the popularity of rags-to-riches stories, just about everybody in the owning class, including those high-ranking politicians, bureaucrats, and military officers, was born into it, inheriting immense amounts of wealth. When individuals are born into wealth, that wealth is often referred to as "old money." "New money" refers to the wealth of a smaller percentage of people in the owning class: individuals who were born outside of the owning class, but accumulated enough wealth to become part of it. In either case, owning class people often have multiple homes in exclusive neighborhoods and send their children to elite private schools and universities. Owning class households are overwhelmingly, although not exclusively, White (Kivel, 2004).

## Income and Wealth

I refer throughout this book to both *income* and *wealth*, terms that are popularly used interchangeably despite the fact that they are not the same. *Income* refers to the "annual inflow of wages, interest, profits, and other sources of earning" (Taylor et al., 2011b, p. 4), so that *family income* is the annual total of these earned by all members of a single household. *Wealth*, on the other hand, refers to the total value of an individual's or family's assets—bank accounts, property, stocks, automobiles, and so on—after accounting for debt. So when you hear somebody say *Oprah Winfrey is worth two billion dollars*, it does not mean that Ms. Winfrey makes $2 billion dollars a year or that she has $2 billion dollars in a savings account at her local credit union. It means that, after accounting for her debt, all of her assets combined are worth $2 billion dollars.

## THE REMAINDER OF THE BOOK

In Chapter 2, "Imagining Equitable Classrooms and Schools for Low-Income Youth: An Equity Literacy Approach," I describe in greater detail the dimensions and key principles of what my colleague Katy Swalwell (2011) and I have called the Equity Literacy framework for creating equitable learning environments for youth and families in poverty. I draw on this model throughout the rest of the book.

Chapter 3, titled "The Inequality Mess We're In: A Class and Poverty Primer," summarizes basic information about class and poverty and how they operate in the United States. I discuss, for instance, overall and child poverty rates in the United States and how they've changed over the last few decades. I also share basic data on how wealth is distributed in the United States overall and across identities like race and gender.

In Chapter 4, "The Trouble with the 'Culture of Poverty' and Other Stereotypes about People in Poverty," I explain why, despite its popularity, the "culture of poverty" approach to understanding low-income people simply does not work. I also review common myths about students and families in poverty that are based more on stereotype than reality, like the myth that poor people don't value education.

Next, in Chapter 5, I explore the many forms of inequity and bias with which low-income families contend—inequities that happen outside of school, but that play a considerable role in educational outcomes. These include concerns like access to healthcare, access to high-quality childcare, and access to opportunities for recreation and exercise. I titled this chapter "Class Inequities Beyond School Walls and Why They Matter at School."

Chapter 6, "The Achievement—er, *Opportunity*—Gap in School" details the many ways in which students in poverty are denied the sorts of learning opportunities enjoyed by their wealthier peers. Topics include disparities in school funding and pedagogy and experiences with bullying across socioeconomic groups.

Chapter 7, "Been There, Done That, Didn't Work: The Most Popular *Ineffective* Strategies for Teaching Students in Poverty," brings us to practical strategies. That is, it brings us to the most popular practical strategies that remain popular, somewhat illogically, despite the fact that there is no evidence that they work.

We continue an exploration of popular strategies in Chapter 8, "What Works (When Adapted to Your Specific Context, of Course): Instructional

Strategies that Are Effective, Equitable, and Even *Data-Driven*." The strategies discussed in this chapter were identified during a several-year process of reading and synthesizing more than 30 years of research from more than 300 sources. It was a grueling but rewarding several years!

In Chapter 9, "The Mother of All Strategies: Committing to Working *With* Rather than *On* Families in Poverty," I share what that same body of research has to say about the most effective ways to go about building respectful, sustainable relationships with low-income families.

Next, in Chapter 10, "Expanding Our Spheres of Influence: School, District, Regional, and National Change for the Educational Good," I discuss the sorts of things we can do to affect bigger and broader efforts for class equity in schools, outside of our classrooms.

Finally, I wrap things up nice and tightly, but not too tightly, in the Conclusion.

# CHAPTER 2

# Imagining Equitable Classrooms and Schools for Low-Income Youth

## An Equity Literacy Approach

Just as I learned growing up that education is the "great equalizer," I also learned that it is impolite to talk about money. I remember being shushed when I was 10 or 11 for asking my uncle how much money he made teaching at a community college. It was a reasonable question, I thought, for a child who wanted to be a teacher. I was in my thirties before I knew how poor my Grandma Wilma (Figure 2.1), my mom's mom, had been growing up in an Appalachian coal-mining town despite the fact that she always was, for many other reasons, my favorite person in the world. In fact, we never talked about those Appalachian roots even within the family, not, as far as I could tell, because anybody was particularly ashamed about it, but because, well, it just wasn't something we were supposed to do. I became so skittish talking about money and class and poverty that I still feel tinges of discomfort talking about those things today even though I teach and write and speak about them all the time.

I'm not alone. Class and money are taboo topics for many people and communities, often making them difficult to discuss within families or among friends or colleagues. In fact, even in academic circles, where people peel apart every possible topic, class and poverty are taboo and, as a result, discussions about them are exceedingly rare (Kincheloe & Steinberg, 2007). This, I think, is one reason why the conversations we have in the education world about poverty can be so imprecise and simplistic. It's why conversations about poverty among educators often seem to focus, not on poverty (what causes it, how it represses some of our students), but rather on simple, pragmatic strategies that are based more on stereotypes than on evidence-informed practice. (*If only* those people *cared about school . . .* )

Another reason people in general and educators in particular might struggle with conversations about class is that many of us were raised to believe that the United States and its schools represent a *meritocracy*, wherein people achieve what they achieve based solely on their merit, so that all

14

## Figure 2.1. Grandma

achievement is deserved rather than rendered. When we tell students that they can achieve anything they want to achieve if they work hard enough, we're saying, "Hey, this is a meritocracy, so you have just as good a shot as the next person. Everybody has an equal opportunity." This ideal of meritocracy has a long and complex history in the United States that is tied to the Horatio Alger myth (Pascale, 2005) and to notions of rugged individualism and an ethic of self-sacrifice. Plus, the media love a good rags-to-riches story. The trouble is, because the media love rags-to-riches stories, we, the audience, are led to believe that they are more common than they actually are. In the United States they are celebrated as the quintessential American narrative: the low-income child who beats the odds and graduates from college; the working class administrative assistant who starts a small business at home after work hours and makes it big; the janitor at Harvard University who ends up attending the school and graduating with honors. You'd think a majority of people spend their lives sprinting up the economic ladder, always reaching a socioeconomic status well beyond that of their parents. It's a common misperception. As Carol West and Sarah Fenstermaker (2002) explain, "Americans believe that they live in a classless society, that class is a matter of achievement, and that, in theory, anyone can make it to the top" (p. 539).

Of course, if we were living in a society in which financial or other types of success could be predicted by hard work, we'd see a lot more economic upward mobility. We'd see a lot more people, like poor and working class parents and caretakers who are working multiple laborious jobs, blasting their way out of poverty and into the middle class, surpassing the wealth and income levels of previous generations of their families. But if meritocracy and upward mobility are real phenomena, why are poverty rates and wealth and income inequality, trends we'll explore in detail in Chapter 3, *increasing* rather than decreasing? Something's not adding up. And that something is this, according to Teresa Swartz (2008), who studies the relationships between family background and socioeconomic status:

> While social class origin does not determine the next generation's class achievement, the odds are that individuals will end up in the same class as their parents or one adjacent to it. As mobility studies have shown, movement from the lower to the upper class, or vice versa, remains rare. (p. 14)

In other words, rags-to-riches stories, wherein somebody who is born into a poor family becomes wealthy, are far more common on television than they are in real life. It happens, but not nearly as often as we're led to believe (Mazumder, 2005).

The somewhat confounding truth of the matter, given all the rags-to-riches hoopla, is that in the United States upward mobility is becoming less common (Bjorklund & Jantti, 2009). Among Western industrialized countries, the United States has among the lowest instances of upward mobility (Isaacs, Sawhill, & Haskins, 2008). According to the Economic Mobility Project (2012), upward mobility is especially rare among the poorest 20% of Americans. The numbers are staggering. If you were born into a family in the top 10% (or top "decile") of income-earners, you are 23 times more likely to end up with an income in that top decile than somebody born into a family in the bottom decile (Hertz, 2005). So, sure, hard work counts, but not nearly as much as being born into economic privilege.

Why? Because context matters. Because privilege begets privilege. Educators know this. It is, in part, why many (although of course not all) teachers and administrators don't tend to stick around very long in the most underresourced schools and why they choose, instead, to seek work in wealthier schools or districts (Battle & Gruber, 2010; Guin, 2004). Similarly, it is (at least one reason) why merit teacher pay programs are flawed: They fail to take into account the difference between teaching privileged students in well-resourced schools, where parents might pool their resources and pay to hire an additional teacher or two, and teaching low-income students in poorly resourced schools, where the students have just as much potential, but have been cheated through every stage of life out of the opportunities and resources their wealthier peers have enjoyed. In other words, meritocracy assumes a level playing field that, as we learned in Chapter 1 and will explore more fully in Chapters 5 and 6, simply does not exist. Context counts.

The danger of accepting meritocracy as reality is that there is a flip side to believing that people achieve whatever they achieve through hard work, that we all deserve our lots in life, for better or worse. If I fail to keep one eye on that larger context, it can be easy to assume that students who are struggling or disengaged, who receive poor grades or who don't score at grade level on standardized tests, simply don't work hard enough. Or that they're lazy. Or that their parents don't care about their education. It can be easy to assume that some students simply don't deserve a fair shake or that they would be incapable of taking advantage of equal opportunity if it fell in their laps.

The truth is, I believe most of us know, at least in some ways, that the system is rigged and the odds are stacked against the most vulnerable students and families, not because they don't work hard, but because opportunity and access beget opportunity and access. We know at least in some cases which kids' families can afford the exorbitant costs of tutors, music lessons, academic camps, and other forms of "shadow" education, not to mention the costs of computers and high-speed Internet access and bedrooms full of books. We might even know, based on subtle changes in individual students, which families' bouts with poverty are more recent rather than generational. Plus, if you've had parents or grandparents or aunts or uncles who, like mine, worked long, back-breaking, thankless shifts as coal miners or custodians or other sorts of low-pay laborers, you know, like I do, that the suggestion that they are poor because they don't work hard enough is ludicrous. I doubt many of us would agree with that. Working hard is no guarantee, especially not when, on top of your poverty, you're denied equal educational opportunity.

Still, the myth of meritocracy persists. As a result, it can be difficult to free ourselves from the shaky perception that poor people don't do as well in school as their wealthier peers because they just don't work hard enough or because they just aren't capable of doing so. It can be difficult to free ourselves from the dangerous assumption that it's all *their fault*. If we allow ourselves to begin with that perception, we set ourselves up for a hollow conversation in which we more or less blame our most vulnerable students for what, after all, are the symptoms of the inequities they likely have faced since birth. And when our conversations are hollow rather than robust, they inevitably lead to hollow rather than robust strategies for alleviating or eliminating the school and classroom barriers that further impede students' learning.

## INTRODUCING THE *EQUITY LITERACY* APPROACH TO EDUCATIONAL EQUITY

In "Why Students Need 'Equity Literacy,'" an article in *Teaching Tolerance*, my colleague Katy Swalwell (2011) recounted her experience observing middle school students and their teacher visiting an exhibit at the National Museum of Natural History in Washington, DC. In the middle of the exhibit, titled "RACE: Are We So Different?", stood a display that used stacks of money as a sort of metaphorical graph to demonstrate how wealth is distributed by race in the United States. Designers had used data collected by the U.S. Census Bureau between 1997 and 2000, when, to mirror the language used in the display, "White" and "Asian" households, on average, controlled roughly 10 times more wealth than "Black" or "Latino" households. (We'll explore the limitations of these broad racial groupings in Chapter 3.) So while the stacks approximating the relative net worth of Black and Latino households might have reached the students' waist, the stacks approximating the relative net worth of White and Asian families towered over their heads. A placard next to the exhibit described matter-of-factly how the wealth gap is perpetuated by disparities in home ownership and property values and passed down from generation to generation.

A group of African American students had gathered around the display. Then, according to Swalwell (2011, ¶ 4), this happened: "One student read the placard aloud. Then came the indignant exclamations: 'That's not fair!' 'Wait, that represents us?' 'This is crazy!'" The students recognized the inequality, saw themselves reflected in it, and appeared primed for a conversation about it. So, Swalwell continued, "They looked to one of their chaperones for answers. 'This says we have almost nothing compared to everyone else!' Her reply: 'Don't worry—that was the olden days. It's not like that now'" (¶ 5). That's how the conversation ended, prompting Swalwell to argue how important it is that we, as teachers, learn how to talk with students about inequities, including class inequities. We should foster in ourselves and our students, she explained, *Equity Literacy*, a base of knowledge about "the historical trajectories of marginalized and privileged groups" (¶ 15).

Around the same time she was formulating her vision for cultivating equity literacy in students, I was writing, also for *Teaching Tolerance*, a brief introduction to what I also was calling *Equity Literacy* (Gorski, in press). My Equity Literacy grew out of dissatisfaction, for reasons we'll explore momentarily, with many of the popular frameworks for talking about diversity and equity in schools, including cultural competence and, in the case of class and poverty, the "culture" or "mind-sets" of poverty approach. It's not enough to know something about this or that culture, I argued, because that does not ensure that we will know how to respond to, or even to recognize, say, subtle biases in a Language Arts textbook or in a school dress code policy. I came to define Equity Literacy as *the skills and dispositions that enable us to recognize, respond to, and redress conditions that deny some students access to the educational opportunities enjoyed by their peers and, in doing so, sustain equitable learning environments for all students and families.*

Whereas my colleague Katy Swalwell had honed in on the importance of teaching youth about principles of equity, I had focused on the skills and dispositions that we as educators need in order to create equitable learning environments for youth. As we began discussing our respective visions for Equity Literacy, we came to see them as interrelated, both in our own philosophies about school and in research about effective teaching and learning. For example, as educators, our curricular and pedagogical skills and dispositions reflect, more or less, the attitudes, stereotypes, and assumptions, however implicit, we have about our students and their families (Williams, 2009). Meanwhile, one of the most important ways to engage students who are disenfranchised racially or economically or in some other way is to teach explicitly about discrimination and liberation (Kelley & Darragh, 2011). So we combined our models into a single, more holistic Equity Literacy. And it is that approach to Equity Literacy that became the framework for this book.

The Equity Literacy framework borrows some of its principles from other models and approaches for thinking about equity and diversity in schools. For example:

- Equity Literacy shares Resiliency Theory's refusal to associate poverty with deficiency rather than focusing on the strengths that allow poor communities to persevere through challenges related to poverty. It encourages us, like Resiliency Theory, to recognize and build upon "the processes that could account for positive adaptation and development in the context of adversity and disadvantage" (Crawford, Wright, & Masten, 2006, p. 355).
- We also drew inspiration from Diversity Pedagogy Theory (DPT), introduced by Rosa Hernández Sheets (2009) as "a set of principles that point out the natural and inseparable connection between culture and cognition" (p. 11). We were most compelled by the DPT principle that we, as educators, should develop skills that will allow us to foster "optimal learning conditions to enable more children to learn what [we] intend to teach" (p. 11).
- We drew, as well, on *funds of knowledge*, a concept coined by Luis Moll, Cathy Amanti, Deborah Neff, and Norma Gonzalez (1992) "to refer to the historically accumulated and culturally developed bodies of knowledge and skills essential for household or individual functioning and well-being" (p. 133).

- We found helpful some of the elements of *cultural proficiency*, as described by Randall Lindsey, Kikanza Nuri Robins, and Raymond Terrell (2009), especially the capacity for self-assessment. It's not enough, they explain, to familiarize ourselves with a vague notion of poor people's "culture," as the cultural competence or culture of poverty framework might ask us to do. Cultural proficiency also requires us to understand our own biases and how they are tied to privilege and even to societal inequalities, which is embedded in one of the principles of Equity Literacy.

What we believe distinguishes Equity Literacy, broadly speaking, from these and other popular frameworks that commonly are used in conversations about poverty and education is Equity Literacy's recognition that the problem is *not* primarily cultural. The issue before us, as we attempt to create more effective learning environments for low-income students, is not *culture*, but *equity*. I can learn everything I want about this or that culture, but doing so is not going to help me spot subtle bias in learning materials or help me realize the injustice at play when high-poverty schools eliminate arts and music programs, which are known to help low-income students achieve academically. So Equity Literacy, while recognizing that culture, among many other school and classroom dynamics, has a role when it comes to poverty and schooling, nudges it out of the center of the conversation, replacing it with equity.

With equity at its heart, the Equity Literacy framework is comprised of four abilities and ten principles, which I describe below.

## WHAT THE "EQUITY" MEANS IN EQUITY LITERACY

A commitment to equity is, in essence, a commitment to fairness, to equal opportunity, to a fair distribution of resources. *Equality*, a word often and wrongly used interchangeably with *equity*, refers, in essence, to sameness, to an *equal* distribution of resources. Not all equity is created equally. And vice versa.

That is to say, a fair or equitable distribution of resources might not be an equal distribution, and an equal distribution of opportunity might require an unequal distribution of resources, at least in the short term (Samoff, 1996). Let's consider an example. One of my students from last year—I'll call her Tina—is blind, rendering posted readings and in-class handouts largely useless to her without the necessary, and expensive, technologies to scan them and either read them to her or translate them into braille. She also required flexibility with assignment deadlines. Equality, or *sameness* in treatment, would have dictated that I refuse her these and other accommodations, because allowing them would create inequalities in the way time and resources and leeway were distributed to students. I have heard colleagues complain about the expectation that they provide accommodations, usually citing fairness as the reason. Equity, on the other hand, takes context into account. My first priority, when it comes to educational equity, is to ensure every student an opportunity to achieve to her fullest capability. Like the larger society, the campus, aside from ramps and elevators and staff members in a Disability Services Office, is built to accommodate the conveniences of people with no mobility challenges or disabilities or differences at all, and not to accommodate students like Tina. The playing field is not level. So I, as an educator who strives to be equitable, recognized her individual circumstances and adjusted the allocation of resources accordingly (Espinoza, 2007). I practiced inequality in this case because doing so was, in my estimation, the equitable thing to do and because the results, such as Tina having access to the readings and being able to participate fully in class, gave her a shot at excelling academically that was similar to the shot enjoyed by her peers (Henderson & Kennedy, 2004).

Later, in Chapters 5 and 6, I describe the wide range of ways in which the educational playing field is not level for low-income students and families. Then, in Chapters 8, 9, and 10, I describe what we can do in our own spheres of influence to adjust that playing field by teaching with class equity in mind and by advocating for educational equity for poor and working class youth.

## THE FOUR ABILITIES OF EQUITY LITERACY

The equity-literate educator cultivates in her- or himself four interlocking abilities, each of which are illustrated with examples throughout this book. These abilities include:

1.  the ability to *Recognize* both subtle and not-so-subtle biases and inequities in classroom dynamics, school cultures and policies, and the broader society, and how these biases and inequities affect students and their families;
2.  the ability to *Respond to* biases and inequities in the immediate term, as they crop up in classrooms and schools;
3.  the ability to *Redress* biases and inequities in the longer term, so that they do not continue to crop up in classrooms and schools; and
4.  the ability to *Create and Sustain* a bias-free and equitable learning environment for all students.

In Figure 2.2 I expand on these abilities, providing examples of classroom skills associated with each one.

## Figure 2.2. Equity Literacy Abilities

| Equity Literacy Abilities | Examples of Associated Skills and Dispositions |
|---|---|
| Ability to *Recognize* biases and inequities, including those that are subtle. | Equity-literate educators:<br><br>• notice even subtle bias in classroom materials, classroom interactions, and school policies;<br><br>• know and teach about how notable people in their content disciplines have used their knowledge to advocate for just or unjust actions or policies; and<br><br>• reject deficit views that locate the sources of outcome inequalities (like test score disparities) as existing within the cultures of, rather than as pressing upon, low-income families. |
| Ability to *Respond to* biases and inequities in the immediate term. | Equity-literate educators:<br><br>• have the facilitation skills and content knowledge necessary to intervene effectively when biases or inequities, such as gender bias or sexism, arise in the classroom or school;<br><br>• cultivate in students the ability to analyze bias in classroom materials, classroom interactions, and school policies; and<br><br>• foster conversations with colleagues about bias and equity concerns at their schools. |
| Ability to *Redress* biases and inequities in the long term. | Equity-literate educators:<br><br>• advocate against inequitable school practices, such as racially or economically biased tracking, and advocate for equitable school practices;<br><br>• never confuse *celebrating diversity* with *equity*, such as by responding to racial conflict with cultural celebrations; and<br><br>• teach, in relevant and age-appropriate ways, about issues like sexism, poverty, and homophobia. |

## Figure 2.2. Equity Literacy Abilities (continued)

| Equity Literacy Abilities | Examples of Associated Skills and Dispositions |
|---|---|
| Ability to *Create and Sustain* a bias-free and equitable learning environment. | Equity-literate educators:<br><br>• express high expectations for all students through higher-order pedagogies and curricula;<br><br>• consider how they assign homework and communicate with families, understanding that students have different levels of access to resources like computers and the Internet; and<br><br>• cultivate a classroom environment in which students feel free to express themselves openly and honestly. |

*Source:* Based, in part, on Paul C. Gorski's "Imagining Equity Literacy" (in press).

## THE TEN PRINCIPLES OF EQUITY LITERACY

The principles of Equity Literacy, which also are the guiding principles of this book, are the consciousness behind the framework. Each principle is based on research about congruence between what educators *believe about* and their effectiveness in *working with* diverse ranges of students and families. They are meant to nudge us beyond a simplistic focus on this or that "culture" and toward a more robust and meaningful understanding of what it takes to provide every student access to the best possible education. I have tailored these principles here in order to speak specifically to class and poverty, the core concerns of this book. However, the values underlying them can be applied to any equity concern in classrooms and schools.

The principles of Equity Literacy, as tailored to address class and poverty, are summarized in Figure 2.3, and discussed in greater detail below.

*Principle 1: The right to equitable educational opportunity is universal.*
All people are entitled to basic human rights, including access to equitable educational opportunity. No student should be denied the educational opportunities offered her peers because of where she was born or the economic condition of her family or, for that matter, her family's home language or racial identity or any other condition beyond her control. Unfortunately, too often, our failure to ensure equitable educational opportunity, as evidenced most clearly by enormous gaps in school funding, often between districts that are right next to each other (Kozol, 1992), guarantees that many of the most economically vulnerable youth are denied this basic right.

**Figure 2.3. Principles of Equity Literacy for Educators of Students in Poverty**

| Principle | Commitments of Equity-Literate Educators |
|---|---|
| 1. The right to equitable educational opportunity is universal. | Equity-literate educators believe that every student has an inalienable right to equitable educational opportunity. |
| 2. Poverty and class are intersectional in nature. | Equity-literate educators understand that class is an intersectional identity for students, so we cannot fully understand how class inequities operate, even in our own classrooms, without also understanding how inequities related to race, gender, language, immigrant status, disability, and other identities operate. |
| 3. Poor people are diverse. | Equity-literate educators recognize that poor and working class people are diverse, so that studying a singular "culture of poverty" will not help us understand individual low-income students or families better, and may, instead, strengthen our stereotypes. |
| 4. What we believe, including our biases and prejudices, about people in poverty informs how we teach and relate to people in poverty. | Equity-literate educators know that our teaching philosophies and practices are driven at least in part by our belief systems, so in addition to relying on practical strategies for teaching low-income students, we become equitable educators when we are willing to change fundamentally what we believe about low-income students and their families. |
| 5. We cannot understand the relationship between poverty and education without understanding biases and inequities experienced by people in poverty. | Equity-literate educators, in addition to changing what we believe about low-income students, are committed to developing deeper understandings of the biases and inequities faced by low-income families both in and out of school, and how these biases and inequities affect their performance and engagement in school. |
| 6. Test scores are inadequate measures of equity. | Equity-literate educators are aware that equity or its absence cannot be captured by standardized test scores because test scores, which measure, as much as anything, levels of prior access to educational opportunity, cannot capture student experience. Raising test scores is not the same thing as creating an equitable learning environment. |

**Figure 2.3. Principles of Equity Literacy for Educators of Students in Poverty (continued)**

| Principle | Commitments of Equity-Literate Educators |
|---|---|
| 7. Class disparities in education are the result of inequities, not the result of cultures. | Equity-literate educators understand that educational disparities primarily result not from cultural conflicts, but from inequities, so that the goal of eliminating disparities requires us to eliminate inequities rather than changing students' cultures. |
| 8. Equitable educators adopt a resiliency rather than a deficit view of low-income students and families. | Equity-literate educators recognize and draw upon the resiliencies and other funds of knowledge accumulated by poor and working class individuals and communities, and reject deficit views that focus on fixing disenfranchised students rather than fixing the things that disenfranchise students. |
| 9. Strategies for bolstering school engagement and learning must be based on evidence for what works. | Equity-literate educators, aware of the magnitude of societal bias against poor and working class people, are committed to basing instructional decisions, not on what's popular or what popular biases might dictate, but on evidence of what works. |
| 10. The inalienable right to equitable educational opportunity includes the right to high expectations, higher-order pedagogies, and engaging curricula. | Equity-literate educators demonstrate high expectations for all students, including low-income students, in part by offering them the same sorts of higher-order pedagogies and engaging curricula commonly found in classrooms or schools with few or no low-income students. |

The equity-literate educator understands that inequities in, for example, levels of educational attainment reflect, for the most part, inequities in opportunity rather than deficiencies in the characters or capabilities of people at the lower end of the economic hierarchy (Breen & Jonsson, 2007). The primary purpose of any conversation about poverty and education, in the view of Equity Literacy, ought to be how to ensure a more equitable distribution of that opportunity, whether in a single classroom, in a single school building, or in the larger society.

*Principle 2: Poverty and class are intersectional in nature.* Socioeconomic status does not exist in a vacuum. In fact, class is linked inextricably to race, gender, (dis)ability, and a wide range of other identities (Kezar, 2011), as depicted in Figure 2.4 and as we will explore in detail in Chapter

3. If we hope to understand and respond to the implications of poverty on childhood and schooling we must also be willing to consider a wide variety of other forms of inequity and how they relate to class. It is important to understand, too, that the elimination of class inequities does not guarantee the elimination of racial, gender, or other inequities. In this sense, conversations about class and poverty are not meant to *replace* conversations about, say, racial inequities, but instead to *complement* those conversations.

*Principle 3: Poor People Are Diverse.* In Chapter 4 we will explore the trouble with the "culture of poverty" notion, which suggests, incorrectly, that poor people, simply by virtue of being poor, share a predictable and consistent culture; that all I have to know is that a person is poor and I can assume, based on that knowledge, what he will think, how he prefers to learn, how he feels about education and money and relationships, and nearly everything else. As I discuss in more detail later, that view never made sense to me. Could I assume that my poor White Presbyterian Appalachian grandmother in North Carolina was the same culturally as equally poor displaced Muslim Ethiopians in Minnesota, or even the same as poor White coastal North Carolinians?

The truth is, like every big and widely dispersed group of people, low-income people are extremely diverse (Turpin, 2009). They vary by race and ethnicity and nationality; by religion and language; by political affiliation, vocation, and value system. "There is no single class identity," as Susan Borrego (2008) explains, "class is only experienced through multiple lenses" (p. 2). In fact, most of what poor people have in common has nothing to do with their cultures or dispositions. Instead, it has to do with what they experience, such as the bias and lack of access to basic needs.

## Figure 2.4. A Partial List of Intersecting Identities

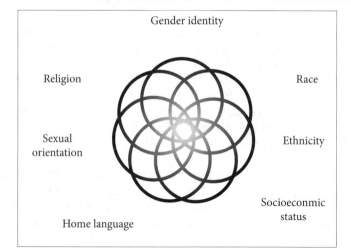

As a practical, educational matter, this means that there is no silver bullet, no magic list of *10 easy strategies for teaching every low-income student* (Lindsey, Karns, & Myatt, 2010), which makes our pursuit of equitable schools considerably more complicated than a "culture of poverty" can explain. Despite the popularity (and marketability) of the 10 easy strategies approach, the solutions, or at least the most effective solutions, are not quite so simple given the vast diversity of poor and working class people.

*Principle 4: What we believe, including our biases and prejudices, about people in poverty informs how we teach and relate to people in poverty.* The fourth principle of Equity Literacy is that, because our attitudes about poverty and our assumptions about why poor people are poor drive our beliefs about and even our behaviors toward people in poverty, practical strategies are not enough. Research has shown, for example, that our beliefs about who or what is to blame for the very existence of poverty pretty well predicts the sorts of interventions and practices we will use to address class inequities (Bullock, Williams, & Limbert, 2003; Williams, 2009). What we believe about poverty and why it exists even affects our expectations of and attitudes toward low-income students, as J. Gregg Robinson (2007) found in his analysis of data from 400 schoolteachers. Complicating matters, low expectations aren't always the result of rabid bias; sometimes they come from a well-intended savior syndrome or a genuine desire to "protect" from school pressures students who are assumed, often incorrectly, to have difficult home lives.

These beliefs are shaped by ideology, by how we are socialized to see and interpret poverty (Bradshaw, 2007). This is why learning about this or that practical pedagogical strategy is not a sufficient approach for creating or sustaining an equitable learning environment. We also need to examine our own class biases by developing deeper understandings of poverty and its effects on youth. It's also why, in addition to describing the sorts of practical strategies that have proven effective in engaging and teaching low-income youth, I focus in this book on challenging common myths about poverty and helping readers develop robust understandings of the experiences of poor and working class families both in and out of schools.

*Principle 5: We cannot understand the relationship between poverty and education without understanding the biases and inequities experienced by people in poverty.* The deepest understandings of poverty and schooling begin with an acknowledgment that poverty is not merely a personal or individual issue that can be solved by fixing the cultures or behaviors of poor people (Brady, Fullerton, & Cross, 2009). Rather, it is a public, structural condition related directly to all sorts of bigger social problems like unequal access to healthcare, the lack of living wage work (especially near poor and working class neighborhoods), and unequal access to educational opportunity (Milbourne, 2010; Rank, Yoon, & Hirschl, 2003). So in order to truly understand poverty and schooling, we need to examine not only the impact of class inequity or economic injustice on low-income students and their families, but also the systems and structures, including educational systems and structures, which perpetuate class inequity. (I have dedicated Chapter 6 to this very purpose.)

This is not to say that every schoolteacher or assistant principal necessarily is responsible for taking up the banner of global poverty eradication. I try to make this point in different ways throughout the book. The question is, What can I do within *my sphere of influence* to make that sphere as equitable as possible? Perhaps your sphere is a classroom or school or district. Whatever we consider our spheres of influence to be, the equity-literate educator understands that we cannot do our best jobs helping low-income students reach their full potentials as learners if we're stuck on their "cultures" or dispositions while failing to recognize how even the most subtle biases and inequities disrupt student learning and engagement.

*Principle 6: Test scores are inadequate measures of equity.* I often worry that all the fuss over standardized test scores has drawn our attention away from a more fundamental conversation about educational opportunity. Test scores represent one sort of outcome, and not even a very robust one. They don't speak at all to other important matters, such as whether students feel affirmed at school or whether their parents or guardians feel welcome and respected by teachers and administrators (Ostrove & Long, 2007). I'm reminded of this powerful line from Mistilina Sato and Timothy Lensmire (2009): "Children from poverty are being identified and labeled with grossly overgeneralized, deficit-laden characteristics that put them at risk of being viewed as less capable, less cultured, and less worthy as learners" (p. 365). We can't capture that with a test score. Perhaps test score disparities demonstrate one implication of this reality, but they can't capture other important implications, like how these conditions affect low-income students' engagement, abilities to relate to teachers, or feelings of belonging in school.

Throughout this book I refer to studies that use test scores as imperfect proxies for this bigger picture, but I also try, as often as possible, to take a more holistic view of educational opportunity. Who has access to what sorts of instructional approaches? Who has access to school nurses and the most wondrous school libraries? Who sees themselves reflected in their curricula? These questions are bigger than test scores. In fact, in many ways it appears as though the high-stakes testing culture of today's schools is impeding progress toward equal educational opportunity. The equity-literate educator, while being realistic about the current testing climate in today's schools, does not limit herself to a vision of educational equity that only values raising test scores.

*Principle 7: Class disparities in education are the result of inequities, not the result of cultures.* Gloria Ladson-Billings (2006), upon receiving the 2004 George and Louise Spindler Award for lifetime achievement in educational anthropology, delivered a speech in which she raised compelling concerns about the tendency in education circles to attribute every possible educational phenomenon to vague notions of culture, especially when it comes to poverty. She explained, "Culture is randomly and regularly used to explain everything . . . from school failure to problems with behavior management and discipline" (p. 104). One problem with this tendency, according to Ladson-Billings, is that the attribution of every challenge or disparity to "culture" almost always results in, or results from, a related tendency to characterize the cultures of low-income students in stereotypical, and often deviant, ways. She refers to this as the "poverty of culture," a not-so-subtle reminder of the flimsiness of the "culture" or "mind-set" of poverty approach to understanding low-income youth and their school experiences.

The other problem with the cultures obsession, as I mentioned earlier in this chapter, is that it can dim our senses to the many inequities that are at the roots of class disparities in educational opportunity and outcomes. It can be all too easy, when looking for fault in the families of economically disadvantaged students, to lose sight of the fact that, at almost every stage of schooling, poor and working class youth are denied the opportunities and resources many of their wealthier peers take for granted. We can begin that conversation in preschool, and the quality of preschool to which students from different economic backgrounds have access—if, that is, low-income youth have any access to preschool at all. In fact, we might begin even earlier, by looking at disparities in access to prenatal care. Throughout the educational experience, we might compare levels of access to the best-resourced schools, the most reasonable class sizes, the most engaging pedagogies, the most consistent access to music and art programs, and on and on. More on this in Chapter 6.

The primary trouble with approaches to addressing outcome inequalities that focus predominantly on culture is that they rarely acknowledge, much less address, these inequities. Unfortunately, not a single thing I can learn about the cultures of low-income students will, in the end, give me the skills and the knowledge I need to recognize, respond to, or redress the sorts of inequities and biases they face. I wouldn't argue, of course, that we shouldn't learn about the individual cultures of individual low-income students and families. We should. But we shouldn't stop there. Equity Literacy requires us to recognize, respond to, and redress inequities because they, and not culture, play the most prominent role in sustaining class disparities in schools.

*Principle 8: Equitable educators adopt a resiliency rather than a deficit view of low-income students and families.* Yet another risk of focusing on stereotypical notions of the cultures or mind-sets of poverty rather than on addressing inequities and biases is slipping into a deficit view of poor and working class people. According to the deficit view, low-income families are to blame for the very class disparities that weigh most heavily on them (Gorski, 2011; Yosso, 2005). They are, the deficit argument goes, intellectually, culturally, and even spiritually inferior, and their poverty is the best evidence of these deficiencies (Carreiro & Kapitulik, 2010; Valencia, 2009).

Of course, referring, again, to Principle 7, the only way to buy into the deficit view is to ignore the inequities, including educational inequities, experienced by low-income families. Unfortunately, that reality is of little mitigating consequence against mass perception, which is on the side of the deficit view. Research since roughly the late 1970s has shown that most people in the United States believe that poor people are poor because of their own deficiencies (Brady et al., 2009; Finley & Diversi, 2010; Marotz-Baden, Adams, Bueche, Munro, & Munro, 1979). And, unfortunately, research even shows that the deficit view remains the dominant view of teachers, including those of us who imagine ourselves as advocates for low-income students (García & Guerra, 2004; Garza & Garza, 2010; Lindsey et al., 2010). For example, in their study of high school teachers who professed an appreciation for racial and economic diversity, Jean Patterson and her colleagues (2008) found that the same teachers, while abstractly recognizing the inequities with which low-income students contended, still blamed them and their parents for not caring about education or for lacking persistence. Of course, when it comes to teaching students in poverty, the deficit view also is known to weaken teachers' academic expectations (Sleeter, 2004) and instructional rigor (Bomer, Dworin, May, & Semingson, 2009). Mary Amanda Graham (2009), a former school counselor who grew up in poverty, described the effects of the deficit view this way:

> Growing up in poverty, I learned some hard lessons about life. These lessons were taught to me not by my family but rather by system "helpers." I learned that being poor offended people. I learned people had rage and anger toward me and others like me. I learned that people thought being poor equated to lacking intelligence, creativity, motivation and desire. I learned that people felt sorry for me. In the process, I also learned to be weary (and wary) of helpers. (p. 46)

## Figure 2.5. A Resiliency View of Overcoming Identities

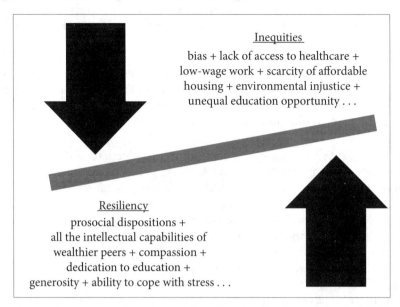

Inequities
bias + lack of access to healthcare +
low-wage work + scarcity of affordable
housing + environmental injustice +
unequal education opportunity . . .

Resiliency
prosocial dispositions +
all the intellectual capabilities of
wealthier peers + compassion +
dedication to education +
generosity + ability to cope with stress . . .

An equity-literate educator, on the other hand, champions the resiliency view, recognizing student and community strengths and funds of knowledge (Gonzalez, Moll, & Amanti, 2005), including the ability to persist in the face of bias, inequity, and other obstacles (Seccombe, 2002), as depicted in Figure 2.5. Low-income families are seen, in the words of Mistilina Sato and Timothy Lensmire (2009), as "robust . . . and worthy" (p. 368) rather than deficit-laden. The strengths and funds of knowledge are many, and they can be assets, not just to low-income students, but to *all* students, if we are inclined to shift our own preconceived notions about people in poverty. For example:

- despite a plethora of stereotypes to the contrary, people in poverty are, on average, *more prosocial* than their wealthier counterparts and more attuned to the needs of others (Kraus & Keltner, 2009);
- poor people are more generous and charitable than people with more economic resources, giving higher proportions of their incomes to charities and causes that help other people (Greve, 2009; James & Sharpe, 2007; Johnston, 2005);
- people in poverty are, on average, more kind to strangers, more likely to help others with onerous tasks, and more compassionate than their wealthier peers (Piff, Kraus, Cote, Cheng, & Keltner, 2010); and

- despite experiencing more stressors than wealthier people, people in poverty report, on average, lower levels of perceived stress (Krueger & Chang, 2008), demonstrating skills at adapting to challenging conditions.

Obviously, every low-income student and family has unique gifts and resiliencies and funds of knowledge. Our role is to identify and draw on those strengths and put them at the center of our perceptions of economically disadvantaged youth, nudging out the deficit view.

*Principle 9: Strategies for bolstering school engagement and learning must be based on evidence for what works.* There is no lack of evidence about the sorts of strategies that tend to help low-income students learn and remain engaged in school. Decades of research, much of which I describe in Chapters 8, 9, and 10, can be our guide, with two caveats: (1) that any strategy should be modified for our particular contexts and for individual students and families, and (2) that no set of strategies will work for every student. Evidence exists, and this is why it is strange that so much of what schools do these days to bolster the achievement of low-income students appears to be based on, well, precisely the *opposite* of what the evidence tells us to do.

I provide several examples of the most popular strategies that schools use despite their contrary nature to what evidence says we ought to be doing in Chapter 7, but one example—one particularly illogical example—has to do with art and music programs, which are quickly disappearing from high-poverty schools. These programs are being downsized or chopped entirely to save money or to create more time in the school day for reading, writing, math, and, sadly, even test-taking instruction. In some cases art and music are disappearing for combinations of these and other reasons. Even in economically diverse schools, low-income students and other students who are more likely than their peers to perform below the narrow standards of high-stakes tests often are denied art, music, physical education, and other components of a robust education, even if their peers still have access to these experiences.

I suppose this would make perfect sense if we had evidence that some students do not perform as well on standardized tests because they spend too much time learning art and music and not enough time learning reading, writing, and math (and if everyone agreed that standardized test scores ought to dictate what it means to provide a robust, holistic education). This might even sound like common sense. But the evidence says that if this *is* common sense, we're in big trouble. Students, and particularly poor and working class students, who have access to art and music education actually perform better on a wide range of academic measures across virtually every subject area (Pogrow, 2006; Tranter & Palin, 2004). Research also shows that, in most cases, student achievement improves at the highest rates not when we extend instructional time, but when we improve instructional quality (Joyner & Molina, 2012).

The Equity Literacy framework urges us to choose our strategies by considering evidence of what works. We might consider the results of formal research, but other important sources of data for our data-driven approach include our own careful observations and what we know about the communities in which we teach and the individuals in those communities. Being equity-literate means not relying on what is trendy. It means having a sense of urgency such that we refuse to spend any more effort on "commonsense" strategies that do not work or, worse, that, like cutting art and music programs, actually deepen the inequities we ought to be washing away.

*Principle 10: The inalienable right to equitable educational opportunity includes the right to high expectations, higher-order pedagogies, and engaging curricula.* High expectations: It's one of the mantras of today's education world. If nothing else, we should dedicate ourselves to having high expectations for all of our students. It might be difficult to find a single person who works in a school who would take issue with this point. So what sense do we make of the fact that, when compared with their wealthier peers, low-income students disproportionately are subject to the kinds of rote, disengaging pedagogies that demonstrate low expectations for their intellectual capabilities?

The equity-literate educator demonstrates high expectations through higher-order teaching and learning methods. This is not mere "student-centered" fluffiness. Research shows clearly that low-income students are more engaged in school and perform better on a wide variety of academic measures (and, yes, even get higher standardized test scores) when we teach them in ways that illustrate for them that we believe they can think creatively, complexly, and critically (Hoy, Tarter, & Hoy, 2006; Kennedy, 2010). I enthusiastically return to this point in Chapter 10.

## CONCLUSION

A wide variety of frameworks and models can help us better understand the challenges low-income families face and the gifts they bear. I chose to build this book around the Equity Literacy framework because of its emphasis on both understanding low-income people and understanding what it means to create an equitable learning environment, even if that means creating it within a larger context that is full of bias and inequity. You will see that for the remainder of the book I indicate at the beginning of each chapter which principles of Equity Literacy are discussed in that chapter. In several cases I discuss principles in more than one chapter.

Next, in Chapter 3, I provide an overview of patterns and conditions related to poverty and class in contemporary society. I describe how income and wealth are distributed, how poverty rates are changing, and how poverty is distributed across a variety of identities like race and gender.

# The Inequality Mess We're In

## A Class and Poverty Primer

Principles of Equity Literacy discussed in this chapter include:

Principle 2: Poverty and class are intersectional in nature.

Principle 3: Poor people are diverse.

Principle 4: What we believe, including our biases and prejudices, about people in poverty informs how we teach and relate to people in poverty.

As anybody who has worked in a public school knows, no educational experience is worthwhile without at least one multiple-choice standardized assessment. I'm kidding, of course. Still, I thought I'd begin our exploration of class and poverty in the United States with a brief quiz. There is no particular reason why you should know the answers to any of these questions, so be gentle with yourself if you do not do well. The purpose of the quiz is not to measure which statistics you've memorized, but instead to provide a broad picture of how your general perceptions about class and poverty in the United States do or do not jibe with reality.

### POVERTY AND CLASS AWARENESS QUIZ

1. According to the Children's Defense Fund (CDF, 2010), how often is a child born into poverty in the United States?

    a.  Every 32 seconds

    b.  Every 3 minutes and 2 seconds

    c.  Every 32 minutes

2. According to the Center for American Progress (2007), what proportion of U.S. citizens will live at least 1 year of their lives in poverty?

    a.  One-fifth

    b.  One-third

    c.  One-half

3. Most poor people in the United States live (Sherman, 2006):

    a.   In inner cities
    b.   Outside of inner cities

4. Which sorts of areas are seeing the greatest increases in poverty rates (Freeman, 2010)?

    a.   Urban areas
    b.   Rural areas
    c.   Suburban areas

5. One in ten White children in the United States is poor according to the CDF (2008). What proportion of Latino children in the United States is poor?

    a.   One in four
    b.   One in six
    c.   One in ten

6. According to a study sponsored by the Pew Research Center (Taylor et al., 2011b), the median wealth of White households in the United States is how many times larger than that of African American households?

    a.   Five times larger
    b.   Ten times larger
    c.   Twenty times larger

7. According to the National Coalition for the Homeless (NCH, 2009), what proportion of homeless men in the United States are military veterans?

    a.   Two in ten
    b.   Four in ten
    c.   Six in ten

8. According to the wealth analysis group WealthInsight (as referenced by Rushe, 2012), during President Barack Obama's first term in office, the number of millionaires in the United States

    a.   decreased by 6,500
    b.   decreased by 154,000
    c.   increased by 49,000
    d.   increased by 1,100,000

9. Identify the source of this quote: "We have deluded ourselves into believing the myth that capitalism grew and prospered out of the Protestant ethic

of hard work and sacrifices. Capitalism was built on the exploitation of black slaves and continues to thrive on the exploitation of the poor, both black and white, both here and abroad."

   a.  bell hooks, author and educator
   b.  Michael Moore, filmmaker
   c.  Martin Luther King Jr., civil rights activist
   d.  Eleanor Roosevelt, human rights advocate

10. In low-poverty U.S. schools, one out of every nine courses is taught by a teacher who is not certified to teach it. In high-poverty schools the proportion is (Almy & Theokas, 2010):

   a.  one in nine
   b.  one in six
   c.  one in four

Answer Key: (1) a, (2) b, (3) b, (4) c, (5) a, (6) c, (7) b, (8) d, (9) c, (10) c

In this chapter I provide an overview of conditions related to class and poverty in the United States, putting some of the information from this quiz into a broader context. We begin by exploring poverty rates, how income and wealth are distributed, and how poverty rates and patterns of income and wealth distribution have changed over the last several decades. We then turn to a different kind of distribution of poverty, looking at ways in which poverty and class interact with other identities, such as race and (dis)ability.

Before we proceed, I want to acknowledge what some readers might feel while reading about some fairly big societal conditions, like the quickening spread of poverty into suburban neighborhoods, growing wealth and income inequality, and distinct connections between race and class in the United States. In some ways, to some readers, the information in this chapter might feel a little outside educators' spheres of influence. *Sure,* you might think, *it's unfortunate that child poverty rates in the United States are growing, but I don't feel particularly empowered to fight that battle. It's enough of a challenge to come to work each day facing growing class sizes of hungry students and to teach them as well as I can in the face of the pressures of high-stakes testing.*

I hear you.

My intention in this chapter, and in this book, is not to suggest that every high school physics teacher or elementary school music teacher should feel immediately responsible for ending global poverty. Instead, my intention is to help us understand poverty and how it operates, to demystify it, to provide a bit of shared understanding of what we and our low-income students are up against. In my experience, conversations about poverty, and frameworks for understanding poverty and education, tend to focus on children and families who are living in poverty, on all that needs fixing about "those people." What's often missing from these frameworks is an ample understanding of poverty itself—of how poverty operates, of who is most susceptible to it, of why it exists at all in the wealthiest countries in the world. I struggle to imagine how I can be the best educator I can be for low-income students without knowing at least a little bit about poverty and class more generally and without pushing myself to reconsider some of my faulty or shaky notions about a society I was raised to believe promised everybody an equal opportunity.

## AN INTRODUCTION TO POVERTY, WEALTH, AND INEQUALITY

You probably remember, following Hurricane Katrina, how the U.S. media heralded the dawn of a new era of poverty awareness and anti-poverty action. As David Grusky and Emily Ryo (2006) put it,

> there was . . . much journalistic intoning in the immediate post-Katrina period about how the disaster forced the public to rediscover poverty, how it unmasked the human cost of poverty, and how it unleashed a newfound commitment among the public to take on issues of poverty and inequality. (pp. 59–60)

Grusky and Ryo call the popular claim that the aftermath of Hurricane Katrina became a sort of mass revelation about the existence or extent of poverty in the United States, which previously had been a big secret that was hidden from the public, the "dirty little secret" (or DLS) hypothesis.

Problem is, when they tested the DLS hypothesis by looking at data on people's awareness of, and engagement in action to address, poverty before and after the hurricane, they learned that the whole thing was more or less produced by the media. In reality, Katrina had far less of an impact on people's attitudes toward poverty than people's existing ideologies. People who chose not to acknowledge the existence or extent of poverty in the United States before the hurricane continued to ignore poverty afterward. Those who blamed poor people for their poverty before Katrina held just as tightly to those views in its aftermath. Nor was there any appreciable increase in anti-poverty activism or advocacy for poor people following Hurricane Katrina (Grusky & Ryo, 2006).

This is an important point: We tend to filter information through our existing belief systems. We might be moved by a story about a homeless child or a YouTube video about bigger-level catastrophes like Hurricane Sandy or the 2011 tsunami that devastated Japan, both of which resulted in homelessness for hundreds or thousands of children. We might even donate money or goods to support displaced victims of a hurricane or tsunami. But chances are that none of this will affect our views on poverty or our attitudes toward poor people unless we have the humility to make our ideologies vulnerable to new ideas. The only place to begin is to acknowledge what we don't know, or at least that there's always something more to know.

I make this somewhat heady point because, when it comes down to it, what we believe about poverty and poor people drives what we are willing to do to in the name of class equity in our spheres of influence. And, unfortunately, what most people in the United States believe about class and poverty is, at best, incomplete and, at worst, very, very biased. We'll dig more deeply into that point in Chapter 4. What's important to consider for now is that sometimes the mythology sounds sweeter than the reality. So we tell ourselves that all children have an equal opportunity to achieve whatever they want to achieve even as we send the wealthiest of them, on average, to the most well-funded and well-resourced schools and the most economically disadvantaged of them, on average, to the most overcrowded, poorly funded, underresourced schools.

The principal purpose of this chapter is not really to upend that mythology per se, but rather to provide a basic primer on poverty and class and how they operate in the United States. However, I can find no honest way to discuss the realities of class and poverty without poking at common beliefs about class inequality. So if anything I share here rubs against the beliefs you had when you opened this book, try to remember that the more we know about poverty, the better equipped we are to support low-income students and families.

## Poverty by the Numbers

A record 47 million people in the United States live in poverty, which is about 15% of the population (U.S. Census Bureau, 2012). Of course, that figure is based on a government standard for a poverty line income, which, for example, is $22,400 for a family of four (Kaufman, 2011). Using the same standard, another 30 million people are living just above the poverty line, in constant danger of dipping below it (Luhby, 2012a). That's about 77 million people at or near the poverty line, a number the enormity of which I admittedly have difficulty comprehending. It's a lot of people, especially considering the total U.S. population is right around 313 million. In fact, the Center for American Progress (2007) estimates that one in every three people in the United States will spend at least 1 year of their lives in poverty. Many of us are just a layoff away.

Complicating matters, many social scientists who study poverty and who have examined the methods the government uses for calculating the poverty threshold have argued that these methods fail to capture the scope and complexity of poverty (Blank & Greenberg, 2008; Meyer & Sullivan, 2012). Part of the problem is that the U.S. government has been using basically the same method for measuring poverty for the last 5 decades. The measure is based mostly on a minimal or subsistence standard of estimated food costs. Why food? A 1955 survey showed that, on average, families were spending roughly one-third of their incomes on food (Blank & Greenberg, 2008). So, multiply that subsistence food cost number by three and—*voilà!*—you more or less have the poverty threshold. Each year hence, the threshold has been modified for inflation. It has not been modified for other significant variables, such as regional cost of living differences. But even more confounding is the fact that, as the threshold has been modified for inflation, it has not been modified to reflect new estimates in the average proportion of family budgets spent on food. Today families spend about one-eighth of their incomes on food rather than one-third (Blank & Greenberg, 2008), and we spend a lot more than we used to spend on things like childcare and transportation, which are not accounted for in government calculations (Gabe, 2012). So government figures tend to underestimate the number of people who don't have sufficient resources to cover basic needs—things like food, housing, healthcare, and clothing (Finley & Diversi, 2010).

Based on most any measure, the poverty rate has been growing steadily in the United States since 2000, when the poverty rate as defined by the government, at 11.3% of the U.S. population, was at an all-time low. The pace of this growth has accelerated since 2007 and throughout the recent recessions or "financial crisis" (Gabe, 2012). As I noted earlier, by 2012, the U.S. poverty rate was 15% and estimated, by the end of the year, to reach its highest point since 1965. These increases, which, notably, are happening even as U.S. corporate profits are at record highs (Rampell, 2012), are the result of a web of economic factors, ranging from job losses to low wages to the bursting housing bubble.

Homelessness is on the rise, too, which should come as little surprise given the millions of people facing foreclosures on their homes over the last several years (Western Regional Advocacy Project [WRAP], 2010). The WRAP (2010) estimates that about 3.5 million people in the United States are homeless on any given day, although homelessness tends to be underreported, too. For instance, people who might be "couch-surfing" or sleeping in cars or tent cities (yes, they *do* exist all over the United States) generally are not counted as homeless (Finley & Diversi, 2010). Perhaps the real "dirty little secret" when it comes to poverty is the lack of attention to who tends to be homeless. For instance, a large percentage of homeless men in the United States are military veterans (National Coalition for the Homeless [NCH], 2009) struggling to readjust to civilian life, often due to serious injuries or post-traumatic stress disorder (commonly called PTSD). Roughly 40% of homeless youth identify as lesbian, gay, bisexual, or queer (Durso & Gates, 2012), and many left home or were thrown out of their homes due to conflict or abuse related to their sexual orientations or gender identities (Ray, 2006). Additionally, many people with mental health challenges become homeless, especially if their families cannot afford to pay for their care at a mental health facility (National Alliance on Mental Illness, 2011).

## Child Poverty

Every 32 seconds, a baby in the United States is born into poverty (Children's Defense Fund, 2010). By the end of 2011, over one in five people under the age of 18, or roughly 15.5 million children, were poor. According to the Children's Defense Fund (2010), both of these figures, like U.S. poverty rates more generally, have been on the rise since 2000. In fact, rates of child poverty are growing at a higher clip than adult poverty rates, as you can see in Figure 3.1. Roughly 12 million U.S. children live with food insecurity (Yu, Lombe, & Nebbit, 2010), defined by Alisha Coleman-Jensen and her colleagues at the United States Department of Agriculture (2012) as lacking adequate nutrition due to poverty.

A whole host of variables put some youth at a greater or lesser risk than others of being poor, such as their racial identities (or racial inequities, to

**Figure 3.1. U.S. Poverty Rates by Age, 2000–2011**

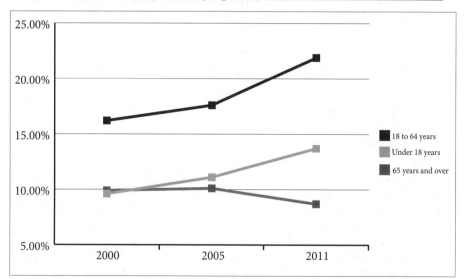

Data from United States Census Bureau (2012), *Current Population Survey: Annual Social and Economic Supplements.*

be more precise) or the region in which they are born. I will discuss those factors in detail shortly.

But among the most important factors that predict the likelihood that a child will be born into poverty is family structure. Approximately 47.6% of children living in families headed by single mothers are poor, whereas 10.9% of children living in families with two parents or guardians are poor (Gabe, 2012). Making matters worse, poor single mothers tend to be targets of a particularly harsh brand of scorn, a trend often traced back to Ronald Reagan's popularization of the term *welfare queen*. If we hope to sustain positive partnerships with single mothers, the first step is to refuse to participate in that scorn and, instead, to try to see the bigger picture, such as cases in which women make a positive choice to leave abusive relationships and raise children on their own, despite the financial hardships. In many ways we might see the high rates of poverty among children being raised by single mothers as a societal failing, as a failure of the wealthiest country in the world to care for some of its most vulnerable citizens. After all, among the world's industrialized nations, the United States ranks first in number of billionaires, first in gross domestic product, 28th in infant mortality rates, and dead last when it comes to relative child poverty (Children's Defense Fund [CDF], 2010).

If low-income students attend your school, chances are that some of those students are, have been, or will at some point be homeless. Child homelessness, like child poverty, is on the rise in the United States. Roughly 1.6 million children were homeless in 2010, roughly 40% of whom were under 5 years old (CDF, 2012). More than 1 million homeless children attended public schools in 2011, according to the Children's Defense Fund (2012).

## Income and Wealth Trends in the United States

Of the hundreds of essays and books I read in preparation for writing this book, one study most definitely stood out. In 2005, Michael Norton and Dan Ariely (2011) asked more than 5,500 U.S. citizens to estimate how wealth is distributed in the country. And this is what they learned: Most of us, including professors of economics, are fairly clueless. Participants were shown three pie charts, one showing the actual distribution of wealth, one showing Sweden's wealth distribution, and one showing an "equal" distribution of wealth, in which every 20% of the population controls 20% of the wealth. A vast majority of participants got it wrong. They chose the pie chart in which the wealthiest 20% of people control about 60% of the wealth—Sweden's wealth distribution. Actually, in 2005 the wealthiest 20% of people controlled about 85% of the wealth. Today, the wealthiest 20% of people in the U.S. control roughly 89% of the wealth (Domhoff, 2012), as illustrated by Figure 3.2.

## Figure 3.2. Distribution of Wealth in the United States, 2010

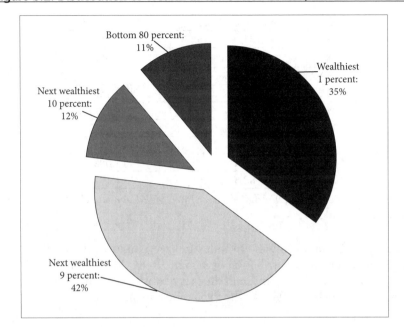

Adapted from G. William Domhoff, *Wealth, Income, and Power* (2012).

Even more interesting, though, is what we tend to believe about the wealth controlled by the poorest Americans. Most of Norton and Ariely's survey responders believed that the poorest 40% of U.S. citizens control something between 8 and 10% of the country's total wealth. Those economists flubbed this one, too, guessing about 2%. Actually, at the time of the survey, the poorest 40% of people in the United States controlled 0.3% of the country's wealth (Norton & Ariely, 2011).

Unfortunately, these disparities have grown since 2005 (Wolff, 2012), as you can see in Figure 3.3. And this is true whether we're talking about wealth—which is net worth, or one's assets minus one's debt—or income. Income inequality has been increasing since 1980 and is now at its highest level in 40 years (McCall & Percheski, 2010). In 2011, for example, the income of middle and working class people, the middle 60% of the income pyramid, *fell* between 1.6 and 1.9% while the income of the wealthiest 20% of people *grew* 1.6%. The wealthiest 1% of Americans saw their incomes grow by 6% (Luhby, 2012b). In other words, even during the recession, the economy was working better for some people than other people, and those other people more likely than not were middle class or poorer.

This might surprise you. People often associate income and wealth inequality with "Third World" countries. And there's some validity to that

**Figure 3.3. Distribution of Wealth in the United States, 1983–2010**

| Year | Wealthiest 20% | Bottom 80% |
|------|----------------|------------|
| 1983 | 81.3% | 18.7% |
| 1989 | 83.6% | 16.5% |
| 1992 | 83.8% | 16.2% |
| 1995 | 83.9% | 16.1% |
| 1998 | 83.4% | 16.6% |
| 2001 | 84.4% | 15.6% |
| 2004 | 84.6% | 15.3% |
| 2007 | 85.1% | 15.0% |
| 2010 | 88.9% | 11.1% |

Adapted from Edward N. Wolff, *The Asset Price Meltdown and the Wealth of the Middle Class* (2012).

association. But among Western industrialized countries the United States has the most unequal distribution of income (Reid, 2006), and it's only getting worse. It's this inequality, and the fact that it's becoming worse, that, in essence, spawned the "We Are the 99%" movement.

## THE UNEQUAL DISTRIBUTION OF POVERTY

Things are about to get a little more complicated. One of the reasons that simplistic approaches to addressing poverty or supporting low-income students don't work is that poverty does not happen in a vacuum. In fact, it's tied to all sorts of other identities and forms of discrimination, including gender and sexism, race and racism, and even disability and ableism. Unfortunately, the popular models for talking about diversity in education tend to limit our attention to one identity at a time, so that we're talking about class *or* race *or* gender *or* disability. The reality, though, is that all of these identities and their respective forms of discrimination are intertwined into one big mess of inequality. What does this mean when it comes to a conversation about poverty and education? It means that, if we desire to have any sort of complex understanding of poverty, we simply must talk about it in relation to race *and* gender *and* disability *and* other factors that are associated with poverty (Hughes, 2010; Luke, 2010).

The gist of the association is this: Poverty is not equally distributed in the United States. We've seen already how children are affected disproportionately by poverty, especially children being raised by single mothers. But gender makes a difference, too, as do race, region, disability status, immigrant status, sexual orientation, and a whole host of other variables (Adeola, 2005; CDF, 2008; Jackson, 2011). Consider a racial example. A whole legacy of discrimination on the basis of race is tied to class inequality today. Generations of families have been denied opportunities to purchase homes in the most economically desirable neighborhoods, something that still happens today, and generations of children in communities of color have been denied access to well-equipped schools, something that also continues today. Consider a regional example, too. People of all racial identities in many parts of Appalachia and people who live on some tribal lands continue to be subject, on average, to underfunded schools and poor technology infrastructure. These, like poverty itself, are legacies of inequity. They are legacies of inequity that all but ensure predictable differences in rates of poverty among particular groups of people.

It would require an additional book or so to describe adequately every way in which poverty is distributed unequally. So, rather than embedding an entire additional book into this book, I chose to describe some of the ways in which class and poverty interact with just a few identities: gender, race, disability, and region.

## Gender

Women attend and graduate from college at higher rates than men today, a reversal that began in the late 1980s (Wang & Parker, 2011). According to the Council for Graduate Schools (2011), women even comprise 59% of all graduate students, 60% of all master's degree awardees, and 52% of all doctoral degree awardees. This phenomenon often is called the "feminization of higher education," illustrating how much of a social and cultural shift it is. After all, nobody referred to the "masculinization of higher education" during the hundreds of years when men dominated college attendance and graduation rates. It's almost as though we, as a society, subtly believe men are *supposed* to have higher attendance and graduation rates than women, so that we need to name our surprise when the tides turn, making it sound a little like an infestation: the *feminization* of higher education.

Despite their credentials, though, women still make only 77 cents for every dollar men make in the United States (DeNavas-Walt, Proctor, & Smith, 2011). And, according to the Women's Legal Defense and Education Fund (2012), they are 34% more likely than men to be poor. Unfortunately, the gap is growing. Among adults in poverty, 59% are women, and the disparity in poverty rates between women and men grew 29% between 2010 and 2011. Sadly, among adults 65 years of age or older, women are 73% more likely than men to live in poverty.

One of the reasons for the growing disparity in poverty rates, according to Paul Taylor and his colleagues at the Pew Research Center (2011a), is that men have recovered more quickly from the economic recession than women. They explain,

> From the end of the recession in June 2009 through May 2011, men gained 768,000 jobs and lowered their unemployment rate by 1.1 percentage points to 9.5%. Women, by contrast, *lost 218,000 jobs* during the same period, and their unemployment rate increased by 0.2 percentage points to 8.5%. (p. 1)

Demonstrating how inequality happens in complex layers, unemployment rates particularly grew, according to the Pew report, "for Hispanic, [B]lack and Asian women" and for "foreign-born women" (p. 5).

## Race

Income and wealth inequality within the United States are among their highest levels when we look at them across race, as illustrated in Figure 3.4. African American, American Indian, and Latina/o people are particularly more likely than White people to be poor (Kochlar, Fry, & Taylor, 2011). Paul Taylor and his Pew Center colleagues (2011b) explain, "The median wealth of white households is 20 times that of black households and 18 times that of Hispanic households." They continue, "These lopsided wealth ratios are the largest since the government began publishing such data a quarter century ago" (p. 1).

As stands to reason, then, African Americans, Latinas/os, and American Indians are significantly more likely than White people to live in poverty (DeNavas-Walt et al., 2011; Muhammad, 2009). And while, as you can see in Figure 3.5, Asian Americans, when counted as a single group, experience less poverty on average than White people, this only is true for *some* groups of Asian Americans, partially predictable by region of origin. Hmong people, 26.9% of whom live in poverty, and other people of Asian ancestry whose families or forebears came to the United States under duress due to repression, many of whom were in poverty on arrival, are much more likely to be in poverty now, according to the Southeast Asia Resource Action Center (2011).

Just as the recession has had a greater impact on women than on men, it has had a greater impact on People of Color than on their White counterparts. For example, just between 2009 and 2010, while the poverty rate for non-Hispanic White people increased one-half of one percentage point, it increased 1.6 percentage points for African Americans (DeNavas-Walt et al., 2011).

**Figure 3.4. Median Net Worth of U.S. Households by Race**

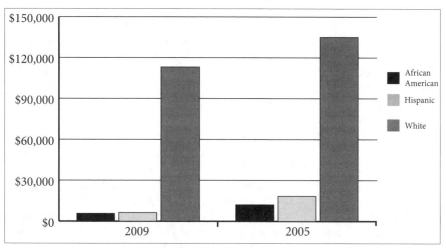

*in 2009 dollars.

Adapted from Rakesh Kochlar, Richard Fry, and Paul Taylor (2011), *Wealth Gaps Rise to Record Highs Between Whites, Blacks, and Hispanics.*

**Figure 3.5. Poverty Rates by Race, 2011**

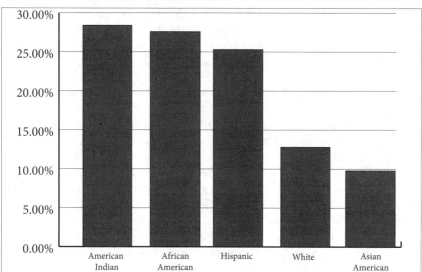

Based on data from Carmen DeNavas-Walt, Bernadette Proctor, and Jessica Smith (2011), *Income, Poverty, and Health Coverage in the United States: 2011.*

## Disability

The topic of disability often is lost in conversations about equity and diversity, despite the fact that people with disabilities, from mobility challenges to autism to depression, face a plethora of inequalities that limit their opportunities. In fact, rates of unemployment and poverty among people with disabilities, and especially among people with two or more disabilities, are among the highest of any identity group (Palmer, 2011; Stapleton, O'Day, Livermore, & Imparato, 2006).

Part of the trouble is that poverty and disability are, in many ways, interrelated. Poor people disproportionately lack access to healthcare, including preventive healthcare and prenatal care; are more likely than their wealthier peers to work dangerous or labor-heavy jobs; and face other challenges that increase the risk of disability (Palmer, 2011). Meanwhile, as Amartya Sen (1992), recipient of the Nobel Prize in Economics, explained in *Inequality Reexamined*, people with some types of disabilities might be limited in the kinds of employment opportunities to which they have access, which, in turn, could limit their income, which, then, might limit their access to other sorts of opportunities. The expenses that some people with disabilities incur, such as the cost of adaptive technologies, increase the likelihood that people who need them will end up in poverty (Glendinning & Baldwin, 1988). You might think that health insurance, for people who have it, would cover those expenses. However, when economist Sophie Mitra and her colleagues (2009) reviewed 8 years of national data on medical expenditures in the United States, they found, after controlling for all sorts of variables, that people who have one or more disabilities spend, on average, 50% more on healthcare *out-of-pocket* than people who have no disabilities. When it comes to people with disabilities who also are poor, in other words, disadvantage begets disadvantage.

Then there's income inequality, which even bears down on people with disabilities who work full-time, year-round. According to DeNavas-Walt and her colleagues (2011), the median income of women with at least one disability in 2010 was $31,851, whereas the median income of women with no disabilities was $37,028. Likewise, the median earnings for men with at least one disability were $41,506 while the median income for their peers without disabilities was $48,031.

Notice, by the way, another example of the intersectionality of inequality here: The median income of women with no disabilities is lower than that of men with a disability. The median income for women with a disability is a full $17,000 less than that for men without a disability.

## Region

In the case of race, gender, and disability, poverty rate inequalities are growing. When it comes to where we live, though, the patterns are changing altogether. Historically poverty has been seen primarily or even solely as an inner-city problem. In point of fact, that view never was completely accurate. Certainly there are high rates of poverty in many city centers, but poverty always has been distributed fairly evenly between cities and rural areas, like parts of Appalachia and the Mississippi Delta, according to Bruce Weber and his colleagues (2005) at the Institute for Research on Poverty. Still, many people in the United States hold onto the doubly troubling perception that poverty is more or less an urban issue and, more precisely, an urban People of Color issue. This perception is doubly troubling in that it (1) strengthens already ugly stereotypes about urban communities of color, and (2) contributes to the invisibility of low-income people, including low-income People of Color, living in rural areas, small towns, and even suburbs (Milbourne, 2010).

Speaking to this invisibility, Marty Strange (2011), policy director for the Rural School and Community Trust, has written, "Rural people remain one of the last groups about whom cultural slurs are considered politically acceptable speech" (p. 9). He goes on to remind us that about 15 million racially diverse students attend schools in small towns and rural areas, and that the poverty rate in those areas is higher than the national average. Neither he nor I would suggest, of course, that we flip the script completely and hone in on rural poverty while ignoring urban poverty. The point, instead, is to recognize that poverty is everywhere. It's even in public schools people think are filled with "upper middle class" students. And increasingly so. It's in every state, from those with large rural populations to those with large cities, as you can see in Figure 3.6.

George Mason University, where I teach future teachers, sits smack dab in the middle of Fairfax County, Virginia, a suburb of Washington, DC, and the second wealthiest county in the United States, according to Francesca Levy (2010) at *Forbes* magazine. Adjacent to campus—literally, across the street from Mason's track and field facilities—sits a housing community run by FACETS, a local nonprofit that provides housing to the county's homeless families. A majority of my students, most of whom grew up in the area (Loudoun, the only wealthier county in the United States, is right next to Fairfax County), also grew up associating poverty and homelessness with DC. Many are shocked that poverty rates, and even more so homelessness rates, are growing right beneath their noses, so close to home.

In fact, for the first time in U.S. history, poverty rates are growing steadily in suburban areas, more quickly than in urban or rural areas or

**Figure 3.6. Percentage of Persons in Poverty by State, 2011**

| State | Percentage | State | Percentage |
|---|---|---|---|
| United States | 15.0 | Missouri | 15.4 |
| Alabama | 15.4 | Montana | 16.5 |
| Alaska | 11.7 | Nebraska | 10.2 |
| Arizona | 17.2 | Nevada | 15.5 |
| Arkansas | 18.7 | New Hampshire | 7.6 |
| California | 16.9 | New Jersey | 11.4 |
| Colorado | 13.2 | New Mexico | 22.2 |
| Connecticut | 10.1 | New York | 16.0 |
| Delaware | 13.7 | North Carolina | 15.4 |
| DC | 19.9 | North Dakota | 9.9 |
| Florida | 14.9 | Ohio | 15.1 |
| Georgia | 18.4 | Oklahoma | 13.9 |
| Hawaii | 12.1 | Oregon | 14.4 |
| Idaho | 15.7 | Pennsylvania | 12.6 |
| Illinois | 14.2 | Rhode Island | 13.4 |
| Indiana | 15.6 | South Carolina | 19.0 |
| Iowa | 10.4 | South Dakota | 14.5 |
| Kansas | 14.3 | Tennessee | 16.3 |
| Kentucky | 16.0 | Texas | 17.4 |
| Louisiana | 21.1 | Utah | 11.0 |
| Maine | 13.4 | Vermont | 11.6 |
| Maryland | 9.3 | Virginia | 11.4 |
| Massachusetts | 10.6 | Washington | 12.5 |
| Michigan | 15.0 | West Virginia | 17.5 |
| Minnesota | 10.0 | Wisconsin | 13.1 |
| Mississippi | 17.4 | Wyoming | 10.7 |

*Source: United States Census Bureau* (2012), Current Population Survey: Annual Social and Economic Supplements.

in small towns (Freeman, 2010). Eric Freeman, who has studied this phenomenon in and around Atlanta, calls it the "redistribution of poverty" (p. 678). No longer are suburbs where people go in order to leave poor communities behind; rather, more and more people are bringing their poverty to the suburbs (Frey, 2005). As urban areas are gentrified, driving up housing costs, Freeman (2010) explains, low-income families are drawn to the suburbs for the most pragmatic reasons: lower-cost housing and a more plentiful supply of low-wage, low-skill jobs in the burgeoning restaurant, lawn care, home and office cleaning, retailing, health industry, and hospitality trades that have vanished from or moved outside the urban core. (p. 676)

Meanwhile, poor and working class immigrants increasingly are settling directly into suburban neighborhoods, also because of these job opportunities. Unfortunately, because most suburban areas are unaccustomed to large numbers of families in poverty, they also tend to lack the sorts of programs and services necessary to support them, as Scott Allard and Benjamin Roth (2010) found in their examination of suburban Chicago, Washington, DC, and Los Angeles. Similarly, many schools in suburban areas, where teachers and administrators might be unaccustomed to working with large numbers of low-income families, are struggling with the transition, which is why Freeman (2010) and others urge us to recognize these shifts and let go of the old perception of the solely *urban* poor.

## CONCLUSION

The kind of information filling the pages of this chapter might seem, to some readers, far removed from the day-to-day joys and challenges of classroom and school life. We, as educators, have plenty to do without somebody coming along and adding increasing rates of child poverty to our agenda of problems to solve. It bears repeating that my intention, in including a sort of class and poverty primer in this book, is not to argue that every teacher must commit her life to ending global poverty, although it's amazing to imagine what we could do if we chose to put our collective energies toward that goal. Rather, the purpose of equipping ourselves with deeper understandings of poverty rates and wealth distribution and various other big patterns and phenomena is to better understand poor and working class students and families and the challenges they are up against.

Considering some of these big patterns also can help us measure what we think we know about poverty and class and how they operate against reality. It can help us see concepts like meritocracy and equal opportunity from new angles. And with this, we segue into Chapter 4, in which we will look at assumptions and ideologies related to class and poverty more carefully. Most particularly, Chapter 4 challenges us to rethink the "culture of poverty" or "mind-set of poverty" approach to understanding and responding to the implications of poverty on the educational experiences of youth.

# The Trouble with the "Culture of Poverty" and Other Stereotypes about People in Poverty

Principles of Equity Literacy discussed in this chapter include:

Principle 3: Poor people are diverse.

Principle 4: What we believe, including our biases and prejudices, about people in poverty informs how we teach and relate to people in poverty.

Principle 7: Class disparities in education are the result of inequities, not the result of cultures.

Principle 8: Equitable educators adopt a resiliency rather than a deficit view of low-income students and families.

When I think about how the "culture of poverty" or "mind-set of poverty" framework has come to dominate conversations about poverty and education, I'm puzzled. I wonder how so many of us have bought into a most preposterous assumption: that we can assume anything at all about somebody's values, dispositions, or behaviors based on knowing a single dimension of her identity. I imagine Grandma, who grew up rural, poor, and Presbyterian, a White woman speaking her distinctly middle-Appalachian dialect, standing next to one of the many urban, low-income, Muslim Somali youth, first-generation U.S. citizens I had the pleasure of knowing while living in St. Paul, Minnesota. *What*, I ask myself, *do these two people have in common culturally?* What can I rightly assume about both of them, knowing only that their families are poor? They and their families do, I concede, have some important life experiences in common: a lack of access to healthcare, for instance, and a lack of access to living wage work. But these similarities are not *cultural*. Rather, they are social conditions. They are barriers and inequities despite which people in poverty must attempt, against considerable odds, to thrive.

In this sense, the culture of poverty idea is nonsensical because the idea that we can know anything about somebody based on a single dimension of her or him is, in the end, nonsensical. There is as much diversity *within* any identity group, whether "tall people" or "women" or "people with disabilities," as there is *between* any two identity groups. But it's nonsensical for a variety of other reasons, too, which we will explore momentarily.

Today, many people associate the culture of poverty or mind-set of poverty paradigm with Ruby Payne (2005), the prodigious professional development guru whose book *A Framework for Understanding Poverty* is among the texts most widely read by teachers. However, it was Oscar Lewis (1959) who introduced that term, the *culture of poverty*, more than 50 years ago in his book *Five Families: Mexican Case Studies in the Culture of Poverty*. The basic idea was, as it is today, that poor people share, more or less, a unique, consistent, and identifiable set of cultural traits. People living in poverty, he argued, have a negligible sense of history. Poor men are violent, often beating their wives. Poor women are promiscuous, favoring instant gratification. He introduced roughly 70 traits in all that constituted, in his view, the culture of poverty. Payne borrowed many of these traits and repackaged them as the "mind-set of poverty."

Lewis and his scholarship are emblematic of a social science paradigm that was becoming more popular in the late 1950s and early 1960s. In this paradigm, personal and community characteristics—attitudes toward education, for instance, or propensities toward peace or violence—were driven more by *culture* than by *biology* (Rosemblatt, 2009). In some ways this was a good development. Lewis rejected the idea that outcome inequalities like differences in IQ test scores were inherent or biological. He suggested, instead, as Payne does today, that they result from learned cultural behaviors and dispositions that can be unlearned. In fact, Lewis, who saw himself as part of a progressive movement in the social sciences (Ortiz & Briggs, 2003), criticized what he interpreted as gross overgeneralizations in his colleagues' poverty scholarship. He once wrote (1950), for example, that anthropologists had "come to deal more and more with averages and stereotypes than with real people in all their individuality" (p. 470). He even claimed that his culture of poverty paradigm was a response to colonialism and the ugliness of contemporary capitalism (Lewis, 1961).

Lewis's "culture of poverty" hypothesis elicited a wide range of responses from his contemporaries. On one end of the continuum were Michael Harrington and Daniel Moynihan, who applied it more or less verbatim in their own work, often honing in on urban African American poverty (Rosemblatt, 2009). Moynihan applied the culture of poverty concept in the now-famous "Moynihan Report," originally titled "The Negro Family: The Case for National Action," which he wrote in 1965 as the U.S. Assistant Secretary of Labor. In the "culture of poverty" tradition, Moynihan suggested that African American poverty could be attributed largely to a "ghetto culture" characterized by single-mother families rather than, as others had argued, the lack of employment opportunities in urban centers. The same type of application of Lewis's work survives today in Payne's (2005) mind-sets of poverty model, which claims that poverty is attributable, not to inequities or to an unequal distribution of opportunity or even to educational access disparities, but to the problematic "culture" of poor families.

On the other end of the spectrum were the likes of Charles Valentine (1968) and William Ryan (1971), who responded vehemently against the culture of poverty model. They argued that attending to a fictitious "culture of poverty" was a diversion, that poverty was the result primarily of the sorts of external factors and repressions that we will explore in Chapters 5 and 6. Are you familiar with the phrase "blaming the victim"? William Ryan coined that idiom, *invented* it, in response to the culture of poverty framework, and particularly to the way it was being applied to the African American community. Concepts like the "culture of poverty," he argued (1971), "concentrate on the [supposed] defects of the victim, condemn the vague social and environmental stresses that produced the defect (some time ago), and ignore the continuing effect of victimizing social forces (right now)" (p. 8). In other words, to use an education example, we deny people in poverty access to equal educational opportunity, access to healthcare, and even access to air unspoiled by environmental hazards. We do this for generations and then, when some low-income youth don't do well on standardized tests or drop out of school or seem disengaged in class, we forget about these inequities and blame it on their "culture."

The most obvious problem with the culture of poverty model is, as I mentioned earlier, its somewhat silly assumption that if we know somebody is poor, we somehow can know all sorts of other things about him such as how he learns, how he communicates, his attitude about education, or his propensity or lack of propensity for violence. It assumes that somehow we can erase the effects of scores of other factors that inform his values, including the many other dimensions of his identity such as his race, religion, ethnicity, sexual orientation, region of residence, and nationality, not to mention the many intersections of these identities.

Another problem, as I mentioned in Chapter 2, is the fact that the education world today is inundated with culture-obsessed approaches to understanding and responding to almost every phenomenon related to equity and diversity. We have cultural competence, cultural proficiency, culturally relevant pedagogy, and intercultural communications, among others. The danger with these approaches or, more specifically, with how they often are implemented is that they conflate "culture" with race, gender, socioeconomic status, sexual orientation, and other identities, thereby suggesting that disparities or conflicts result from *cultural misunderstandings* rather than *biases and inequities*. Describing this conflation, Gloria Ladson-Billings (2006), in her speech "It's Not the Culture of Poverty, It's the Poverty of Culture," explained, "the problem of culture in teaching is not merely one of exclusion. It is also one of overdetermination. What I mean by this is that culture is randomly and regularly used to explain everything" (p. 104).

The intensive and, at times, exclusive focus on culture masks the bigger reality: that, as we will see in great detail in the next two chapters, low-income people face innumerable inequities in and out of schools. These inequities regarding access to everything from adequately funded schools to playgrounds to prenatal care have nothing to do with poor people's cultures and everything to do with what Jonathan Kozol (1992) calls the "savage inequalities" of schools and society. We, as a society, give low-income youth less access to educational opportunity, healthcare, nutrition, and other goods, and then blame the outcomes of these inequities on their "culture of poverty."

It should come as little surprise, then, that studies consistently have shown that *there is no such thing as a culture of poverty*. In the 50 or so years since Lewis introduced the culture of poverty concept, social scientists have not been able to replicate his findings, and it's not for a lack of trying. They've attempted to identify the culture of poverty in a variety of contexts, from countries and cities to individual racial groups (see, for example, Billings, 1974; Carmon, 1985; Jones & Luo, 1999). In fact, several researchers have even reviewed the history of other people's attempts to locate the "culture of poverty," each coming to the same conclusion: Poor people do not share a predictable, consistent culture (Abell & Lyon, 1979; Rodman, 1977).

Nor does research support the broader "culture of poverty" notion that dysfunctionality abounds in poor communities (Baetan, 2004) any more, at least, than it abounds in wealthy communities or, for that matter, in every community. Sure, we can find in low-income communities individual people who are alcohol or drug addicts, who have a propensity for violence or associate with criminals, or who are inattentive parents or guardians. It might be easy, even with the best of intentions, to presume greater instances of these problems in poor communities than in wealthier communities, given the desperation people might feel because of the scarcity of living wage job opportunities and the weak social service infrastructures in many high-poverty neighborhoods. But the presumption would be wrong, more stereotype than insight. In fact, the presumption could reflect the *reverse* of reality, as is the case when it comes to alcoholism. We'll explore this curious reality in a moment. Suffice it to say for now that if it's equitable schools and classrooms we want, if it's places where students from any socioeconomic background will have opportunities to learn and grow to their fullest capabilities, studying a fictitious and stereotypical "culture of poverty" is not going to get us there.

I know what you're thinking: "Okay, then, what *will* get us there?" Fair question, and I promise we are making our way there as we step through the dimensions of Equity Literacy.

We should recognize first, though, that even if we reject the "culture of poverty" approach to understanding and educating low-income students, we still live in a society in which stereotypes about poor people abound. They are demonized in the media, demonized by politicians, and even demonized in some teacher lounges and school hallways. In fact, the stereotypes that make up the "culture of poverty" idea have become, in many ways, part of the "common sense" of achievement gap chatter: how low-income families are lazy, how they don't care about education, and so on.

These messages are all around us. But what of these messages, if anything, is true? How have so many of us bought into the "culture of poverty" mythology despite its nearly 5-decade repudiation?

## A HINT OF TRUTH?: THE NATURE OF CLASS STEREOTYPING

A longtime colleague of mine with a penchant for road rage—I'll call him Frederick—is fond of flinging the word *jerk* at drivers whose driving skills have offended him in some way. That is, he is fond of flinging the word at *male* drivers, or drivers he assumes to be men, and reserves it for them exclusively. When a driver he assumes to be a woman pulls in front of him, neglects to use a turn signal, or drives a few miles per hour under the speed limit, his response is different. Rather than calling her a jerk, he shakes his head, brow furled, and exclaims with exasperation, "Women drivers!"

I have challenged Frederick on what appears, to me, to be a clear case of gender stereotyping, of a biased view that looks a lot like sexism. He responds to my challenges firmly: "That's not a *stereotype*. It's my *experience*. Women are bad drivers." He tends to append to this defense the common refrain, "Plus, there's a hint of truth in stereotypes; otherwise, why would so many people believe them?"

As troubling as his attitude might be, Frederick is not alone in his view or in his tendency to see somebody within his gender group who has offended his sensibilities as an outlier, a *jerk*, while interpreting a female offender, somebody outside his gender group, as representing all women. A long history of psychosocial research details the human tendency to imagine our own social and cultural groups as diverse while we imagine "the other," people belonging to a social or cultural group with which we are less familiar, as being, for all intents and purposes, all the same (e.g., Meiser & Hewstone, 2004).

Cognitively speaking, our stereotyping has been shown to be a natural and necessary human response in the face of limited context-specific knowledge. A woman's stereotype about men might prove to be an overgeneralization in most instances, but her intuition eventually could protect her from sexual assault. However, the *content* of stereotypes is only partially organic, only partially based upon a measured consideration of the totality of our experiences. Stereotypes grow, as well, from how we're socialized (Shier, Jones, & Graham, 2010). They are the result of what we are *taught to think* about poor people, for instance, even if we are poor, through celebrations of "meritocracy" or by watching a parent lock the car doors when driving through certain parts of town. They grow, as well, from a desire to find self-meaning by distinguishing between social and cultural groups with which we do and do not identify (Hornsey, 2008). That's the heady science of it.

One of the keys to distinguishing between stereotyping as a cognitive process for everyday, nonexploitative decision-making (*Where might I find a water fountain in this building?*) and stereotyping as a threat to equity is in determining how much these mechanisms—socialization processes and the drive for group distinction—are in play in any given instance. This is because these mechanisms, in the way they reward a sort of selective evidence-gathering routine, are at the root of group-level biases (Nesdale & Flesser, 2001). In other words, we tend to require less evidence, *and less accurate evidence*, to convince us of the legitimacy of a stereotype about a group to which we do not belong than we require to convince us of a stereotype about a group to which we do belong. Social psychologists have referred to this phenomenon as *in-group bias* because it is based more generally on the tendency to see our social and identity groups more favorably overall than groups with which we do not associate (Gorman, 2005). Certainly Frederick has what he considers good evidence that women are bad drivers. But just as certainly, in order to extrapolate an experience or two into a generalization about all women, he has to suppress considerable amounts of counterevidence, such as the number of women drivers he never notices because they do not ignite his road rage. This suppression protects him because if he generalizes men the way he generalizes women, he also implicates himself.

We all participate in this sort of faulty generalizing in one way or another, usually unconsciously (Gorman, 2005). This is not always a bad thing in the sense that stereotypes can help us make decisions when gaps exist in our knowledge and experience, as when we're looking for a water fountain and know to look near a restroom. However, when we apply stereotypes to groups of people and their relative worth rather than to buildings and the consistency of their plumbing infrastructures, we run the risk of being biased and inequitable. In an interpersonal sense, the socialization behind our stereotypes encourages us to seek evidence to cement existing biases

(Jervis, 2006). We might take, for example, an instance of a low-income parent or guardian missing a scheduled meeting as evidence supporting our view that *those people* don't value education. Meanwhile, we often fail to note evidence that does not support these biases. Gorman (2005) explains, "People are more likely to notice and remember information that confirms an applicable stereotype than information that disconfirms it" (p. 704).

When I teach a class or deliver a workshop about poverty and schools, I often begin by asking participants to reflect on a question: *Why are poor people poor?* Answers vary. However, even when participants believe that societal inequities are responsible for a portion of or even most poverty, they almost always qualify their responses with a litany of stereotypes: Poor people are lazy. They don't care about education. They're alcoholics and drug abusers. They don't want to work; instead, they are addicted to the welfare system. Unfortunately, these are not outlier views. Most people in the United States believe that poor people are poor because of their own deficiencies rather than inequitable access to services and opportunities (Rank et al., 2003).

So what if I told you that some stereotypes commonly associated with poor people, such as a propensity for alcohol abuse, are *truer of wealthy people* than they are of poor people (Galea, Ahern, Tracy, & Vlahov, 2007; Humensky, 2010)? It's true. But how often do we, in the education world, apply this stereotype to wealthy people? How often do we hear, "No wonder so many rich kids don't do well at college; their parents are all alcoholics . . . "?

On the other hand, I might have 5, 10, or 20 low-income students who do not fit a particular stereotype about poor people, but if I have 2 or 3 who do fit it, those 2 or 3 can become, if I'm not aware of my biases, sufficient evidence to confirm my existing stereotype. As Jervis (2006) explains, "Given the complexity and ambiguity of our world, it is unfortunately true that beliefs for which a good deal of evidence can be mustered often turn out to be mistaken" (p. 643). If a low-income student regularly does not turn in homework, am I quicker to attribute it to her socioeconomic status than I would for a student in my own economic bracket?

Let's consider another school-based example. There are many common stereotypes about poor people in the United States that suggest that they are inattentive and, as a result, ineffective parents. Low-income parents or guardians who do not attend parent-teacher conferences can become targets of stereotyping—or worse, targets of blame—by those educators. According to Jervis (2006),

> Judgments . . . can be self-reinforcing as ambiguous evidence is taken not only to be consistent with preexisting beliefs, but to confirm them. Logically, the latter is the case only when the evidence both fits with the belief and does not fit

the competing ones. But people rarely probe the latter possibility as carefully as they should. (p. 651)

So whereas a more well-to-do parent or guardian might be pardoned for missing structured opportunities for family involvement—*she's traveling for work*—a low-income parent or guardian's lack of this sort of involvement might be interpreted as additional evidence of disinterest in her or his child's schooling (Patterson et al., 2008), regardless of whether or not it, too, is related to work.

In our efforts to become equity-literate educators, one of our first tasks is to understand our own socializations and the ways in which we have bought into stereotypes that might hinder our abilities to connect with low-income families, or any families, in the most authentic, open way. It's not easy. It takes an awful lot of humility to acknowledge that we harbor stereotypes. The fact that many of us have been trained as teachers and administrators with frameworks like the "culture of poverty" that *encourage* stereotyping does not help. One important step in this process, though, is to nudge ourselves to rethink some of the most common stereotypes about people in poverty and the extent to which we might have been fooled into believing them.

## MIS-PERCEIVERS ARE WE: COMMON STEREOTYPES ABOUT POOR FAMILIES AND EDUCATION

Poor people in the United States are stereotyped in innumerable ways (Williams, 2009). A vast majority of these stereotypes are just plain inaccurate. In fact, as I mentioned earlier, some are truer of wealthy people than poor people.

I decided several years ago to test a list of the stereotypes about people in poverty that are most common among my teacher education students against social science evidence (Gorski, 2008a), a process I revisited more recently in preparation for writing this book (Gorski, 2012). *Is there a hint of truth in every stereotype?* I wondered.

Here's what I found.

*Stereotype 1: Poor People Do Not Value Education.* The most popular measure of parental attitudes about education, particularly among teachers, is "family involvement" (Jeynes, 2011). This stands to reason, as research consistently confirms a correlation between family involvement and school achievement (Lee & Bowen, 2006; Oyserman, Brickman, & Rhodes, 2007). However, too often, our notions of family involvement are limited in scope, focused only on *in-school* involvement—the kind of involvement that requires parents and guardians to visit their children's schools or classrooms. While it is true that low-income parents and guardians are less likely to participate in this brand of involvement (National Center for Education Statistics, 2005), they engage in home-based involvement strategies, such as encouraging children to read and limiting television watching, *more frequently* than their wealthier counterparts (Lee & Bowen, 2006).

It might be easy, given the stereotype that low-income families do not value education, to associate low-income families' less consistent engagement in on-site, publicly visible, school involvement, such as parent-teacher conferences, with an ethic that devalues education. In fact, research has shown that many teachers assume that low-income families are completely uninvolved in their children's schooling (Patterson et al., 2008). However, in order to assume a direct relationship between disparities in on-site involvement and a disregard for the importance of school, we would have to omit considerable amounts of contrary evidence. First, low-income parents and guardians experience significant class-specific barriers to school involvement, some of which are depicted in Figure 4.1. These include consequences associated with the scarcity of living wage jobs, such as the ability to afford childcare or public transportation or the ability to afford to take time off from wage work (Bower & Griffin, 2011; Li, 2010). They also include the weight of low-income parents' and guardians' own school experiences, which in many cases were hostile and unwelcoming (Lee & Bowen, 2006). Although some schools and districts have responded to these challenges by providing on-site childcare, transportation, and other mitigations, the fact remains that, on average, this type of involvement is considerably less accessible to poor families than to wealthier ones.

Broadly speaking, there simply is no evidence, beyond differences in on-site involvement, that attitudes about the value of education in poor communities differ in any substantial way from those in wealthier communities. The evidence, in fact, suggests that attitudes about the value of education among families in poverty are identical to those among families in other socioeconomic strata. In other words, poor people, demonstrating impressive resilience, value education just as much as wealthy people (Compton-Lilly, 2000) *despite* the fact that they often experience schools as unwelcoming and inequitable.

For example:

- In a study of low-income urban families, Compton-Lilly (2000) found that parents overwhelmingly have high educational expectations for their children and expect their children's teachers to have equally high expectations for them, particularly in reading.

**Figure 4.1. Challenges to On-Site School Involvement for Low-Income Families**

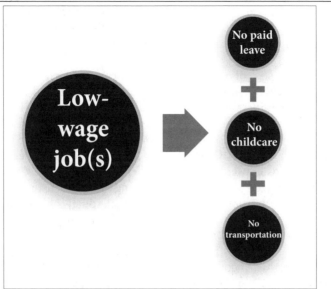

- In their study focusing on low-income African American parents, Cirecie West-Olatunji and her colleagues (2010) found that they regularly reached out to their children's schools and stressed the importance of education to their children.
- Similarly, Patricia Jennings (2004), in her study on how women on welfare respond to the "culture of poverty" stereotype, found that single mothers voraciously valued and sought out educational opportunities for themselves, both as a way to secure living wage work and as an opportunity to model the importance of school to their children.
- Based on their study of 234 low-income parents and guardians, Kathryn Drummond and Deborah Stipek (2004) found that they worked tirelessly to support their children's intellectual development.
- During an ethnographic study of a racially diverse group of low-income families, Guofang Li (2010) found that parents, including those who were not English-proficient, used a variety of strategies to bolster their children's literacy development.
- A recent study shows, in contrast to popular perception, that poor families invest just as much time as their wealthier counterparts exploring school options for their children (Grady, Bielick, & Aud, 2010).

- Finally, using data from the more than 20,000 families that participated in the Early Childhood Longitudinal Study, Carey Cooper and her colleagues (2010) found, quite simply, that "poor parents reported engaging their children in home-learning activities as often as non-poor parents" (p. 876).

As with any stereotype, the notion that people in poverty don't value education might have more to do with some well-intended misinterpretations of social realities than with *their* disinterest in school. For example, some low-income families, and particularly low-income immigrant families, may not be as informed as their wealthier counterparts about how educational systems in the United States work (Ceja, 2006; Lareau & Weininger, 2008), an obvious consequence of the alienation from school systems that many people in poverty experience, beginning during their time as students. It can be easy to interpret this lack of understanding, which is a symptom itself of educational inequities, as disinterest. Similarly, it can be easy to interpret lower levels of some types of school involvement, including types that are not scheduled or structured to be accessible to low-income families, as evidence that low-income parents simply don't care about school. But these interpretations, in the end, are based more on stereotype than reality. They are, for the most part, just plain wrong.

The challenge for us, then, is to do the difficult work of considering what we are apt to misinterpret, not simply as a fluffy attempt at "inclusion," but as a high-stakes matter of student success. After all, research also shows that when teachers perceive that a student's parents value education, they tend to assess that student's work more positively (Hill & Craft, 2003). Bias matters.

***Stereotype 2: Poor People Are Lazy.*** Another common stereotype about poor people, and particularly poor People of Color, is that they are lazy or have weak work ethics (Kelly, 2010). Unfortunately, despite its inaccuracy, the "laziness" image of people in poverty and the stigma attached to it has particularly devastating effects on the morale of poor communities (Cleaveland, 2008).

The truth is, there is no indication that poor people are lazier or have weaker work ethics than people from other socioeconomic groups (Wilson, 1996). To the contrary, all indications are that poor people work just as hard as, and perhaps harder than, people from higher socioeconomic brackets (Reamer et al., 2008). In fact, poor working adults work, on average, 2,500 hours per year, the rough equivalent of 1.2 full-time jobs (Waldron, Roberts, & Reamer, 2004), often patching together several part-time jobs in order to support their families. People living in poverty who are working part-time are more likely than people from other socioeconomic conditions to be doing so involuntarily, despite seeking full-time work (Kim, 1999).

This is an astounding display of resilience in light of the fact that low-income people are concentrated in the lowest-paying jobs with the most negligible opportunities for advancement, in jobs that require the most intense manual labor and offer the fewest benefits, such as paid sick leave (Kim, 1999). If you are thinking, *Well, then they should find better-paying jobs*, consider this: More than one out of five jobs in the United States pays at a rate that is below the poverty threshold (Waldron et al., 2004). And prospects are growing dimmer, as more and more new jobs pay a poverty-level or lower wage (Reamer et al., 2008). According to the National Employment Law Project (2011), following the growing unemployment rates over the last several years, the "recovery" brought back over a million jobs, but a disproportionate number of them were low-wage jobs, which accounted for 23% of job losses prior to 2010, but nearly half of newly available jobs as of 2011. Meanwhile, less than half of the jobs the Department of Labor predicts will be added to the U.S. economy by 2018 will pay enough to keep a two-worker, two-child family out of poverty (Wider Opportunities for Women, 2010).

*Stereotype 3: Poor People Are Substance Abusers.* As I mentioned earlier, low-income people in the United States are *less likely* to use or abuse alcohol than their wealthier counterparts (Galea et al., 2007; Keyes & Hasin, 2008; National Survey on Drug Use and Health, 2004). Interestingly, this pattern is consistent internationally. Around the world, alcohol use and addiction are associated positively with income; in other words, the higher somebody's income, the more likely he is to use alcohol or to be an alcoholic (Degenhardt et al., 2008).

Patterns of alcohol use among youth are a little less definitive. Some studies suggest that, as with the broader population, alcohol consumption and addiction are positively related to income. For example, in their study of two populations of high school students, one predominantly White and economically privileged and the other predominantly African American and low-income, Kevin Chen and his colleagues (2003) found significantly higher alcohol consumption in the former than the latter. Studies by the National Survey on Drug Use and Health (2004) and Monitoring the Future (2008) suggest that alcohol use among youth is equally distributed across socioeconomic strata. However, using data from the National Longitudinal Survey of Adolescent Health, Jennifer Humensky (2010) found that "Higher parental education is associated with higher rates of binge drinking, marijuana and cocaine use in early adulthood. Higher parental income is associated with higher rates of binge drinking and marijuana use" (p. 1).

What is certain is that alcohol use and addiction are less prevalent overall among low-income people than among their wealthier counterparts. This is particularly astounding, and an indication of tremendous resiliency among low-income communities, when we consider that alcohol abuse can be a side effect of discrimination and social deprivation, such as inequitable access to social services (Lee & Jeon, 2005).

Similarly, there is little evidence that low-income people are more likely than wealthier people to use illicit drugs. Drug use in the United States is distributed fairly evenly across income levels (Degenhardt et al., 2008; Saxe, Kadushin, Tighe, Rindskopf, & Beveridge 2001), regardless of age and other factors. Monitoring the Future (2008), for instance, found that socioeconomic status does not predict rates of drug use and abuse among youth.

It is true, of course, that alcohol and drug abuse exist in poor communities, just as they exist in wealthier communities. It also is true that substance abuse is a serious issue that has deleterious effects on youth regardless of their socioeconomic status. I certainly am not making the point that we should not attend to drug and alcohol use among low-income people or consider how it affects students' opportunities to achieve in school. We should. We also should realize that when these problems do exist in low-income families, they have the potential to be particularly devastating because people in poverty who are struggling with substance abuse generally do not have access to the sorts of recovery opportunities available to wealthier families. Nor do they have access to preventive medical attention that might catch and treat growing dependencies before they become full-fledged addictions. This is one of many reasons to advocate for universal health care as one way to ensure equitable educational opportunity.

What we must try *not* to do is falsely associate drug and alcohol use and addiction with a "culture of poverty" or think of it as yet another example of why poor people are poor.

***Stereotype 4: Poor People Are Linguistically Deficient and Poor Communicators.*** Mirroring attitudes in the broader society, many educators have been led to believe erroneously that poor people, like my grandma, are linguistically deficient (Collins, 1988; Miller, Cho, & Bracey, 2005). This is a particularly dangerous stereotype given the extent to which students' identities are associated with their languages (Gayles & Denerville, 2007; Grant, Oka, & Baker, 2009). Criticizing a person's language means criticizing her or his deepest self. It can lead students targeted in this way to feel disconnected from school (Christensen, 2008).

Fortunately, there is good reason *not* to criticize. When teachers assume that language is a marker of intelligence, the stereotype that people in poverty also are language-poor negatively affects their assessments of low-income students' performance (Grant et al., 2009). This stereotype is built upon two shaky assumptions: (1) that children in poverty do not enter school with the volume or type of vocabulary they need to succeed (and that this is a reflection of parent disinterest in education), and (2) that the use of particular variations of English reflects inferior language capabilities.

The idea that children from low-income families enter school linguistically deprived, with smaller or less complex vocabularies than their wealthier peers, and that this condition is a result of family "cultures" that devalue learning, has become part of the "common sense" of education reform. What you might not know is that the idea that low-income students are linguistically deficient is based largely on a single study of a few dozen economically diverse families in the Kansas City area (Hart & Risley, 1995), as described in great detail by Curt Dudley-Marling and Krista Lucas (2009) in their essay "Pathologizing the Language and Culture of Poor Children."

Studies have shown, indeed, that low-income and working class children begin school with less developed reading skills on average than their wealthier counterparts (Children's Defense Fund, 2008). This initial discrepancy can foreshadow lags in reading proficiency that can last throughout students' school lives (Duncan, Ludwig, & Magnuson, 2007). However, there is no evidence that this discrepancy in reading skills is connected to a language *use* deficiency or that it reflects parental disinterest in education. Similarly, based on their study involving a sample of 1,364 racially diverse public school children, Veronique Dupere and her colleagues (2010) concluded that reading score differences between low-income and wealthier students could be explained largely by discrepancies in the sorts of institutions to which they had access throughout early childhood. For example, poor and working class families, unlike many of their wealthier counterparts, rarely have access to high-quality early childhood education programs that support children's language learning in intensive, engaging ways (Kilburn & Karoly, 2008; Temple, Reynolds, & Arteaga, 2010).

The second shaky notion, that particular variations of English reflect superior or inferior language capabilities, incorrectly assumes the existence of "superior" and "inferior" language varieties (Miller et al., 2005). Linguists roundly reject this superior/inferior dichotomy. Some call it "standard language ideology" in reference to the presumptuous and familiar term "standard English" (Lippi-Green, 1994). According to Kathryn Woolard and Bambi Schieffelin (1994), "Moral indignation over nonstandard forms [of language] derives from ideological associations of the standard with the qualities valued within the culture, such as clarity or truthfulness" (p. 64). In fact, since at least the early 1970s linguists have bemoaned the ways in which students are taught to misunderstand the nature of language, including the false dichotomy of "correct/proper" and "incorrect/improper" language varieties (Baugh, 1983; Burling, 1973).

In linguistic reality, all variations of a language and all dialects, from what some people call "Black English Vernacular" (Gayles & Denerville, 2007) to the Appalachian English spoken by my grandma (Luhman, 1990), are highly structured, with their own sets of grammatical rules. These variations of English, like so-called "standard" English, are not indicators of low intelligence or deficient cultures. Instead, they are indicators of the regional, cultural, and social contexts in which somebody has learned to speak. Among linguists this is no revelation. More than 100 years of linguistic research points to the fact that all languages and language varieties are communicatively equal because they are, in their contexts, equally complex and coherent (see, for example, Boas, 1911; Chomsky, 1965; Labov, 1972; Newmeyer, 1985; Terry, Connor, Thomas-Tate, & Love, 2010). As James Collins (1988) explains, "languages are *systems*, of formidable and roughly equal complexity, whether classic 'world languages' or the speech of economically simple societies, whether prestige standards or stigmatized dialects" (p. 301).

Another common language stereotype is that children in poverty primarily speak with an "informal" register or style, as I might speak with my sister or a close friend, while their middle class and wealthier peers speak with a "formal" register, as I might speak during a job interview. However, like other forms of code-switching—the ways we modify behavior based on the context in which we find ourselves—*all people* use a broad range of language registers, regardless of the variety of language we speak (Brizuela, Andersen, & Stallings, 1999). The false association, for instance, of middle-Appalachian English with the informal register mistakes "formal" ways of speaking with what we call "standard" English.

To be clear, I do not mean to suggest that students, low-income or not, do not need to learn the varieties of English that will help them gain access to the fullest range of educational and vocational opportunities. I believe, in fact, that I, as an educator, have a responsibility to help all students develop a firm understanding of, and ability to use, what some people mistakenly call "standard" English. But I believe that I should do so without denigrating the language varieties spoken in students' homes and communities and without wrongly assuming that students' language varieties are indicators of their intelligence.

A related stereotype, and one that is featured prominently in the "culture of poverty" or "mind-set of poverty" model, is that low-income people are ineffective communicators. Ruby Payne has suggested, incorrectly, that people in poverty often fight with each other because they do not have the necessary verbal communication skills to resolve conflicts. "Words are not seen as being very effective in generational poverty to resolve differences; fists are," she wrote in her brief essay "Reflections on Katrina and the Role of Poverty in the Gulf Coast Crisis" (2006, ¶ 3).

Contrasting this stereotype, studies have shown that low-income people communicate with the same sophistication as their wealthier peers. For example, Mary Ohmer and her colleagues (2010) studied the communication strategies used by members of a low-income, predominantly African American community who had assembled to address a variety of neighborhood problems. They documented how people at these gatherings discussed and modeled complex communication techniques that could help them effectively address community challenges with their neighbors. They talked, for instance, about using language to de-escalate conflict, being conscious of their tone of voice, and approaching their neighbors in an inviting, non-hostile manner.

Their study reminded me of the time I spent as a child with my grandma's people in the mountains of Appalachian western Maryland, where I never heard so much as a raised voice nor saw a single person lay anything other than a friendly hand on anybody else. This doesn't mean, of course, that people in poverty never scream at each other, and it certainly doesn't mean that violence is not a problem in some low-income neighborhoods. It does mean that we risk the authenticity of our relationships with low-income students and their families when we assume that because they are low-income students and families, they must prefer shouting and fighting to peaceful and loving communication.

*Stereotype 5: Poor People Are Ineffective and Inattentive Parents.* In my experience, the bad parent stereotype is based largely on other false assumptions, like the ones we've already debunked: Poor parents don't value education, poor parents are substance abusers, and so on. It also is based on decontextualized considerations of other sorts of evidence. For instance, when I hear that children in poverty watch television and participate in other sedentary activities at higher rates than their wealthier peers, my initial reaction might be, *Aha! Further evidence that poor parents are inattentive to children's well-being.* In order to reach that conclusion, though, I would have to ignore the fact that low-income youth have considerably less access to a whole range of afterschool and extracurricular activities, as well as to recreational facilities, than their wealthier peers (MacLeod, Gee, Crawford, & Wang, 2008; Shann, 2001).

Researchers routinely have found that low-income parents and guardians are extremely attentive to their children's needs despite the many barriers they must overcome to provide for their families. This is no less true for poor single mothers, who often are the most scorned targets of the "bad parent" stereotype. We already established, for instance, that poor single mothers overwhelmingly claim a sense of responsibility for inspiring their children to pursue higher education. More broadly speaking, when Robert Hawkins (2010) used a variety of qualitative research techniques to examine how 20 formerly homeless single mothers used their social networks to improve their lives, he found that they prioritized the well-being of their children in virtually every decision they made. He also found that they were not shy about seeking the help they needed to provide a good life for their children, even when doing so made them vulnerable or uncomfortable.

In fact, following their longitudinal study of low-income families, a follow-up to Annette Lareau's (2000) now-famous study of how socioeconomic class affects children's home lives, she and Elliot Weininger (2008) unequivocally denounced the "bad parent" stereotype. They concluded that "working class and poor parents are no less deeply committed . . . to the well being of their children than are middle class parents" (p. 142).

## THE DANGERS OF STEREOTYPES AND STEREOTYPE THREAT

*Why*, you may be wondering, *are we spending so much time on stereotypes? Why are we focusing on all of this negativity rather than talking about what we can do to strengthen educational opportunities for all students?*

I hear you. And we are working our way toward some practical strategies, which will be discussed in great detail later in this book. However, there is no strategy for creating equitable and welcoming classrooms and schools that is more practical or immediate than this: We *must*, above all else, commit to losing the stereotypes that paint poor people as the problem. This might be the single most important thing any of us, as educators, can do in our commitments to equity and diversity. In the end, our understandings of poverty and our attitudes toward families in poverty play an enormous role, and perhaps the *most* enormous role, in how we see and treat low-income students (Robinson, 2007; Williams, 2009), not to mention the lengths to which we will or will not go to advocate for them and their educational rights.

The dangers of not doing so are plentiful. Stereotypes can make us unnecessarily afraid or accusatory of our students, including our most disenfranchised students, and their families. They can misguide us into expressing low expectations for poor youth and their families or blaming them for the very ways in which the barriers they face impede their abilities to engage with schools the way some of us might engage with schools.

Complicating matters, according to Claude Steele (2010), an expert on stereotyping and its dangers, people who are stereotyped are attuned to the ways in which they are stereotyped. As a result, the *accuracy* of a stereotype about people in poverty might be irrelevant to the *toll* the stereotype exacts on low-income students. He explains:

> This means that whenever we're in a situation where a bad stereotype could be applied to us—such as those about being old, poor, rich, or female—we know it. We know what "people could think." We know that anything we do that fits the stereotype could be taken as confirming it. And we know that, for that reason, we could be judged and treated accordingly. (p. 5)

The weight of this "knowing," of imagining the very *possibility* that somebody might target them with a stereotype, can affect students' school performance and emotional well-being, as research on stereotype susceptibility and stereotype threat has demonstrated (McKown & Weinstein, 2003; Steele, 2010). Stereotype threat, according to Bettina Spencer and Emanuele Castano (2007), occurs when people who share a particular identity such as race or socioeconomic status perform below their potential on an assigned task due to fear that their performance will confirm negative stereotypes people already have about them. The stereotype threat hypothesis might sound like a far-fetched idea, particularly for those of us who never have been consistent targets of bias. We might wonder how stereotypes can have such an immediate and measureable effect on students. But stereotype threat is real, as evidenced by a robust and constantly growing collection of studies demonstrating its effects (Steele, 2010). Most of the researchers studying stereotype threat have focused on its impact on students of color and young women. However, stereotype threat also affects low-income students. For example, when informed that their socioeconomic status is relevant to a task they are being asked to complete, such as by being told before a test that students in poverty do not do as well on it as wealthier students, low-income students perform worse than they do when nobody names the disparity (Spencer & Castano, 2007).

So our understandings of and attitudes about people in poverty, even if we don't believe we are applying them to individual students, have an effect on low-income students' school performance. Like I said earlier, stereotypes and biases matter. They matter in an extremely practical and immediate way. And no amount of resources or pedagogical strategies will help us provide the best opportunity for low-income students to reach their full potential as learners if we do not attend first to the stereotypes, biases, and assumptions we have about them and their families. Our first practical task, then, is to identify, then work on expunging, what we thought we knew about poor people if what we thought we knew paints families in poverty with broad, negative, stereotype-ridden strokes.

## CONCLUSION

If we can expunge that negativity, we position ourselves well to do a better job recognizing and building on the strengths and resiliencies of poor and working class students and families. When we let go of the "culture of poverty" stereotypes, we position ourselves to see more clearly the barriers faced by low-income families in their pursuit of educational equity. It's a difficult but critical shift, but one at which, in my experience, teachers and other school workers are especially adept, given our propensities for seeing the gifts and strengths in every student. If we're willing to make that shift, and start to see educational disparities in light of bigger contextual factors rather than seeking their sources in the cultures of economically disadvantaged students, we can begin to relate to our students in new, deeper ways.

We turn, in the next two chapters, to exploring those bigger contextual factors. First, in Chapter 5, I present the sorts of inequities faced by students in poverty outside of school and how those inequities relate to school readiness and performance. Then, in Chapter 6, I explore all the ways in which schools, as presently structured, compound those inequities.

## NOTE

Parts of this chapter were adapted from my article, "Perceiving the Problem of Poverty and Schooling," which appeared in *Equity & Excellence in Education, 45*(2), 2012, pages 302–319.

# CHAPTER 5

# Class Inequities Beyond School Walls and Why They Matter at School

Principles of Equity Literacy discussed in this chapter include:

Principle 5: We cannot understand the relationship between poverty and education without understanding biases and inequities experienced by people in poverty.

Principle 7: Class disparities in education are the result of inequities, not the result of cultures.

I started Kindergarten in 1976, a decade before personal computers were en vogue for families that could afford them, 2 decades before most people had heard of the World Wide Web. The image of largesse imprinted in my mind from my elementary school years is the 64-count box of Crayola crayons, the one with the built-in sharpener. I didn't have precise language for it at the time, but I knew that box was a symbol of privilege in my elementary school in the same way I knew that Air Jordan basketball shoes and Starter jackets signified economic might in my middle and high schools.

I also remember when poster board was a hot commodity, how some students would tremble when teachers assigned projects requiring its use. I recall the faces of classmates like Melissa, Jake, and Russell, who were shamed into "outing" themselves as "poor" when the teacher asked, *Who needs help getting poster board?* The teachers I most admired, and this was *most of my teachers*, were subtler, collecting everybody's crayons at the beginning of the school year and dumping them into community-owned bins or keeping a stash of poster board tucked behind a filing cabinet, distributing it discreetly to students whose families, as best they knew, could not afford it. My own working class family fell somewhere in between. We could afford poster board, the occasional Hong Kong Phooey spiral notebook, or a pack of National Football League pencils, but I settled for the 16-count box of Crayola crayons.

Today I can, if I choose, order 100 sheets of poster board from Amazon. com—10 sheets each in 10 vibrant colors—for $31.03 with shipping and handling. That's 31 cents per sheet. I don't know, all these years later, how much we paid for the poster board back in the mid- to late 1970s. A dollar, maybe? Seventy-nine cents?

My point is this: Even when the hot commodity was poster board, Russell, Melissa, Jake, and other students who had no say in the financial conditions of their families and no control over the affordability of school supplies were at a disadvantage. So too were the students who couldn't afford poster board and who, to an even greater degree, couldn't afford the stigma that marks students when, from their earliest school experiences, they are asked by adults to perform their disadvantage by publicly acknowledging their inability to afford poster board. That's when poster board was the commodity. Now it's computers. And high-speed Internet access. And software. And a printer.

During a recent visit to a high-poverty middle school, I had an opportunity to speak with a group of about 40 8th-grade students. I had worked with their teachers, an energetic and committed team, earlier in the day. I asked the students how many of them had a functioning computer and Internet access at home. Only a few raised their hands. I then asked how many had been assigned homework requiring the use of computers and the Internet since the last grading period ended. All of them raised their hands.

Today I can, if I choose, buy a computer from Amazon.com for $1,040.79, the average cost of the site's five best-selling desktops. These computers do not come with Internet access or a printer and include only the most rudimentary software, making them the rough equivalents of one of those boxes of 16 crayons without the sharpener in the back. Despite these limitations, the $1,040.79 price tag amounts to approximately 3,354 sheets of poster board. And unlike poster board, which our teachers might have required of us once or twice a year when I was in elementary school, many students today, including the Melissas and Jakes and Russells, are expected to have access to computers and the Internet and software and a printer on a regular, if not daily, basis.

It can be difficult, as somebody who *does have* home access to these commodities, and who, like me, has come to take these resources for granted, to remember that many poor and working class families simply cannot afford them. In fact, some families, particularly those who live in the most rural communities, might not even have access to the necessary technological infrastructure for high-speed Internet access. Others might own a computer, but cannot afford to repair it when it breaks down or purchase up-to-date software.

Regardless of the particulars, if we truly want to understand the lives of all of our students, we must remember that low-income youth simply do not have access to the sorts of resources and experiences that their wealthier peers, on average, enjoy. We must remember, too, that their lack of access to these resources and experiences is not an indicator of their attitudes about education, their levels of intelligence, or their potentials as learners and citizens, and it has nothing to do with their cultures. Rather, these disparities mark logical, if unjust, outcomes of a society in which access begets access and opportunity begets opportunity, so that advantage and disadvantage compound themselves into ever-widening disparities in access and opportunity (Noguera, 2011).

Of course, many of these disparities fall outside of what traditionally has been considered the purview of public schools. As I mentioned in Chapter 1, I do not believe that it is the responsibility of each individual educator to dedicate their lives to the elimination of global poverty or economic injustice; rather, it is our foremost responsibility to commit to addressing the effects of these disparities in our own teaching, in our own spheres of influence, and, when manageable, to grow our spheres of influence so that, perhaps, we can help take on some of the underlying issues. However, even modest attempts to quell class disparities in my own classroom are destined to fail if I do not understand how they came to be. I am destined to fail if I don't acknowledge how, in Worpole's (2000) words, "disadvantaged communities often get penalized twice. Not only do they have to live with fewer economic resources, they . . . almost always live in environments which exact an additional toll on their well-being" (p. 9).

In order to illustrate this point, I describe in this chapter many of the resources and experiences commonly accessible to middle class and more economically advantaged families and youth, but often unavailable to working class and poor families and youth. I focus here on out-of-school types of resources before turning, in the next chapter, to school or educational access.

## THE UN-LEVEL PLAYING FIELD OF POVERTY

Obviously, working class and poor youth do not have the same level of economic support as their wealthier peers. This also means that they do not enjoy the same sorts of options as their wealthier peers enjoy because, as Herbert Gans (1995) explained in *The War Against the Poor*, having options is a symptom of wealth. As a result, their access to a wide range of resources and experiences is limited, not, as the stereotypes go, because they *choose* not to pursue them or because they are *too lazy* to pursue them, but because they simply cannot *afford* them. I have divided these resources and experiences into seven imperfect and overlapping categories:

1. access to healthcare;
2. access to healthy living and working environments;
3. access to recreation options;
4. access to community and social services;
5. access to quality childcare;
6. access to cognitive enrichment resources; and
7. access to a validating society.

## Access to Healthcare

Obviously, access to healthcare and opportunities to interact with physicians greatly influence families' health and mortality (Cutler & Lleras-Muney, 2010). Our health depends on our access to healthcare and, as a result, on the affordability of that healthcare. Unfortunately low-income families are less likely than their wealthier counterparts to be able to afford consistent access to healthcare professionals (Koenig, 2007). As a result, in addition to being less likely to receive care when they become sick or injured, poor and working class people have less access to regular checkups and preventive health screenings (Pampel et al., 2010), putting them at higher risk of developing more serious ailments from undiagnosed health problems. So, for instance, what appear in some students to be reading troubles or learning disabilities might simply be undiagnosed vision problems, easily remedied by corrective eyewear (Gould & Gould, 2003).

Disparities in access to health insurance, as summarized in Figure 5.1, account for part of this fissure. According to the Children's Defense Fund (2008), one in five poor children do not have health insurance, a rate double that of their non-poor peers. Unfortunately, although closing or eliminating the gap in access to health insurance might alleviate these discrepancies to some extent, other complexities are in play. For example, simply having health insurance does not guarantee one's ability to afford a co-pay or to secure transportation to a clinic. Nor does it make up for lost wages if somebody who has a job without paid leave must take time off of work in order to visit, or take their children to visit, a doctor. Imagine, if you haven't experienced it, having to choose between keeping the heat turned on or visiting the doctor because you cannot afford to do both.

The implications of these disparities are plenty, and they take hold even before low-income children are born. For instance, economically disadvantaged children are more likely than their peers to have been born prematurely

## Figure 5.1. Uninsured Rate by Family Income, 2010

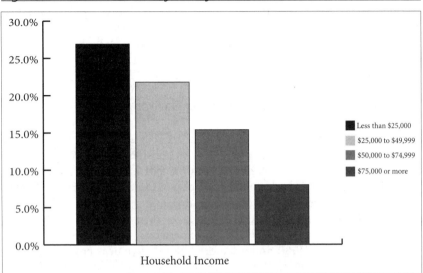

Data from Carmen Denavas-Walt, Bernadette D. Proctor, and Jessica C. Smith (2011), *Income, Poverty, and Health Insurance Coverage in the United States: 2010.*

and with lower than normal birth weights (Temple et al., 2010; Wadsworth et al., 2008), largely due to their mothers' lack of access to prenatal care. As a result, they are born with increased respiratory health risks, a condition exacerbated by their disproportionate exposure to environmental hazards and poor-quality housing (Davis, Gordon, & Burns, 2011). The unfortunate outcome of these disparities is that working class and poor children suffer from asthma and respiratory infections at higher rates than their wealthier peers (Bloom et al., 2006; Simoes, 2003), cutting into school attendance and focus, a phenomenon with which anyone who has worked in a high-poverty classroom is probably well familiar.

Lack of access to healthcare affects low-income families' mental and emotional health as well. As Kimberly Fulda and her colleagues (2009) found, based on their analysis of data from 40,000 participants, low-income youth are significantly more likely than their peers to have unmet mental health challenges such as depression or anxiety, also putting them at risk of missing school and having trouble concentrating at school. Their finding is especially troubling in light of research demonstrating causal links between stress related to stigma and isolation commonly experienced by people in poverty and a wide range of other health concerns (Lantz, House, Mero, & Williams, 2005). In fact, studies have shown that children in poverty experience increased levels of chronic stress, affecting other spheres of their emotional and physical health (Almeida, Neupert, Banks, & Serido, 2005; Wadsworth et al., 2008). For example, poverty is related to an increased threat of depression (Najman et al., 2010; Vericker, Macomber, & Golden, 2010), particularly among children and teenagers (Denny, Clark, Fleming, & Wall, 2004; Hammack, Robinson, Crawford, & Li, 2004).

## Access to Healthy Living and Working Environments

These disparities in healthcare access are exacerbated by the fact that people in poverty contend, on average, with considerably more health risks than people with greater economic security. For example, they are more likely to live in poorly built and structurally unsafe housing (Evans, 2004), putting them at greater risk of unintended injury, as Leanne Whiteside-Mansell and her colleagues (2010) found in their study of families with children in Head Start programs. They experience greater exposure to lead poisoning (Crooks, 1995) and are more likely to live near environmentally hazardous sites, largely because toxic waste dumps and production and storage facilities for hazardous materials are disproportionately located near poor neighborhoods (Walker, Mitchell, Fairburn, & Smith, 2005), increasing their exposure to toxic levels of radon and carbon monoxide. Overall air and water quality in poor neighborhoods is lower than in areas where wealth is more concentrated (National Commission on Teaching and America's Future, 2004).

Making matters worse, poor people are more likely than their wealthier counterparts to have jobs in which they are exposed to hazardous materials (Pampel et al., 2010). However, as Glorian Sorenson and her colleagues (2004) found, they are less likely to have benefit packages that reward or encourage healthy behaviors. They also are at higher risk of work-related injuries, concentrated, as they are, in jobs requiring dangerous forms of manual labor (Villenas, 2001). Milbourne (2010) found that these sorts of conditions, despite targeting poor people, often embolden stereotypes against them, which, in turn, can contribute to feelings of disempowerment in low-income students and their families.

Poor and working class families also, as stands to reason, are more likely to suffer from nutritional deficits, hunger, and food insecurity (Coles, 2008; Siefert, Heflin, & Corcoran, 2004), conditions that affect students' reading and math performance (Jyoti, Frongillo, & Jones, 2005). Eating healthily, such as by consuming organic foods, lean meats, and fresh vegetables, is cost-prohibitive for many low-income families and, increasingly, a challenge for middle class families as well (Cutler & Lleras-Muney, 2010). Foods more readily available and affordable to families in high-poverty neighborhoods tend to be highly processed with refined grains and large amounts of sugars and fats (Drewnowski, 2004). This is due, in part, to the absence of larger grocery stores in poor communities, which often means that low-income families have to purchase groceries at convenience stores, which, in turn, means they pay more for their groceries than those of us who have access to Trader Joe's or Costco. DeNeen Brown (2009), who studied this problem in the Washington, DC, metro area, explained,

> You don't have a car to get to a supermarket, much less to Costco or Trader Joe's, where the middle class goes to save money. You don't have three hours to take the bus. So you buy groceries at the corner store, where a gallon of milk costs an extra dollar. . . . A loaf of bread there costs you $2.99 for white. For wheat, it's $3.79. The clerk behind the counter tells you the gallon of leaking milk in the bottom of the back cooler is $4.99. She holds up four fingers to clarify. The milk is beneath the shelf that holds beef bologna for $3.79. A pound of butter sells for $4.49. In the back of the store are fruits and vegetables. The green peppers are shriveled, the bananas are more brown than yellow, the oranges are picked over. (pp. 7, 8)

Meanwhile, fast food restaurants and liquor stores disproportionately are located in poor neighborhoods, where those grocery stores with large selections of healthy foods are scarce (Pampel et al., 2010), inhibiting low-income families from investing in nutritional diets. Poor communities are subject, as well, to a disproportionate amount of advertisements for fast food (Boggs, 2007). Due, in large part, to these disparities, working class and poor people struggle with obesity at higher rates than wealthier people (Scharoun-Lee, Kaufman, Popkin, & Gordon-Larsen, 2009; Wells, Evans, Beavis, & Ong, 2010). This, in turn, contributes to an increased risk for a variety of health problems, from heart conditions to diabetes. In fact, in their 2010 study, Sharon Saydah and Kimberly Lochner found that living in poverty is "associated with a twofold higher mortality rate [from diabetes] . . . compared with adults with the highest family incomes" (p. 377).

Intensifying these threats to wellness, low-income families are more exposed to advertisements promoting other unhealthy habits, such as smoking, than wealthier families (Pampel et al., 2010). However, due, in part, to their lack of regular access to healthcare, they experience significantly *less* exposure to warnings about the effects of smoking, poor diet, and a lack of exercise (Siapush, McNeil, Hammond, & Fong, 2006). And even when they are aware of the severity of these risks, they are more likely than their wealthier counterparts to be unable to afford not only healthier food options, but also tobacco cessation aids or memberships to organized weight-loss programs or exercise clubs (Cutler & Lleras-Muney, 2010).

The working class child who comes to school overweight: Would you tend to interpret this as irresponsible parenting or an unfortunate effect of limited options? It is important to remember, as Fred Pampel and his colleagues (2010) point out, that what somebody with more economic stability might interpret as unhealthy choices among healthier options—*Why do they stay in that neighborhood if it's so unhealthy? Why do they send potato chips as a snack rather than fresh fruit?*—are less markers of bad decision-making than of disparities in access to healthier options.

## Access to Recreation Options

Exacerbating health risks associated with poverty, working class and poor families have less access than their wealthier counterparts to physically enriching activities (Brann-Barrett, 2010; Swartz, 2008). As I mentioned earlier, they often cannot afford to pay for access to organized sports leagues or to the equipment necessary to participate in them. Poor youth sometimes struggle to find time for recreational activities; they are more likely than their wealthier peers to need to work to help support their families and to be charged with caring for younger siblings while their parents or guardians are working. Meanwhile, they are less likely to live near playgrounds or other recreational areas. Unfortunately, according to a recent study (Macpherson, Jones, Rothman, Macarthur, & Howard, 2010), parks and recreation centers that are located in low-income communities are more likely than those in wealthier areas to be in disrepair, putting poor youth at greater risk of injury while using them.

Tanya Brann-Barrett (2010), reflecting on her study of low-income youths' responses to these sorts of conditions in their neighborhoods, explains,

> What was painful for many was that they remembered when the parks and playground in their neighborhoods were cared for and functioned as places to play and have fun. The now neglected basketball courts with no nets and defunct playgrounds with rusted remnants of equipment are perceived as a visual reminder of how it used to be. These physical illustrations are read by participants as an indication that their communities are forgotten. (p. 11)

Making these realities all the more devastating, schools in lower-income communities increasingly are cutting recess and physical education programs. (More on this in the next chapter.)

## Access to Community and Social Services

According to a study by the National Commission on Teaching and America's Future (NCTAF, 2004), low-income neighborhoods have, on average, lower-quality municipal and social services than wealthier neighborhoods. Even the most basic services—water, electricity, or roads, for instance—are more poorly run in high-poverty communities than in wealthier communities. Public spending on these sorts of services is considerably lower in high-poverty communities than in low-poverty communities, according to the NCTAF. This can be especially true in poor rural communities, where populations are sparser and, as a result, they receive relatively little funding to update and maintain services.

Although these disparities are well documented with regard to a wide range of services, one in which we, as educators, might be particularly interested is the class-tinged disparity in access to libraries. Literacy scholars long have bemoaned the fact that low-income children have access to fewer books than their wealthier peers, whether at home or in their communities (Krashen, 2004). After all, access to books is related directly to reading proficiency (Lindsay, 2010). The good news is, in a recent multinational study, Stephen Krashen and his colleagues (2010) found that public libraries can play a mitigating role in this disparity, offering children access to a wide variety of texts and media as well as computers and the Internet, at least during the school year. Unfortunately, poor and working class families have less access than wealthier families to libraries, which are less likely to be located in poor neighborhoods. When libraries *are* located nearby, they tend to have shorter hours and fewer resources than libraries in wealthier communities.

## Access to Quality Childcare

Childcare programs vary widely. Some offer organized educational experiences for children, while others are group babysitting services, more or less. Those that do prioritize learning and are staffed by certified preschool or early childhood educators sometimes are referred to as "high-quality" programs. These programs, which usually are thriving in wealthier communities, are scarce, if they exist at all, in most poor communities (Burchinal, Nelson, Carlson, & Brooks-Gunn, 2008). Even when high-quality childcare programs exist in close enough proximity to poor communities (where people are more likely than their wealthier peers to not own a functioning automobile) to be *physically* accessible to low-income families, they generally are *financially* inaccessible, even to most working class families. In fact, Eric Freeman (2010), who calculated the average cost of high-quality childcare for children 13 months to 3 years old, found that they cost about $7,800 annually, as much as tuition at some colleges and universities.

Based on their study of 1,364 racially and economically diverse families, Veronique Dupere (2010) and her colleagues concluded that children raised in advantaged neighborhoods appear to receive higher quality child care . . . even when family characteristics, such as the quality of the home environment, are held constant. In turn, access to advantaged institutions may explain why children in comparatively advantaged neighborhoods tended to have higher vocabulary and reading scores than their peers in less advantaged neighborhoods. (p. 1241)

Notice, again, that this disparity cannot be understood as a marker of desire or commitment or parenting effectiveness. It only can be understood as a marker of *access* and *opportunity*. Unfortunately, conversations about school readiness and class-related gaps in students' vocabularies entering school rarely, at least in my experience, take into account the fact that the gaps are attributable largely to the quality of institutions, such as childcare programs, to which low-income families have access. As a result, disparities are attributed to low-income families' parental practices or assumed lack of enthusiasm about learning, further alienating the families that are attempting to overcome these disparities.

## Access to Cognitive Enrichment Resources

I struggled with what to call this kind of access, largely because the "common sense" about young people's access to "cognitive enrichment" resources sometimes lacks a satisfying level of complexity. People in all socioeconomic conditions have access to a variety of opportunities for cognitive enrichment. For example, from a young age I developed an ear for the poetic beauty of language listening to my grandma tell stories about her childhood in Appalachia; today I am a published creative writer. I had early opportunities to practice deconstructing complex social conditions hearing her talk about why she pursued a nursing degree the year she turned 50, an experience that continues to inspire my equity work in and out of schools. Of course, some forms of enrichment, including these, do not necessarily align with the kind of enrichment most valued in traditional school settings, where mastery of the mechanics of writing, reading, and math are rewarded more than creative prowess or critical thinking.

What is undoubtedly true, though, is that working class and poor people have less access than their wealthier peers to the sorts of cognitive enrichment opportunities that reflect the notions of cognitive ability most rewarded in today's public schools. This is especially true for the kinds of experiences that require access to financial resources. It stands to reason, then, that low-income youth perform below national averages on standardized measures of cognitive development, and that this chasm persists throughout their school years (Gottfried, Gottfried, Bathurst, Guerin, & Parramore, 2003). After all, poor and working class families often cannot afford to participate in out-of-school academic training or tutoring, music lessons, athletics, or other extra-curricular activities (Avery, Fairbanks, & Zeckhauser, 2003; Bracey, 2006), whether because the activities themselves are too expensive or because they do not have access to adequate amounts of time or to dependable sources of transportation. What makes this disparity in access especially frustrating is that participation in all of these activities has been correlated with higher levels of academic achievement and lower rates of truancy.

Low-income youth also are less exposed to reading than their wealthier peers for similarly complex reasons. In fact, Richard Coley (2002) found that only 36% of low-income parents with children in Kindergarten read to their children each day compared with 62% of wealthy parents. According to a report from the Children's Defense Fund (2008), poor youth are three times as likely as non-poor youth not to have a parent read to them. Additionally, they are less likely to be able to identify the letters of the alphabet or spell their names. Poor youth have fewer books at home and receive less help on their homework, on average, than their wealthier peers (Kumanyika & Grier, 2006).

It could be easy, given these conditions, to assume that poor parents and guardians simply do not care as much about their children's literacy development as their wealthier peers. You might be thinking: *Why not make time to read to your child?* But again, in order to understand these conditions, it is helpful to consider *why* they exist.

For example, one privilege associated with wealth is *time*. Low-income parents and guardians are more likely than their wealthier peers to work multiple jobs and to work into the evening, a symptom of the scarcity of living wage work in most lower-income communities (Flessa, 2007; Rank et al., 2003). They are less likely, of course, to be able to afford "help" with house cleaning, lawn maintenance, and home repairs, which could give them more leisure time to read with their children. They are less likely, as well, to have been surrounded with books when they were kids. Meanwhile, they are more likely to have experienced challenges with their own literacy. A growing percentage of poor people in the United States are immigrants for whom English is a second or third or fourth language; they likely are in the process of learning English—research shows that immigrants to the United States today are learning English faster than any previous generation of immigrants—but may not have the fluency needed to read to their children in English. Remember, too, that, as we learned in Chapter 4, research has shown that, despite popular belief, low-income parents and guardians do find ways to bolster the literacy skills of their children, even if they do not have access to books, and even when, as is the case for some immigrants, they are not yet proficient in English (Li, 2010).

In addition to having less access to reading materials, youth in poverty have less access to computers and the Internet at home and in their communities than their wealthier peers (Evans, 2004; Thomas, 2008). Economically disadvantaged children, and particularly those of color (another example of the race-class intersection), are more likely than their wealthier (and Whiter) counterparts to grow up in households without a computer or Internet access (Judge, Puckett, & Cabuk, 2004). Studies have shown, as well, that the newest and most efficient technologies, like high-speed Internet access, reach poor people, and particularly rural poor people, last, even if they desire access to these resources (Clark & Gorski, 2002; Gorski, 2009). These conditions limit many young people's access to a slew of learning resources, such as online or computer-based educational games and other interactive media that also could strengthen their fine motor skills.

And when poor people do have access to these technologies, they tend to use them in less sophisticated ways (Evans, 2004)—this, again, is a symptom, not of lower cognitive potential, but of less access. Not having grown up immersed in the digital world like many of their wealthier peers, whom Marc Prensky (2010) calls "digital natives," poor youth might resemble, like those of us who are scrambling to figure out these technologies, "digital immigrants," lacking the skills, familiarity, and, at times, confidence needed to build and construct and interact with digital platforms. It doesn't help, of course, that low-income families generally cannot afford the growing variety of children's technology camps and programs that could help mitigate these gaps.

## Access to a Validating Society

If bearing the brunt of these deprivations—*opportunity* deprivations, I mean—is not enough, low-income youth also must weather a fairly constant storm of bias and bigotry (Lantz et al., 2005). Often this bias and bigotry carry with them an underlying message that *they* are to blame for the very inequities that repress them. For example, we have seen in recent years a growing tide of attention to bullying and its implications for the bullied in and out of schools. But how much of that attention has gone to class-based bullying, which, according to over a decade of research, is just as prevalent as any other form of bullying (Due, Holstein, & Jorgensen, 1999; Due, Lynch, Holstein, & Modvig, 2003; Nordhagen, Nielsen, Stigum, & Kohler, 2005; von Rueden et al., 2006)? Interestingly, a rise in "classed" bullying has been tracked, not only in the United States, but also in Canada and Europe (Due et al., 2009). Low-income youth are more susceptible than their wealthier peers to other forms of class-based harassment, as well (McLaughlin et al., 2008), such as police harassment or unprovoked suspicious treatment by store clerks.

Certainly working class and poor people have little, if any, access to positive reflections of themselves in the mainstream media (Comber, Nixon, Ashmore, Loo, & Cook, 2006). Most often, they are portrayed, if they are portrayed at all, as intellectually deficient or morally deviant (de Goede, 1996; Kelly, 2010), as in "reality" shows like *Cops* or "talk" shows like *Jerry Springer*. Heather Bullock and her colleagues (2001) found that stories featuring poor people and their concerns are rare on national newscasts. When poor people were featured, the stories were most likely to run during daytime interview or reality shows or police live-action programs and to portray their subjects as dysfunctional, promiscuous addicts. Similarly, based on analyses of media coverage of welfare reform, Marieke de Goede (1996) found that poor people overwhelmingly were associated with laziness, amorality, criminality, and irresponsibility. Nearly 15 years later, Maura Kelly (2010), studying television news portrayals of women in poverty, found the exact same thing.

## WHY THE "ACHIEVEMENT GAP" IS REALLY AN *OPPORTUNITY* GAP

Healthcare, safe recreational facilities, supermarkets, Internet access: Which of these resources, if any, do you take for granted? How might your life be different without them? How might they have affected your ability to achieve to your fullest potential in school?

I have come to think of these disparities in terms of a metaphorical toolbox. All people, regardless of their families' economic conditions, begin gathering tools literally from the moment of conception. Some are material, such as access to financial support or the Internet. Some are service-oriented, like access to prenatal care or a speech pathologist. Others are experiential, such as access to the arts, or educational, like access to tutors or preschool. Still others, such as resilience or a feeling of interconnectedness, are dispositional, relating to what somebody has learned from family and community.

Those dispositional tools are important. They equip us with the attitudes and understandings that will help us thrive in an often-limiting world. Consider, for example, how important it is for students to value education. Despite popular belief, research for decades has shown that poor families value education as much as their wealthier counterparts, which is quite remarkable given that poor families do not have the same access to education as those counterparts. This valuing goes a long way in keeping many low-income students in school, persisting through all of the other disparities they face.

The trouble is, even if a low-income student has all of the "right" dispositions, those dispositions will not make these other disparities disappear. A positive attitude about schooling is not enough to overcome disadvantages faced disproportionately by low-income youth in access to health care, quality childcare, or healthy food options. This is why, as far as I can tell, the thing we tend to call an "achievement gap" ought to be understood, first and foremost, as an *opportunity* gap. After all, these disparities have nothing to do with student effort or intelligence or families' attitudes about school. They only reflect low-income students' levels of access to the kinds of opportunities that other students, no smarter or more dedicated to school than they are, enjoy.

## CONCLUSION

So when we hear the common refrain that poor students enter school already behind their wealthier peers in reading, say, or cognitive functioning more generally, we need to understand that this discrepancy reflects, not some inherent flaw in low-income families, but a lack of access to a lifetime's worth of opportunities afforded to other kids (Crosnoe & Cooper, 2010). If I really want to understand my students in poverty, I have to understand this key aspect of their experience: not only do they not have access to computers and the Internet, but they carry the weight of shame for not having that access in a society that equates technologies with social evolution.

Next, in Chapter 6, I describe the various dimensions of the opportunity gap in schools and how the inequities we explored in this chapter are reproduced almost exactly within school walls. Equipped with that knowledge, we move, in Chapters 7, 8, and 9, into strategy mode, considering how we might respond to these inequities.

# CHAPTER 6

# The Achievement—er, *Opportunity—* Gap in School

Principles of Equity Literacy discussed in this chapter include:

Principle 1: The right to equitable educational opportunity is universal.

Principle 5: We cannot understand the relationship between poverty and education without understanding biases and inequities experienced by people in poverty.

Principle 6: Test scores are inadequate measures of equity.

Principle 10: The inalienable right to equitable educational opportunity includes the right to high expectations, higher-order pedagogies, and engaging curricula.

One reason multiple-choice standardized tests don't work particularly well for assessing the aptitudes of students, besides the fact that it doesn't make sense to assess people the same way we assess widgets, is that the tests don't measure what we think they measure (Toch, 2011). More than one's ability or aptitude or potential as a learner, they measure the *opportunity* and *access* test-takers have enjoyed in their lives up to the point of taking their tests. A considerable portion of the opportunity has to do with students' out-of-school access to the sorts of resources and experience described in Chapter 5. How many academic enrichment camps could their families afford? How many books? Did their parents or guardians enjoy ample leisure time to read to them or help with their homework, or were they working evening hours at a second or third job, a result of the scarcity of living wage work?

Another portion of the opportunity gap has to do with educational access, or differences between school and school-related experiences available to families in different economic situations. As Pedro Noguera and Antwi Akom (2000) explained in their article, "Disparities Demystified," "An analysis of test scores . . . reveals a close correspondence between the scores children obtain and broader patterns of social inequality. With few exceptions, children of the affluent outperform children of the poor" (p. 29). I think we do a pretty good job acknowledging their second sentence. It's the message in their first sentence that seems so infrequently acknowledged.

Complicating attempts to understand these sorts of access inequities is the popularly held notion I discussed briefly in Chapter 1: that education is the "great equalizer" and that public schooling is meritocracy in its most fundamental form. Access to public schooling, this line of thinking goes, counteracts the piles of disadvantages experienced by many low-income people, assuming they work their buns off to achieve "academic success." The trouble with the "great equalizer" notion, though, is that it presumes a level playing field, where working class and poor students have access to all the sorts of educational opportunities their wealthier peers enjoy. Unfortunately, as we will see, this is a terribly faulty presumption (Lareau & Weininger, 2008). In fact, as we also will see, there is more evidence to the contrary, illustrating that the inequities and indignities many low-income youth face outside of school largely are reproduced *inside* schools. According to this view, schools, as they have operated since the birth of public education, are sites of social *reproduction* rather than egalitarianism (Bourdieu, 1982). In other words, if we don't start doing things differently, schools will continue to *contribute* to, rather than mitigate, existing patterns of poverty and class inequity (Rouse & Barrow, 2006).

Researchers for decades have documented the relationship between socioeconomic status and a variety of measures of academic achievement and educational attainment, including standardized test scores and graduation rates. For example, Selcuk Sirin (2005), having analyzed a decade's worth of studies covering more than 100,000 students and nearly 7,000 schools, found that socioeconomic status is a good predictor of a variety of measures of reading achievement; in other words, the wealthier the student, the better, on average, she will perform on reading assessments. On the other hand, the poorer the student, the more likely she will experience reading difficulties (Kieffer, 2010), a pattern that is even more pronounced for low-income students who speak languages other than English at home (NCES, 2009). No big surprise there, right? As we learned in the previous chapter, these conditions reflect, in part, inequities in working class and poor families' access to a wide variety of opportunities and resources outside of school, such as resources that support reading development (Kieffer, 2010). They reflect, not an *achievement gap* or an *intelligence gap* or a *capability gap*, but an *opportunity gap*.

In this chapter we turn our attention to the educational opportunity gap: the many troubling ways in which youth in poverty, on average, are denied the level of educational access granted to more affluent youth. I try to paint a picture of the kinds of disparities against which many low-income students must struggle in order to succeed academically once they enter a classroom or school. In that sense, this is one of those bad-news chapters.

But hold tight, because later, in Chapters 8 and 9, I discuss research-driven strategies for eliminating, or at least mitigating, the very inequities I describe in this chapter.

## THE GREAT UN-EQUALIZER?

Low-income students do not perform as well in school on average as their wealthier counterparts, and they are considerably less likely to earn a high school diploma. In fact, according to the Children's Defense Fund (2008), roughly 15% of low-income 8th-graders perform proficiently in reading, a rate less than half that of their wealthier classmates, 39% of whom are proficient grade-level readers. Similarly, around 15% of low-income 8th-graders are proficient in math, about a third of the rate of their wealthier classmates, 42% of whom are proficient. Additionally, low-income youth are four times more likely to drop out of school than their wealthier peers.

The question is, *Why?*

It might be easy, or even tempting, to lean on some of the popular, if faulty, assumptions I refuted in Chapter 4 in order to answer that question: *Poor people are lazy. Poor people don't care about education. Poor people do not have positive role models at home.* The problem, though, is that none of these assumptions are true. There is no evidence that suggests that poor people on average are lazier, care less about education, or are less likely to have positive role models than anybody else. Something else must be amiss.

The National Commission on Teaching and America's Future (NCTAF, 2004) points us in a particularly troubling direction in search of that something:

> The evidence . . . proves beyond any shadow of a doubt that children at risk, who come from families with poorer economic backgrounds, are not being given an opportunity to learn that is equal to that offered to children from the most privileged families. The obvious cause of this inequality lies in the finding that the most disadvantaged children attend schools that do not have basic facilities and conditions conducive to providing them with a quality education. (p. 7)

In other words, just as socioeconomic status and school performance are correlated, so, too, are socioeconomic status and educational opportunity (Loughrey & Woods, 2010). So here we are, back at that pesky reality. Opportunity begets opportunity, even at school.

The socioeconomic demographics of schools, as Gregory Palardy and his colleagues (Palardy, 2008; Rumberger & Palardy, 2005) have demonstrated through complex statistical analysis, have a larger effect on student performance than students' individual socioeconomic backgrounds. In fact, a school's economic composition, according to Palardy (2008), may be more strongly correlated with student achievement than any other individual school-related variable. Illustrating this point, a recent analysis of math score data from the National Assessment of Education Progress exam uncovered something both fascinating and troubling: Low-income students attending low-poverty schools (identified as those in which a small percentage of students receive free or reduced-price lunch) score 20 points higher on average than low-income students attending high-poverty schools (Kahlenberg, 2007). The gap of 20 points, the author explained, represents roughly a two-grade-level difference in math proficiency. And this is just the tip of the iceberg, as we will see.

First, though, it's important to acknowledge here, again, that there will be dimensions of this educational opportunity gap that some, if not many, readers might consider outside their spheres of influence. Some readers might feel that, for example, they do not decide which schools individual students attend or how those schools are resourced. And, again, the immediate goal here is to think about our current spheres of influence. However, as with all those out-of-school challenges described in Chapter 5, one important way to understand and forge authentic relationships with students and families in poverty is to understand, with as much complexity as possible, how they experience schools. Unfortunately, there is no way to do that without considering some harsh realities. Fortunately, equipping ourselves with these understandings means that we're also equipping ourselves to do something informed and effective about those harsh realities.

For example, examining elements of the educational opportunity gap can help us better understand the complex relationship between poverty and school performance. It can be easy to imagine the relationship as a simple cause-and-effect sort of thing: Poverty causes low levels of reading proficiency. However, this view is too simplistic; it fails to consider several contextual factors related to class and poverty that affect school performance. Instead, as we consider educational access disparities, we might try, as Joseph Flessa (2007) urges us to do, to understand the relationship between poverty and school performance as a chain of conditions. He explains:

> One might link poverty to lack of employment opportunities that pay a living wage, in turn to a family's need to move frequently, in turn to inconsistent school attendance, in turn to low reading scores; or one might link poverty to economically segregated neighbourhoods to low school quality to novice teachers to low reading scores. (p. 10)

With these complexities in mind, we turn now to the many dimensions of the educational opportunity gap, including disparities in access to:

- preschool;
- well-funded schools;
- adequately resourced schools;
- shadow education;
- school support services;
- affirming school environments;
- high academic expectations;
- well-paid, certified, and experienced teachers;
- student-centered, higher-order curricula and pedagogies;
- opportunities for family involvement; and
- instructional technologies.

## Access to Preschool

Few areas of educational research have blasted onto the educational scene over the past few decades with the same force as brain research. Thanks to this research, we have new sorts of details regarding what many of us rightly presumed. We know, for instance, that brain development during children's earliest years is critical, that it influences their rates of cognitive development throughout their entire lives (Duncan et al., 2007). This does not mean, of course, that children who have been denied early access to, say, opportunities to build literacy skills lack the *potential* to excel academically. It only means that they will begin that pursuit at a disadvantage, and through no fault of their own. And because disadvantage only begets more disadvantage when not answered by some form of opportunity intervention, early intervention is essential to eliminating the educational opportunity gap (Duncan, Magnuson, Kalil, & Ziol-Guest, 2012).

Unfortunately, just as families in poverty have less access than their wealthier counterparts to quality childcare programs, they also have less access to high-quality preschool programs, if they can afford any preschool at all (NCES, 2008). Recent studies show that about 84% of preschool-age children living in homes with family incomes between $75,000 and $100,000 attend preschool, compared with only 55% of children whose family incomes fall between $20,000 and $30,000 (Barnett & Yarosz, 2007). In another example of intersectionality, poor immigrant children have even less access to quality early childhood education than their poor non-immigrant peers (Karoly & Gonzalez, 2011). Moreover, when low-income families do have access to formal preschool programs, the programs to which they have access tend to be of lower quality than the programs attended predominantly by wealthier children. As part of a policy analysis on early childhood education, Travis Wright (2007) concluded that preschool programs attended by lower-income children were, on average, of lower quality on measures related to everything from student-teacher ratios to the quality of instruction.

It might be easy to cite these conditions, like so many of the social conditions we've discussed so far, as further evidence that poor people simply don't value education. *Why don't the parents enroll their kids in a better preschool?* you might be asking yourself. *Why don't they make preschool a top priority?*

Like childcare, preschool, and especially high-quality preschool with certified and experienced teachers, well-equipped learning centers, and advanced pedagogical frameworks, simply is cost-prohibitive for most poor and working class families when it is not provided universally by their local school systems. Because many preschools do not provide a busing service, the simple act of transporting children to and from a preschool program is a challenge for many low-income families, particularly if it is not within walking distance of their homes (Karoly & Gonzalez, 2011), which is extremely unlikely, especially in rural areas. Other barriers exist as well. For some low-income immigrant families, language is a considerable barrier to enrolling their children in preschools (Matthews & Ewen, 2006). Sometimes they contend, as well, with cultural ignorance among early childhood education staff (Matthews & Jang, 2007), part of a larger pattern of documented alienation from educational institutions experienced disproportionately not only by many low-income people, but also by many People of Color, people with disabilities and learning differences, and lesbian, gay, bisexual, and transgender people, among others.

## Access to Well-Funded Schools

In his landmark book, *Savage Inequalities: Children in America's Schools*, former teacher and longtime advocate of equitable schooling Jonathan Kozol (1992) detailed the many ways in which schools attended predominantly by children from families in poverty were grossly underresourced, even when compared with wealthier schools a couple miles away. Even today, high-poverty schools, generally identified as those in which a majority of students are eligible for free or reduced-price lunch programs, receive significantly less overall state and local funding on average than schools with wealthier student bodies (Baker & Corcoran, 2012; Baker, Sciarra, & Farrie, 2010). They also receive lower per-pupil funding (Barr & Parrett, 2007).

These disparities result, in large part, from the popular but inequitable practice of funding schools with property taxes (Kozol, 2005), a tradition that all but ensures an opportunity gap. In fact, the United States is unique among "developed" democratic countries in its failure to centralize school funding and to rely, instead, on state and local funding, both of which are unequal. So even when we look at the investments different states make in their public school students, inequalities abound (Dixon, 2012), as you can see in Figure 6.1. What makes these conditions especially troubling is that research has shown that the equalization of education funding, particularly at the elementary level, can, at the very least, mitigate persisting inequalities in access to upward mobility between poor youth and their wealthier counterparts (Bergh, 2005; Mayer & Lopoo, 2008).

For many of us, the notion of high-poverty schools evokes images of urban students and perhaps, more particularly, urban students of color. But the savage inequalities of underfunding, like all dimensions of the education opportunity gap, similarly wreak havoc on high-poverty rural schools. Rural communities, like their inner-city and predominantly of-color counterparts, often do not enjoy educational funding levels that are comparable with non-rural districts, even within their own states (Strange, 2011). Consider, for instance, the case of Lake View, Arkansas, a rural school district comprised almost entirely of families in poverty. In 2001, 18 years after the state claimed to have changed its school funding policy after its existing policy had been ruled unconstitutional by the Arkansas Supreme Court, the community took the state, under Governor Mike Huckabee, back to court for its continued practice of cheating poor, rural families out of the same educational funding it granted wealthier districts. The case, *Lake View*

**Figure 6.1. Top Five and Bottom Five Average Per-Pupil Spending in Public Schools by State, 2009–2010**

| Geographic Area | Per-pupil spending |
|---|---|
| United States | $10,615 |
| *Top Five* | |
| District of Columbia | 18,667 |
| New York | 18,618 |
| New Jersey | 16,841 |
| Alaska | 15,783 |
| Vermont | 15,274 |
| *Bottom Five* | |
| Tennessee | 8,065 |
| Oklahoma | 7,896 |
| Arizona | 7,848 |
| Idaho | 7,106 |
| Utah | 6,064 |

*Based on data from Mark Dixon* (2012), Public Education Finances: 2010.

*v. Huckabee,* ascended back to the Supreme Court, which found in Lake View's favor. Testimony showed, for instance, that the Lake View schools could afford only one mathematics teacher. The teacher was unlicensed and paid as a long-term substitute teacher while doubling as a school bus driver, earning roughly $15,000 per year. Unfortunately, Arkansas responded, not by equalizing funding, but by closing the district altogether, merging it with other nearby districts (Strange, 2011).

According to Deborah Meier and George Wood (2004), contemporary federal education policy often exacerbates these challenges faced by low-income families. For instance, No Child Left Behind requires all schools, regardless of who attends them, to meet the same benchmarks of "adequate yearly progress" (AYP). The legislation, though, does not require equitable school funding (Barr & Parrett, 2007), often leaving the most economically distressed schools all the more vulnerable to sanctions for not meeting those benchmarks.

You might be thinking, *What about Title I (of the Elementary and Secondary Education Act)?* Title I, like some other programs, does, indeed, provide supplemental funding to schools and districts that serve large numbers of working class and poor families. However, these funds provide, on average, less than a 5-percentage-point boost to school funds (Baker et al., 2010), hardly offsetting the many other inequitable conditions with which high-poverty schools contend, such as lower levels of overall funding or the need to commit more resources to the basic maintenance of their buildings, which are more likely to be outdated and dilapidated than schools in wealthier neighborhoods (NCTAF, 2004). Also, as Goodwin Liu (2008) demonstrated in his analysis of allocation of Title I funds, there are serious inequities even in how these funds are dispersed. He explained, "In particular, small or mid-sized districts that serve half or more of all poor children in areas of high poverty receive less aid than larger districts with comparable poverty" (p. 973).

## Access to Adequately Resourced Schools

It stands to reason, of course, that lower-funded schools will tend to be less adequately resourced when compared with the more well-funded schools disproportionately situated in wealthy neighborhoods. In fact, based on its analysis of schools, the NCTAF (2004) found that students in high-poverty schools were more likely than their peers attending low-poverty schools to be taught using insufficient or outdated classroom materials in inadequate learning facilities, such as science labs. Kozol (1992, 2005) mentions these sorts of disparities as well among the "savage inequalities" of public schooling in the United States.

The disparities are captured most powerfully, perhaps, in the Educational Video Center's film *UnEqual Education: Failing Our Children* (Weinberg, 1992), in which a film crew follows two New York City public school students during 7th grade, one attending a school in a wealthy, predominantly White neighborhood, the other attending a school in a poor, predominantly African American neighborhood. The schools sit only miles apart, but the opportunities they offer students are vastly different. For example, whereas students in the wealthier school have fields where they can play, music classes with orchestral instruments, and a fully equipped science lab, the youth assigned to the poorer school have no fields, only keyboards in their music classes, and no science lab at all.

It might be hard to imagine how such obvious inequities persist in public education even as we continue to call it the great equalizer. The explanations are many and varied. For example, schools in higher-income neighborhoods tend to be newer than those in low-income neighborhoods, requiring fewer resources for general upkeep and maintenance. Parents and guardians in wealthier districts are more likely to have the resources and leisure time to pool their energies and raise money for everything from state-of-the-art learning materials to additional teachers. They also have more power to lobby and exert pressure on school boards and other decision-making bodies. Additionally, because parents and guardians from more affluent families are more likely than their lower-income peers to have the time, resources, and paid leave, if necessary, to volunteer in their children's schools, they can help create time for teachers and other school workers to spend some of their energies on grant-writing and other activities that might increase their students' access to learning resources and opportunities.

The disparities in resources between schools affect students at lower-income schools in several other ways as well. For example, as we learned in Chapter 5, libraries can play a mitigating role, shrinking the portion of the opportunity gap created by the fact that working class and poor students have less access to books at home than their wealthier peers (Krashen et al., 2010). They *can*. Unfortunately, they largely *don't*. In fact, libraries in high-poverty schools have fewer books, on average, than libraries in wealthier schools (American Library Association, 2010; Constantino, 2005). Sadly, in a study conducted in the Los Angeles metro area, Rebecca Constantino (2005) found that in some communities, wealthy families had access to more books at home than their economically disadvantaged peers had access to at home and at school combined. Meanwhile, based on its nationwide study, the American Library Association (2010) determined that the recent spate of school budget cuts has hit libraries in high-poverty schools harder than those in wealthier schools, widening the educational opportunity gap.

Certainly, all students in poverty do not attend dilapidated, falling-down schools with Mini-Me libraries and no microscope in sight. In fact, as increasing numbers of poor families move into the suburbs, a trend we explored in Chapter 3, a growing population of economically disadvantaged students are attending schools that, until recently, might have been seen as bastions of economic privilege. However, despite shifting demographics in some districts, research shows that, overall, a *re*-segregation of public schools along class lines has been in full effect over the last 20 years (Michelson, 2010), mirroring simultaneous trends toward racial re-segregation (Orfield & Frankenberg, 2008). Starting in preschool (Wright, 2011), students in many parts of the country attend schools that are more class- and race-segregated than local schools were *before Brown v. Board of Education*. This is no mistake; it is not coincidental. These patterns reflect growing numbers of instances in which school districts, often with support from powerful parent groups, redraw school boundary lines in ways that *increase* class and race segregation (Frankenberg, 2009; Herbert, 2010).

This means a double whammy for low-income students of color, and even disproportionately affects students of color who are not poor. Salvatore Saporito and Deenesh Sohoni (2007), who studied this trend by comparing Census poverty rates and school boundary lines, concluded,

> Members of all racial groups typically live in neighborhoods in which the majority of children are *not poor*. Yet, unlike the typical white child, who attends a public school in which most of the children are above the poverty line, the typical black or Hispanic child attends a public school in which most children are below the poverty line. This is a troubling finding given the strong correlation between school-level poverty rates and the academic achievement of individual students. Poor and non-white students are less likely to perform as well than their more affluent and white counterparts because, in part, they attend public schools with elevated concentrations of poverty. (p. 1246)

We see here, again, evidence of the strong link between race and class in the United States, even as it pertains to educational opportunity.

## Access to Shadow Education

The term *shadow education* refers to informal educational programs designed either to remediate or support formal schooling (Buchmann, Condron, & Roscigno, 2010). The SAT or ACT test prep course you took, if your family could afford to sign you up for one, is shadow education. The academic camps for kids at the local college or university are examples of shadow education, too. Another example, and perhaps the most common form of shadow education, is the local private tutoring program (Bray, 1999) with its fancy brochures and rates upwards of $100 per hour.

Although it has grown into an extensive industry, particularly since the enactment of No Child Left Behind (with its requirement, for instance, that "failing" schools provide tutoring to students who request it), I rarely hear references to shadow education in conversations about the achievement gap or adequate yearly progress. This, in part, is why it's called *shadow* education: It takes place in the shadow of formal schooling, out of public sight lines. We do not always know which of our students are participating in shadow programs. Systemically speaking, nobody is weighting schools' test scores or adequate yearly progress based on who can afford summer academic camps and private tutoring. Perhaps they should, though, because these programs can make a considerable difference, not only in student performance, but also in student cultural capital.

The problem, of course, is that some families, by virtue of their wealth, have greater access to shadow education than others. Considering the cost of some of these programs—private tutoring, for instance—some families do not have access to any form of shadow education, not because they don't want their children's learning to be bolstered by a summer writing or math camp, but because they just can't afford the cost (Avery et al., 2003). This discrepancy begins in elementary school with camps, tutors, and, perhaps, music lessons. It grows throughout students' educational careers, particularly as they approach high school graduation. Unfortunately, as Jenny Stuber (2010) found in her study of students' access to extracurricular activities in college, the discrepancy can continue into higher education, for those who can afford postsecondary schooling.

As with many dimensions of the opportunity gap, we as teachers have little control over whether our students' families can afford shadow education programs. We do have control, though, about whether we take this and other access discrepancies into account when we are forming our perceptions of low-income students. Certainly we never *intend* to mistake gaps in opportunity for gaps in intelligence or ability. Is it possible, though, that we sometimes are susceptible to false impressions, confusing the fruits of access, such as the academic boosts shadow education provides to students whose families can afford it, with intellectual superiority?

## Access to School Support Services

All students, regardless of socioeconomic status, ought to have access to basic support services during the school day, like the services provided by school counselors and nurses. Low-income students are more likely to need these sorts of services more often than their wealthier peers, not because they are inherently "deficient," but because their families are less likely to be able to afford physical or mental healthcare, counseling, and other types of services that many wealthier families take for granted. Unfortunately, in many cases, poor and working class students have less access to these services at school than their wealthier peers.

For example, high-poverty schools commit fewer resources, on average, to college counseling than wealthier schools. As a result, students in poverty, who disproportionately attend high-poverty schools, have less access to college counseling than their wealthier peers (Bergerson, 2009; Perna, Rowan-Kenyon, Bell, Li, & Thomas, 2008). *This stands to reason*, you might be thinking. *Students from families in poverty attend college at a much lower rate than wealthier students.* The observation is true; there is a discrepancy in college attendance rates across class. The question, though, is, *Why?*

Cost, or perceived cost, is one barrier, of course. Research has shown that even if they want to go to college, low-income students are less likely to see doing so as a realistic possibility, financially speaking (Bloom, 2007; Paulsen & St. John, 2002). In this sense, their lack of access to college counseling, a service that could mitigate these concerns by helping students and their families explore financial aid options, is an equally formidable barrier. Ellen Amatea and Cirecie West-Olatunji (2007) extend the conversation beyond college counseling by urging school counselors to imagine a wide variety of ways they can support low-income students, from challenging deficit views in schools to helping to foster a family-friendly school culture. Unfortunately, school counselors have not been immune to job cuts, so they are becoming scarcer and scarcer in schools.

Students attending high-poverty schools also have less access to school nurses than their peers at wealthier schools. High-poverty schools are more likely than wealthier schools to have no nurse on staff at all, and if they do have a nurse on staff, they tend to have greater pupil-to-nurse ratios (Berliner, 2009). This disparity has important implications. The American Academy of Pediatrics (AAP) Council on School Health (2008) has reported that school nurses play a key role in addressing student health concerns that affect learning and school performance. Studies have shown that access to school nurses improves school attendance rates by minimizing lost time due to illness (De-Socio & Hootman, 2004). Similarly, a recent study of more than 16,000 elementary school students (Baisch, Lundeen, & Murphy, 2011) showed that access to school nurses has a positive effect on students' immunization rates and schools' management of health concerns among students.

Recognizing the importance of student access to school nurses, several healthcare associations, including the AAP, the American School Health Association, and the National Association of School Nurses, have advocated placing a nurse in every school (Baisch et al., 2011). Unfortunately, school

nurses often are casualties of budget cuts, a trend disproportionately affecting the lowest-income schools and districts. The trend even affects low-
income students in mixed-class schools adversely, as they are much more
likely to depend on school nursing services than their more economically
advantaged classmates (Fleming, 2011).

## Access to Affirming School Environments

A popular theme in conversations about diversity in schools is safety.
We as educators are responsible, at the very least, for ensuring that every
student has access to a safe and affirming learning environment, free from
bias, harassment, and bullying. Do low-income students even have access
to that?

Certainly, some do. On average, though, there are many reasons to believe that low-income students feel less connected and affirmed at school
than their wealthier peers. The challenge for individual educators is that
although we might be trying as hard as we can to be affirming and provide
that safe, equitable learning environment, we are not always aware of, or
we do not always see, the ways in which students are being invalidated or
experiencing bias.

For example, we aren't always privy to students' school-day social interactions. As we learned in Chapter 5, students in poverty, in what appears
to be an international phenomenon, are more likely than their wealthier
peers to be bullied (Due et al., 2009; von Rueden et al., 2006). Much, and
perhaps most, bullying in schools happens beyond the earshot of adults.
Additionally, in an ethnographic study of poor and working class youth,
Tanya Brann-Barrett (2010) learned that many of them struggled to fit in
at school because they couldn't afford what their peers considered to be the
most fashionable clothes, an experience about which they would be unlikely
to talk with their teachers. (This, by the way, is one among many reasons
I discourage teachers and administrators from complimenting students on
expensive outfits or name-brand clothes. Another reason to avoid doing
so is the research showing that these sorts of compliments from teachers,
which focus on students' appearance rather than their intelligence, disproportionately are meted out to young women, while compliments regarding
intelligence disproportionately go to young men.)

On the other hand, students in poverty experience other forms of bias
to which we *are* privy, sometimes of our own doing. Consider, for example,
class bias in learning materials. This brand of bias begins in the earliest
grades, according to Stephanie Jones (2008), who synthesized research on
picture books and found consistently biased portrayals of poor and working class families. She also pointed out an example of what some people

call the *null* or omitted curriculum, explaining that there is a "great void in children's literature," a lack of "everyday stories of working-class and poor families' lives that validate and value daily living experiences including the happy, sad, ecstatic, tragic, and the mundane" (p. 46).

In another example of the intersectional nature of class and race, Jones's review of decades of scholarship showed that White people, who represent the numerical majority of poor people in the United States, were underrepresented in depictions of poor people in children's books, while People of Color were overrepresented. Illustrating yet another example of intersectionality, literature published for students who are English Language Learners contains a particularly egregious amount of class bias (Sano, 2009).

If bias in learning materials isn't enough to make low-income students feel disconnected from school, the conditions of the schools they attend could do so. For example, low-income students are more likely than their wealthier peers to attend schools with cockroach and rat infestations or with dirty or inoperative student bathrooms. They are more likely to have large numbers of substitute teachers, insufficient or outdated classroom materials, and inadequate or nonexistent learning facilities such as science labs (NCTAF, 2004).

Teachers, too, who choose or who are assigned to work in high-poverty schools often face these discouraging conditions and yet persist in their commitments to do all they can do to facilitate equitable learning environments for their students. That's why teachers are my heroes.

## Access to High Academic Expectations

In fact, in my experience, people who choose education as a career overwhelmingly are committed to helping every student thrive academically. Why work in a school otherwise? Unfortunately, over a decade of research shows that despite this commitment, educators in a variety of roles regularly show lower academic expectations for working class and poor students than they do for more economically privileged students. Sometimes low expectations are a matter of bias or preconceived notions about who is capable of what kinds of learning. These sorts of low expectations might reflect our attitudes about why poor people are poor in the first place. Sometimes, though—and I find this fascinating—low expectations actually can emanate from good intentions, such as when we desire not to put too much pressure on students whom we worry are overburdened in other areas of their lives.

Unfortunately, whatever our intentions, low teacher expectations are bad for students, and high expectations breed stronger student performance (Horvat & Davis, 2011) regardless of socioeconomic status. Patterns of low expectations help explain some of the behaviors popularly assumed to be associated with poor and working class families. For example, low-income students are less likely than their wealthier peers to experience positive reinforcement from their teachers (Evans & English, 2002). They regularly are steered, intentionally or not, into less rigorous classes, even when their grades do not necessarily warrant it (Futrell & Gomez, 2008). They disproportionately are labeled learning-disabled (Blair & Scott, 2002; McDermott, Goldman, & Varenne, 2006) as well. And, in another intersection of racial and class inequity, in their study of teacher expectations for low-income Mexican American students, the Garzas (2010) found that teachers regularly expressed high expectations for them in the short term, mostly around standardized test performance. However, their teachers tended to display low long-term expectations for them around their abilities to succeed in college or secure anything more than a minimum wage job. These sorts of long-term low expectations, according to Rebecca and Encarnacion Garza (2010), result in the most economically disadvantaged students being subject to the most lower-order curricula and pedagogies.

You might be thinking, *Well, yes, they disproportionately do not perform as well as wealthier students, so it makes sense that they are more likely to be placed in more remedial classes and academic tracks with less rigorous curricula.* Consider, though, how the cycle works. First, consider that this sort of tracking, whether formal or informal, often is tinged with bias. For instance, in their study of nine elementary schools, Jay Gottlieb and Sharon Weinberg (1999) found that one-eighth of the teachers make roughly two-thirds of special education referrals. In a broader study of the same phenomenon, the U.S. Department of Education (2003) learned that 10% of teachers make about 80% of all special education referrals. It might be easy, even commonsensical, to interpret the disproportionate number of working class and poor students in special education or remedial academic tracks as evidence of lower academic ability, lower levels of interest in education, lower levels of motivation, or other perceived weaknesses attributed to low-income communities. If low-income students are less motivated academically as a group than their wealthier peers—and this is a big if, because research on this matter is inconclusive at best, findings largely dependent on whether phenomena such as tracking and lower expectations are taken into account—we must ask ourselves to what extent this is a reflection of who the students are or of how some educators treat them.

## Access to Well-Paid, Certified, and Experienced Teachers

Like most of their colleagues in wealthier schools, teachers who work in high-poverty schools overwhelmingly are determined to help their students succeed academically. It would be quite easy to argue, in fact, that teachers who choose to stay in high-poverty schools, even when they have opportunities to leave for wealthier schools or districts, demonstrate a unique sort of determination and commitment to ideals of educational equity. Unfortunately, most teachers with an opportunity to leave high-poverty schools for a job in a low-poverty school choose to do just that. This often leaves schools in the most economically repressed communities struggling to hire and retain fully certified, experienced teachers. The result is a disproportionately high proportion of 1st-year teachers being assigned to high-poverty schools (Almy & Theokas, 2010) and a disproportionately high teacher turnover rate in low-income schools that, as you might imagine, can be quite disruptive to student learning (Guin, 2004) and to families' relationships with their children's schools (Sepe & Roza, 2010).

Similarly disruptive, at least potentially, is the disproportionately high rate of principal turnover at low-income schools. As recently as the 2008–2009 school year, principals in schools in which 75% or more of the students qualified for free or reduced lunch were significantly less likely to stay at their schools, more likely to take a job at a different school, and more likely to leave their administrative roles altogether than their colleagues at schools where less than 35% of students were eligible for free and reduced lunch (Battle & Gruber, 2010). Sadly, teacher and principal stability is just one of many challenges students in poverty face when it comes to who is teaching them.

According to Gregory Palardy (2008), who analyzed national data on the matter, "Teachers at low social class schools earned significantly lower salaries, were less likely to have earned an advanced degree, were less likely to have earned a bachelor's degree in the subject area they teach, were less experienced, and were less likely to be fully certified" (p. 31). More specifically, for example, high-poverty high schools are twice as likely as low-poverty high schools to have uncertified teachers teaching core subject courses (Almy & Theokas, 2010). To be sure, pay and experience and even certification are not always the best predictors of effective teaching. I never would make a judgment about an individual teacher based on these factors alone. However, the cumulative effect of inequalities in the distribution of teachers is that throughout their educational lives, low-income students are considerably more likely than their wealthier peers to experience a steady stream of teachers teaching outside their certification areas and teachers with little formal teacher training.

Then there's the issue of teacher pay. Due to inequities in school funding, districts with high concentrations of low-income students are not able to pay teachers the sorts of salaries offered by wealthier districts (Miller, 2010). In fact, in his study of school expenditures, Gregory Palardy (2008) found that teacher salaries, which constitute the largest expenditure for schools, are significantly lower, approximately $2,500 per year lower on average, in high-poverty schools and districts than in wealthier schools and districts. Often, teachers with provisional licenses or with, at least initially, no licenses at all are concentrated into these districts, in part because it costs less to pay them and partially because of teacher shortages in high-poverty communities.

This, of course, means that low-income students, on average, do not enjoy the same level of access to certified and experienced teachers as their wealthier peers, which is among the best-documented educational inequities in the United States (Chambers, Levin, & Shambaugh, 2010; Orfield, Frankenberg, & Siegel-Hawley, 2010). In fact, not only are teachers in predominantly low-income schools more likely than their colleagues at wealthier schools to be uncertified in the subjects they teach (Rouse & Barrow, 2006), they also have less education on average (Cooper, 2010). Again, a lack of certification or lesser amounts of formal teacher education are not necessarily worthy lone measures of the effectiveness of individual teachers, but their cumulative effects for poor and working class students are, at the very least, notable.

Palardy's (2008) study uncovered other, slightly messier inequities as well. He explained, for instance, that

> Compared with teachers at high social class schools, teachers at low social class schools were rated by students as being of lower quality, were confronted with significantly greater levels of class disruptions, were less likely to coordinate their curriculum with other teachers in the school, had a lower sense of control over their work environment, and had a lesser locus of control. (p. 31)

It might be tempting to see these results as an implication of the teachers themselves. However, these conditions, as far as I can tell, are not the results of inattentive teachers, but rather, in many cases, of *disaffected* teachers who share with their students the difficulties of being in underresourced schools. Remember, too, that teachers in low-income schools are more likely to have imposed upon them the kinds of curricular and pedagogical models, like direct instruction, that stifle their creativity.

## Access to Student-Centered, Higher-Order Curricula and Pedagogies

In fact, students in poverty have less access overall than their wealthier counterparts to the kinds of student-centered, higher-order curricula and pedagogies that encourage deep and complex learning (Barr & Parrett, 2007). They are assigned disproportionately to schools that offer few, if any, college preparatory or honors classes (Gándara, 2010), the types of classes in which higher-order, constructivist, engaging pedagogies are most likely to be used. Meanwhile, low-income students are more likely than wealthier students to be subject to rote-like or "skills-and-drills" instruction, the kinds of instruction that students themselves report as less engaging and less effective (Dudley-Marling & Paugh, 2005; Tivnan & Hemphill, 2005). These disparities exist not only *between* low-income and higher-income schools, but also *within* mixed-income schools, where lower-income students are disproportionately assigned to lower academic tracks (or "ability groups") as illustrated in Figure 6.2.

The overemphasis on direct instruction in high-poverty schools and classrooms is only one example of this phenomenon, but it's a particularly pertinent example. We know, based on a decade or so of research on the effectiveness of various pedagogical models, that *some* direct instruction or skills-and-drills sorts of pedagogies can be helpful to students who are attempting to acquire basic skills or knowledge, especially if that instruction is followed by opportunities to *apply* what they have learned in ways that make it relevant to their lives. However, we also know that an *overemphasis* on direct instruction robs students of opportunities to learn deeply and comprehensively. For example, according Stephen Krashen and his colleagues (2010), direct instruction can improve, at least in the short term, the mechanics of student reading, but it

## Figure 6.2. Higher- and Lower-Order Thinking Activities

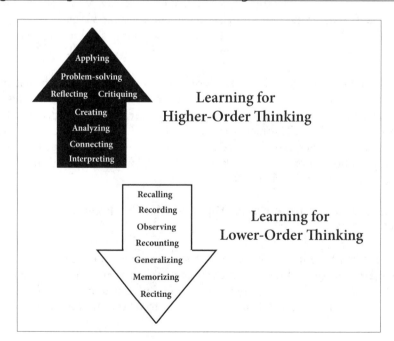

does not improve reading comprehension or scores on tests that actually "require children to understand what they read" (p. 28).

It's worth mentioning again, I think, that these pedagogical disparities are not, as one might suspect, purely an indication of the abilities or commitments of teachers of low-income students. We must remember that, due to the AYP aspect of No Child Left Behind and other federal mandates, teachers in low-income schools often feel heightened pressures to *teach to the test* or rely heavily on direct instruction, sometimes based on orders from their administrators. Teachers who teach predominantly low-income students also contend with larger class sizes than their colleagues at higher-income schools (Barton, 2004), which could make them feel more uneasy about implementing higher-order pedagogies than, say, their colleagues who teach 12 students at a time at the wealthiest independent schools in the United States. In other words, in my experience working with teachers in a variety of schools across the United States, this is less an indication of teacher capacity and desire than an indication of a combination of the other inequities I discuss in this chapter.

## Access to Opportunities for Family Involvement

Family involvement. Are any two words identified as often and earnestly as the panacea for educational woes? I rarely participate in a conversation about student learning or the achievement gap or school reform without hearing impassioned and repeated attempts to blame almost everything imaginable on "disinterested" or "lazy" parents, particularly when they are poor, of color, or both. Certainly, there is ample evidence that family involvement can play a considerable role in student engagement and academic success, at least when "success" is measured in traditional ways (Ceja, 2006). But before we use this evidence to excuse ourselves and our schools from any part in these disparities, we might consider asking ourselves a couple of important questions.

First, are opportunities for on-site family involvement accessible to poor and working class parents and guardians like they're accessible to wealthier parents and guardians? What kinds of obstacles might exist for poor or working class families who want to be involved in, say, on-site family involvement opportunities like classroom volunteering or even parent-teacher conferences or Back to School Nights? What sorts of time constraints might they face to which their wealthier counterparts are more or less immune? We explored some of these questions in Chapter 4, so this time I'll take a bit of a different approach.

Imagine now, if you haven't already experienced it, that you are a low-income parent of a couple of elementary school children. You *want* to attend events at your children's school, but you work the evening shift at your second job, and because you're a wage employee, missing work means losing wages, which, by extension, could result in another late electricity payment: bad news with winter approaching. You don't have the "paid leave" perks enjoyed by your supervisor, after all.

Remember, now, that as a low-income parent or guardian, you are much more likely than your wealthier counterparts to work multiple jobs, including evening jobs (Van Galen, 2007). In fact, in one of her groundbreaking studies, Annette Lareau (1994) found, upon comparing families from two 1st-grade classes (one in a low-income neighborhood and the other in a middle class neighborhood), that, likely because you work multiple jobs, you have less free time and less time flexibility than middle class parents. This, unfortunately, is just one of many obstacles you face in your attempts to engage with your children's school (Howard, Dresser, & Dunklee, 2009).

Still, you're committed to being involved in every possible way, so you hope that finally, this year, the school will be a little more flexible when scheduling parent-teacher conferences and other events. Usually, as you know, schools—not just your children's school, but all schools—schedule these events at times that just don't make sense for people who are likely to work nights or multiple jobs (Amatea & West-Olatunji, 2007): people like you. Then there are the other expenses, such as public transportation and childcare. *Have the people scheduling these events ever had to rely on public transportation?*, you wonder, trying to calculate the least expensive and most time-efficient bus route from your first job to the school, then to your second job.

You attended school as a low-income student as well, and experienced it at times as an unwelcoming environment, so on top of the expenses is the trepidation you feel about the psychological toll that visiting the school might take on you (Finders & Lewis, 1998; Graham, 2009). Many of the teachers, you worry, with good reason, too, based on previous interactions with your children's schools, assume, perhaps implicitly, that you don't care about your children's education.

What will you do?

## Access to Instructional Technologies

The term *digital divide* usually refers to inequities in physical access to computers and the Internet among various groups of people. For example, poor and working class students have lower levels of access to computers and the Internet at home than their wealthier peers. Despite considerable progress over the past 10 years toward eliminating the digital divide at school, gaps persist there, too (Thomas, 2008), as low-income schools continue, on average, to stock classrooms and computer labs with fewer computers per student than wealthier schools. This disparity is significant, for sure, but it tells only part of the story. Even as gaps in physical access to these technologies have begun to close, more insidious disparities have emerged, not just in physical access to the technologies, but in the ways teachers are using them in the classroom.

When we consider the matter from the point of view of a broader notion of "access," as those in the digital equity movement have attempted to do, we find that computer and Internet technology use in high-poverty schools tends to mirror other pedagogical trends. For example, teachers in low-poverty schools, and especially low-poverty, predominantly White schools, most often use these technologies to support the development of critical or creative thinking. Students in these schools are encouraged, on average, to engage with computer and Internet technologies in constructivist and creative ways, doing research, constructing multimedia projects, and practicing critical thinking skills. On the other hand, as both localized and national studies have shown, computer and Internet technologies tend to be used in high-poverty schools to support the rote and skills-and-drills learning already prevalent in those contexts (Gorski, 2009; Judge et al., 2004). As a middle school teacher at a high-poverty school just outside of Washington, DC, once told me, "We're encouraged to use these machines as if they are big digital flash cards." In their study of these trends, Sharon Judge and her colleagues (2006) found that they begin in early childhood classrooms.

As with other examples of educational inequities, it would be a gross oversimplification to suggest that teachers are at fault when it comes to these digital discrepancies. After all, teachers at high-poverty schools are provided with less in-service training than their colleagues at low-poverty schools on how to use these technologies and their sometimes complex software applications in pedagogically sophisticated ways. In addition, low-income schools are less likely than wealthier schools to have on staff a full-time instructional technology specialist to provide pedagogical supports to teachers who wish to use these technologies for higher-order learning activities (Gorski, 2009). As a result, whereas teachers in high-poverty schools are most likely to use computer and Internet technologies for record-keeping and administrative tasks, their colleagues in low-poverty schools are most likely to use them for creating new learning materials and otherwise strengthening their instruction (Valadez & Duran, 2007).

## THE PROBLEM WITH NCLB, VOUCHERS, AND SCHOOL "CHOICE"

Unfortunately, many of the school reform initiatives pitched as efforts to equalize educational opportunity have had the opposite effect, growing these sorts of inequities. Consider, for example, the standardized testing regimens of No Child Left Behind and Race to the Top. We've long known that the tests themselves are class-biased as well as race- and language-biased. In fact, analyses of standardized tests have shown that between 15 and 80% of test items are class-biased, depending on subject area (Popham, 2004). Imagine, for example, being a poor student from urban Minneapolis required to answer a series of word problems about camping and boating in the rural Minnesota Northwoods: word problems full of words like *portage*, words you've never heard about activities your family can't afford to do. It's bad enough—isn't it?—that students have to endure these tests and that youth in lower-income schools are more likely than their wealthier peers to be subject to hours of test-taking lessons during class time, increasingly in place of physical education, art, and music classes. They also have to manage tests designed with somebody else's life experiences in mind.

Equally troubling, cross-group, cross-school, and cross-district score comparisons rarely take into account the many inequities that affect students' performance on high-stakes tests. Of course, many of these inequities (access to equitable healthcare, for instance) are beyond schools' control. As a result, the most vulnerable schools often are punished again and again for the implications of the very inequities that hamper them and their students (Toutkoushian & Curtis, 2005). In essence, these testing regimens, along with AYP mandates, place an additional burden on schools with high percentages of low-income students rather than alleviating or mitigating educational inequities. William Cunningham and Tiffany Sanzo (2002), among others, are concerned that this pattern hurts people associated with low-income schools in other ways, such as by making teachers who choose to teach in high-poverty schools despite the inequities vulnerable to ruthless criticism and by deteriorating the self-image of low-income students and their families.

Similarly, despite the fact that vouchers and other school "choice" initiatives often are pitched as solutions to class inequities, they have, for the most part, provided families who already have the widest-reaching access with even greater access (Barr & Parrett, 2007; Paquette, 2005). For example, a district might provide transportation for low-income students who choose to attend a charter school outside their neighborhoods, but they almost universally do not provide transportation for students who want to get to school early for extra help or stay at school late to use the computer lab or participate in an extracurricular activity. The disparities are elevated, as you might imagine, in poor, rural, areas (Zhang & Cowen, 2009), where many youth already have to travel considerable distances to attend their "neighborhood" schools. It should be little surprise, then, that less than 1% of families who are eligible to take advantage of the NCLB choice option actually do so (RAND, 2008) and that those who do so are disproportionately affluent and White (Holme & Richards, 2009; Rutgers University, 2006).

Step back a bit further, and the picture becomes a wee bit bleaker. Because choice programs generally do not guarantee the option to "choose" schools outside of a student's home district, many poor families, especially if they live in rural or urban districts, are free to "choose" only among a sample of segregated high-poverty schools (Holme & Wells, 2008). When interdistrict choice options do exist, again, they generally provide greater choice to those who already have the most choice and, as a result, actually exacerbate racial and class segregation and stratification (Clotfelter, 2004; Holme & Richards, 2009).

We must remember, of course, that unlike their wealthier counterparts, who might have the ability to move into a neighborhood based solely on its schools (Grady et al., 2010; Marks, Cresswell, & Ainley, 2006), poor families often are forced to move under duress, seeking work or fleeing unsafe housing (Schafft, 2006). Obviously, this mobility can affect the academic progress of students in several ways as well (Killeen & Schafft, 2008).

## CONCLUSION

So maybe the education system, as presently constituted, is not the great equalizer it's cracked up to be. Maybe, in fact, it's just the opposite, bestowing on the most privileged families additional privilege and denying the least privileged families access to what they and their children deserve. The evidence leans heavily in that direction.

Trying to consider all of these conditions at once can be a little overwhelming, I know, especially for those of us who don't feel much control over big-level education policy or individual students' access to preschool. The idea, remember, is not necessarily to feel guilty or fully responsible for the existence of these inequities, but instead to ask ourselves what they mean for us and our students within our spheres of influence. At the very least, they should help us better understand why some low-income students might feel disengaged from school or why, on average, they might seem so far behind their wealthier peers academically. They should remind us that it's not their fault. The odds are stacked against students whose families are in poverty, and particularly for those whose families are in generational poverty. They might remind us to ask ourselves what we're willing to do to make sure we aren't reproducing these disadvantages in our own classrooms and schools.

Next, in Chapter 7, we begin our exploration of strategies for alleviating the class inequity mess in our schools. We begin it, though, by examining some of the most popular *ineffective* ways in which schools and school districts have attempted to respond to class disparities in school outcomes.

# CHAPTER 7

# Been There, Done That, Didn't Work

## The Most Popular *Ineffective* Strategies for Teaching Students in Poverty

> **Principles of Equity Literacy discussed in this chapter include:**
>
> Principle 9: Strategies for bolstering school engagement and learning must be based on evidence for what works.
>
> Principle 10: The inalienable right to equitable educational opportunity includes the right to high expectations, higher-order pedagogies, and engaging curricula.

In some ways it's difficult to figure. Even as we are sold the virtues of data-driven decision-making, a vast majority of common responses to the economic achievement gap, disproportionate dropout rates, and the like reflect more or less the *opposite* of what research data suggest we ought to be doing. In some cases they reflect the opposite of what research has demonstrated for generations about what does work when it comes to academic success for low-income families.

I say that it's difficult to figure only in some ways because in other ways it's sadly predictable. Schools, like most complex organizations, are slow to change. This is especially true when strategies for creating equitable schools are based on misunderstandings about the nature of poverty or the deficit views about poor people that so easily follow those misunderstandings. If I believe, for instance, that students from poor families are educationally deprived at home, it might be easy to assume that higher-order pedagogies and high academic expectations would overwhelm them or that they would learn better in a hypercontrolled environment, through direct instruction and rote lessons. This would be a mistake according to analyses of vast amounts of data, which show that low-income students thrive on the same higher-order, deeply engaging, interactive pedagogies usually denied them but enjoyed by their wealthier peers (Kennedy, 2010; Patterson et al., 2008). More on this in Chapter 8.

Similarly, if I base my understanding of student success purely on test scores, I might endorse initiatives that strip physical education, art, and music from the school experiences of low-income youth in favor of more traditional instructional time for reading, writing, and math. Again, according to mounds of data, this would be a mistake. All students, and particularly low-income students, perform better in almost every subject area, feel more engaged in school overall, and are less likely to drop out of school when physical education, art, and music are integral parts of their educational experiences (Landsman & Gorski, 2007; Tranter & Palin, 2004; Wetz, 2004). More on this in Chapter 8, too.

In this chapter I review some of the most popular and most *misguided* initiatives meant ostensibly to ensure equitable educational opportunity for low-income students. Some of these are big, system-level sorts of reforms—the kinds of thing you might think are outside your sphere of influence. Others are pedagogical in nature. All of them do damage to low-income youth.

## MISDIRECTION IN SCHOOL REFORM

First, though, consider this: Why, given what we know, would anybody with the best interests of low-income students at heart think it's a good idea to eliminate art and music education as a strategy for bolstering their academic achievement? Why do schools and school systems ostensibly committed to data-driven decision-making do all sorts of things in the name of leaving no child behind or racing to the top or being more equitable that we know, when we look at the data, simply do not work?

Obviously there are many factors at play here and no easy answer to these questions. For example, as we learned in Chapter 4, the deficit view, which unfortunately remains the dominant view, of low-income students and families misdirects a lot of well-intentioned efforts to create equitable schools by leading us to believe we solve the problem of unequal educational outcomes by "fixing" poor people rather than the conditions that are unfair to poor people (Gorski, 2012). This misdirection of our individual and collective energies is somewhat easy to remedy. I can refuse to take the deficit view. I can challenge myself to see a bigger picture, to recognize what low-income families have to overcome in and out of schools in order to succeed academically. I can refuse to have low expectations for poor families. I might not be able to eliminate poverty or class inequity from an entire district—although it would be wonderful if we pooled our energies to give it a shot—but I can amend the policy and practice in my own classroom or unit or department to be more equitable.

More insidious, though, are some of the societal factors that misguide efforts to close the economic achievement gap and mask the very existence of the economic opportunity gap. Chief among these, perhaps, is the growing influence of neoliberal ideology on education policy and practice, ideology that is easy to spot in many of today's most active school reform initiatives once you know what to look for. What makes neoliberal school reform initiatives dangerous is that they are sold, with language like *No Child Left Behind* and *school choice* and *merit pay*, as efforts to create more equitable educational opportunity despite the fact that by almost every measure, they intensify existing inequities. We will return to this point in a moment.

Neoliberalism, in the most general sense, is a political movement or ideology that imposes free enterprise or free market ideals on every aspect of social and political life. This includes, and perhaps *especially* includes, community resources, like public education, once considered the domain of government, part of the common social good, not to be soiled or controlled by the interests of profiteers. Pauline Lipman (2011), in an essay detailing neoliberalism's growing hold on public education, describes it as "the commodification of all realms of existence" (p. 116). The telltale signs of neoliberalism include arguments in favor of the privatization of public goods and services, for turning public roads, the prison system, schools, parks, and even the military into profit-driven, rather than public-service-driven, commodities. They also include the adoption of corporate-style reforms in the public sphere. Evidence of this process in education can be found in the very language we use to talk about school reform: *standardization, adequate yearly progress, accountability*, and even *data-driven decision-making*. Often it begins with efforts to defund or underfund public services, like public schools, and to redirect once-public funding to private enterprise, as with school voucher programs and charter schools. Does any of this sound familiar?

It is as though the language of neoliberal school reform has become so pervasive that it drives conversations about education today. Think of the way so many of us, knowing how the obsession with standardized testing—an obsession so out of whack that, in some states, *Kindergartners are given standardized tests*—deteriorates our own agency as educators and, as a result, students' access to fulfilling learning experiences, still somehow get sucked into talking about student success on the basis of test scores. Today I hear much, much more about raising low-income students' test scores than about creating equitable schools. Worse, I often hear school officials using the goal of "raising test scores" as a proxy for creating equitable educational opportunity. I rarely hear this from teachers, though, probably because teachers know better.

To be clear, I know why this happens. I understand that all this talk about test scores is a setup for teachers and administrators. I recognize that livelihoods are at risk, especially for people who work at high-poverty schools.

In Chapter 9 I further discuss deficit ideology, the view that low-income youth and families are intellectually, morally, or spiritually deficient, that poor people are "the problem." Suffice it to say for now that deficit ideologies fail or refuse to see low-income people as resilient, as citizens who have to overcome a lot, including the denial of basic rights like healthcare, in order to survive in a society in which the odds are stacked against them.

Well, I believe that schoolteachers and administrators, particularly when they choose to work in low-income schools, also are targets of a kind of deficit ideology. The media, informed mostly by people who never have experienced the challenge or delight of engaging a roomful of 30-some young people with all manner of gifts and needs and curiosities, love to target teachers and ignore shrinking budgets and the pressures of high-stakes testing, not to mention the re-segregation of schools by socioeconomic status. Political commentators and policy wonks love to compare test scores between schools that are resourced at vastly different levels while remaining remarkably silent on the inequitable distribution of pristine science labs, Advanced Placement programs, athletic fields, school nurses, and computer labs. Do we hear about the studies showing how devastating the high-stakes testing craze has been on the morale of teachers who are committed enough to poor youth to teach at high-poverty schools (Byrd-Blake et al., 2010; Cunningham & Sanzo, 2002), where they, too, are denied the sorts of resources and opportunities provided to their colleagues at wealthier schools? Do we hear about the anxiety these testing regimens cause teachers and principals (Gurr & Drysdale, 2007; Ramalho, Garza, & Merchant, 2010), who often are compelled by the pressure to *raise test scores* (as opposed to bolster *learning*) to teach and lead in ways they know are not ideal for youth? How often, when newspapers print those charts comparing school or district test scores, do they present the data in ways that account for disparities in school funding, students' preschool attendance, or students' access to preventive healthcare?

Given this scorn, I worry that some of us might buy in as a matter of survival. One such friend, an elementary principal at a high-poverty school, recently explained to me, "If we don't raise those scores, we risk the state taking over our school, firing our teachers, and stealing from us whatever integrity we have left in the face of this No Child Left Behind and Race to the Top craziness." Test scores, test scores, test scores.

Obviously, a vast majority of us want students from every background to succeed. Really, who would dedicate their lives to teaching if they weren't committed to so basic a goal? Not an ounce of me questions the desire of teachers, teacher aides, counselors, administrators, and others who spend their lives surrounded by youth to create equitable schools. There are plenty of careers whose workers are better paid and appreciated for people who once thought they wanted to be teachers, but then decided they just aren't invested enough in the well-being of disenfranchised youth to stay in the profession. Those folks don't tend to stick around education very long, at least not in low-income schools.

However, after spending the past several years studying low-income families' experiences in public schools, I am concerned with what we are and are not doing when it comes to realizing the goal of equitable schools for poor youth. The problem, as I have come to see it, is not that we don't *want* to create more equitable classrooms and schools, but that we spend tremendous amounts of resources pursuing initiatives for doing so that either do not work or that, worse, widen the gaps we so desperately want to eliminate.

My intention for the remainder of this chapter is to identify a few of these popular but ineffective initiatives before turning, in the next chapter, to what research has shown in a variety of contexts to be *effective* strategies for strengthening engagement and learning among low-income youth. I am careful, in both cases, to cite studies from the hefty and growing mounds of research on poverty and schooling in order to demonstrate, first of all, that there *is* evidence for what does and does not work. But I also do so in order to show how popular perceptions and even "common sense" often conflict with reality, so that we can't always rely on what "feels right" or on what we might think is common sense when we're formulating our teaching strategies. In fact, sometimes common sense or what "feels right" are more reflections of our biases than a blueprint for effective teaching.

## A SMALL SAMPLE OF INEFFECTIVE
## (BUT POPULAR) STRATEGIES

I was incredulous when my friend Susan, the principal of a middle school, told me that she was being forced by the district to cut her art and music programs. "Test scores," she lamented. "Our scores are not where we want them to be, and certainly not where the district wants them to be." As a result, the district insisted that Susan share her music and art teachers with two other middle schools. "It should work out," she told me, "because more than half of our students will be spending an extra hour each day in math and writing instruction. We're trading art and music for math and writing, like almost every other school on this side of the district."

By "this side of the district," Susan meant the *poor* side of the district. Nearly 80% of her students were eligible for free and reduced lunch. Their parents and guardians epitomized the working poor, often piecing together two, three, or four minimum wage jobs just to pay the rent and put food on the table.

The district's decision to cut the art and music programs in its lower-income middle schools illustrates what to me is the most formidable barrier to the realization of class equity in schools: a serious, if somewhat delirious, case of beneficent shortsightedness. Susan, like the individuals in her district office, is no ravaging "classist." In fact, she's an outspoken advocate for low-income students and their families. Why, then, was she willing to deny her most struggling, most economically disadvantaged students access to art and music education—important components, by almost any measure, of a holistic education?

In fact, in-school access to art and music education is especially important to poor and working class students (Heath & Roach, 1999; Pogrow, 2006). This stands to reason, of course, because families in poverty are less likely than their more economically advantaged counterparts to be able to afford to provide their children with these experiences outside of school (Bracey, 2006). So this is bad strategy. It's bad, unjust strategy, more likely to inspire students who feel its effects to disengage from school than to help them engage and thrive.

Unfortunately, this is only one of many ways schools and districts are attempting to bolster the "achievement" of low-income students with illogical initiatives. A few particularly egregious examples of the many such initiatives include: (1) foregoing engaging pedagogical approaches for lower-order pedagogies, (2) tracking or "ability grouping," and (3) opening charter schools.

## Direct Instruction and Other Lower-Order Pedagogies

*Teaching to the test*: What does it say about the state of public schooling when a phrase like this becomes part of the popular lexicon? As with most bad pedagogical approaches, low-income students are more subject than their wealthier peers to teaching to the test and the equally troubling practice of spending class time teaching test-taking strategies. As a matter of fact, poor youth are subject disproportionately to disengaging, rote, and skills-and-drills pedagogies (Barr & Parrett, 2007; Luke, 2010)—what Martin Haberman (1991) has called the *pedagogy of poverty*.

Especially prevalent in low-income schools and low-track classes in economically diverse schools (usually comprised predominantly of low-income students) is direct instruction. The direct instruction model, according to the National Institute for Direct Instruction (2012), replaces "teacher creativity and autonomy as high priorities" with "a willingness to follow certain carefully prescribed instructional practices" (¶ 2). Notice in this description the double whammy deficit ideology. An implicit assumption appears to be that students need their teachers to follow "carefully prescribed" practices in order to learn. An explicit assumption is that teachers are incapable of teaching effectively when given the latitude to use their expertise and creativity.

More to the point, research shows that although some amount of direct instruction can be effective for teaching initial skills, an overreliance on direct instruction simply does not produce deep learning. For instance, as previously mentioned, Stephen Krashen (2009) found that while direct instruction can improve reading mechanics, it fails to improve reading comprehension or scores on tests that "require children to *understand what they read*" (emphasis added; Krashen et al., 2010, p. 28). And this, teaching for lower-order rather than higher-order learning, is the common denominator for instructional practices that comprise the pedagogy of poverty (Haberman, 1991). Just like eliminating art and music programs, embracing these approaches is simply irrational, as explained by Stanley Pogrow (2009):

> Reteaching specific discrete skills all the time creates a sense that learning means memorizing. So more advanced learning skills and cognitive processes aren't developed, and . . . students never understand what learning actually is—even though they have as much potential for academic success as others. (p. 409)

On the other hand, as we will learn in Chapter 8, there are few certainties in the education world that are as certain as this certainty: Low-income students thrive academically, remain more engaged in school, and even have fewer behavioral challenges when they are given access to the same sorts of student-centered, higher-order, interactive pedagogies their wealthier peers have come to expect from their schools.

## Tracking and Ability Grouping

Tracking, or organizing students into groups or classes based upon perceived or assumed capabilities, has become so much a part of the common sense of schooling that some of us might struggle to imagine the possibility of organizing students in any other way. In fact, scholars concerned with educational equity began to study tracking practices, not out of concern that the overall approach couldn't work, but rather out of a concern that the approach, in effect, was being used to segregate students within schools (Losen, 1999). They were right to worry, as tracking and ability grouping have been found almost universally to be inequitable by class and race, among other things (Oakes, 2005; Orfield et al., 2010). Sometimes all it takes for somebody to be tracked into low-ability classes or groupings is tattered clothes, brown or black skin, or an accent or dialect stereotypically associated with an immigrant or rural community.

Beyond these obviously unjust tracking practices, though, research has shown since the 1980s that tracking simply does not work for a vast majority of students (Van de Werfhorst & Mijs, 2010). There is some evidence that the practice can be just a bit beneficial to a tiny percentage of the highest-achieving students, but the overall effect is null or negative, especially for low-income students, who most often are placed in lower tracks (Oakes, 2005). In fact, and not surprisingly, considering the discrepancies in access to engaging instruction described earlier, tracking *increases* gaps in rates of student achievement and engagement (Hattie, 2002; Huang, 2009; Van de Werfhorst & Mijs, 2010).

On the other hand, research has shown that a vast majority of students, and especially students who otherwise would be assigned to lower tracks, benefit from learning in mixed-ability groups (Thrupp, Lauder, & Robinson, 2002).

## Charter Schools

Among the many school reform initiatives that redirect resources out of neighborhood public schools are the charter school movement and voucher programs. Charter schools, which turn out to be just as segregated as, or more segregated than, public neighborhood schools, and whose students perform no better on average than public neighborhood school students (Carnoy, Jacobsen, Mishel, & Rothstein, 2005), draw students and, as a result, resources out of the most needy schools. To make matters worse, the factors that reflect an unequal distribution of resources between poor and better-off public schools are replicated in almost identical fashion in charter schools.

Kim Bancroft (2009), who studied charter schools in California, came to the same conclusion. Just like public neighborhood schools, she explained, "charters situated in resource-rich communities can provide more opportunities for students and teachers alike" (p. 250). She also pointed out that charter schools in low-income areas struggle more than those in wealthier communities to raise money, and because they don't have the same public financial supports as neighborhood public schools, they struggle with many of the same challenges as high-poverty non-charter public schools.

## CONCLUSION

There are other examples of illogical responses to the economic achievement gap, many of which I discussed in previous chapters or will discuss in upcoming chapters. The major failing they share, as far as I can see, is just that: They are responses to the *achievement* gap rather than the *opportunity* gap we peeled apart in Chapters 5 and 6. And they don't empower teachers to draw on their considerable skills and creativity. I never understood how stifling teachers helps students.

The good news is that there are just as many strategies that teachers and schools are using successfully to engage and educate students in poverty. I describe them, and the research behind them, next in Chapter 8.

# What Works (When Adapted to Your Specific Context, of Course)

## Instructional Strategies That Are Effective, Equitable, and Even *Data-Driven*

Principles of Equity Literacy discussed in this chapter include:

Principle 8: Equitable educators adopt a resiliency rather than a deficit view of low-income students and families.

Principle 9: Strategies for bolstering school engagement and learning must be based on evidence for what works.

Principle 10: The inalienable right to equitable educational opportunity includes the right to high expectations, higher-order pedagogies, and engaging curricula.

Despite the disheartening realities of poverty and the inequities experienced by low-income youth and their families, I have hope. During my 15 or so years working intimately with public school educators I have found an almost universal vigilance when it comes to advocating for students in poverty. Plus, while it is unfortunately true that the literature spilleth over with evidence of persistent inequalities in our schools, it also spilleth over with evidence that there is something we can do about them. There are many somethings, actually.

I begin this chapter by describing several such somethings, focusing first on instructional and curricular strategies before I turn, in Chapters 9 and 10, to interpersonal or relational strategies and then to bigger school- and district-level initiatives that have proven effective at bolstering the learning and engagement of low-income students and families.

## A COUPLE CAVEATS

Before diving into the strategies, though, I want to reemphasize a sad but important reality. We never will realize educational equity in any full sense until we address bigger economic justice concerns. The symptoms of economic injustice infest schools in a variety of ways. Those of us who have worked in or with poor communities or their schools tend to be pretty well attuned to this because, in addition to incredible resiliency, we see in low-income youth and their families the effects of food insecurity, the scarcity of living wage work, unequal access to healthcare, and the scars of class bias. In a society that prides itself on being a meritocracy, we haven't even managed to guarantee equitable access to the thing we call the "great equalizer": education. This is a notable failure for the wealthiest country in the world.

As I mentioned earlier, educators should not be held more responsible for the effects of these injustices than anyone else; obviously, the change required to address societal disparities will only come through a series of long-term projects. But it is also true that we can't afford to wait, and poor families can't afford to wait, for a big-level societal change. So I have to commit *now* to doing what I can do *today* to address what low-income families are experiencing in this moment, right before me.

In order to do so, we must remember that there is no simple solution; in Eric Freeman's (2010) words, "there is no one-shot inoculation for neutralizing the consequences of disadvantage" (p. 693). Low-income students and communities are infinitely diverse. You know your students better than I know them and better than any researcher or educator cited in this book knows them. No matter what anybody says and no matter how prettily packaged it might be, no set of perfectly scripted strategies will work for *all* low-income students *everywhere*, as Robert Balfanz and Vaughan Byrnes (2006) found in their study about strategies for raising mathematics achievement in high-poverty schools. There is no magic bullet, no effective cookie-cutter approach to improving much of anything when it comes to poverty and inequality (Thurston & Berkeley, 2010). In fact, aside from advocating in any way we can for the social change necessary to alleviate the very existence of poverty, the most important thing any of us can do in the name of educational equity is to draw on the expertise of people within poor and working class communities—to partner with them in order to identify and implement community-specific strategies for educational equity (Kezar, 2011; Lindsey et al., 2010).

## INSTRUCTIONAL STRATEGIES THAT WORK

In this spirit, the strategies I describe here should not be seen collectively as a prescriptive blueprint for eliminating class inequity or even for bettering test scores (an obsession which itself appears to be part of the problem). Instead, they are a broad swath of strategies that I accumulated during a several-year process of reading and synthesizing mountainous mounds of research and spending a lot of time in schools and immersing myself in communities of teachers, new and veteran. With context-specific adaptations they can be important components of a holistic, inclusive plan for making classrooms and schools more equitable, engaging, and validating for low-income students and families. These strategies include:

1.  incorporating music, art, and theater across the curriculum;
2.  having and communicating high expectations for all students;
3.  adopting higher-order, student-centered, rigorous pedagogies;
4.  incorporating movement and exercise into teaching and learning;
5.  making curricula relevant to the lives of low-income students;
6.  teaching about poverty and class bias;
7.  analyzing learning materials for class (and other) bias; and
8.  promoting literacy *enjoyment*.

As a final caveat, the strategies I describe in this and the next two chapters might seem more or less relevant to you based on your job description and sphere of influence. I encourage you to focus first on the strategies you can adapt and implement immediately, tomorrow, then build toward incorporating the other strategies. Work in teams, across subject areas, whenever possible.

*Strategy One: Incorporate Music, Art, and Theater Across the Curriculum.* In-school access to music, art, and theater education fortifies learning, engagement, and retention for all groups of students, but can be particularly important for poor and working class students (Pogrow, 2006; Wetz, 2004). This stands to reason, of course, because poor and working class families are less likely than more economically advantaged families to have the money to provide their children with these experiences outside of school (Bracey, 2006). In-school access to the arts has a motivating effect on students who generally feel alienated at school. It can make them more likely to show up and stay engaged in all of their classes (Tranter & Palin, 2004).

Unfortunately, as we've seen, art and music programs increasingly are being slashed from public schools, and the fiercest slashing usually happens at the highest-poverty schools, sometimes because of insufficient funding, often in order to carve out additional time for reading, writing, and math instruction. Interestingly, according to Stacey Joyner and Concepcion Molina (2012), who synthesized a broad range of research on how extending instructional time affects student learning for the Texas Comprehensive Center, there is scant evidence that simply lengthening instructional time for math or writing increases student achievement. More important than instructional *time*, they found, was instructional *quality*. This is an important point, and we will return to it momentarily.

Given the potential of arts experiences to bolster the learning and engagement of low-income students, one worthwhile strategy is to find ways to integrate the arts across the curriculum, especially at schools that have reduced or eliminated art, music, and theater programs (Landsman & Gorski, 2007). Whether pointing to Picasso's use of geometric shapes in his paintings as part of an elementary mathematics lesson (Holtzman & Susholtz, 2011) or using Augusto Boal's Theatre of the Oppressed techniques with high school students to teach about community-based environmental science (Sullivan & Lloyd, 2006), the possibilities are endless.

In order to get you started, I have provided in Figure 8.1 several resources and guidebooks full of ideas for incorporating the arts into your teaching.

*Strategy Two: Have and Communicate High Expectations for All Students.* The constant stream of low expectations often experienced by students in poverty can have palpable psychological effects on low-income families. Cecilia Rouse and Lisa Barrow (2006) explain,

> If teachers have lower expectations for children from disadvantaged families, regardless of their ability, and if their perceptions about which children are disadvantaged are on average correct, then the lower expectations for disadvantaged children may raise the psychological costs of education relative to their more privileged peers and thus help explain why children of disadvantaged parents attain less education. (p. 99)

In other words, low expectations become an additional weight on the shoulders of low-income students, helping to create the very outcome inequalities for which low-income families are blamed.

Despite these realities, some people dismiss high expectations talk as self-esteem fluffiness. The reality, though, is that expressing high expectations is fluff only when it is all talk, only when we fail to demonstrate them in real ways during our daily interactions with students. When high expectations are expressed in our instruction—more on what this looks like in a moment—those expectations can have a tremendously positive impact on students'

**Figure 8.1. Resources for Incorporating Arts Across the Curriculum**

*Beginner's Guide to Community-Based Arts* by Mat Schwarzman and Keith Knight (2005, New Village Press)

*Engaging Films and Music Videos in Critical Thinking* by Charlene Tan (2007, McGraw-Hill)

*Handbook for K–8 Arts Integration: Purposeful Planning Across the Curriculum* by Nan L. McDonald (2012, Pearson)

*The Hip Hop Education Guidebook* by Marcella Runnell and Martha Diaz (2007, Hip-Hop Association)

*Integrating the Arts Across the Elementary School Curriculum* by R. Phyllis Gelineau (2011, Wadsworth Publishing)

*Music and Movement in the Classroom* by Greg and Steven Trough (2004, Creative Teaching Press)

*Teaching Music Across the Curriculum* by Valereai Luppens and Greg Formena (2011, Alfred Publishing)

*Theater of the Oppressed* by Augusto Boal (1993, Theatre Communications Group)

intellectual development (Figlio, 2005; Jessim & Harber, 2005). Students learn more, and more deeply, when we demonstrate that we believe in their abilities to do so. This is especially true for students who are unaccustomed to experiencing high expectations from authority figures (Kannapel & Clements, 2005; Kitchen, DePree, Celedón-Pattichis, & Brinkerhoff, 2004).

***Strategy Three: Adopt Higher-Order, Learner-Centered, Rigorous Pedagogies.*** Unfortunately, incongruence often reigns. I hear a lot of talk these days about having high expectations for every student, but the unfortunate reality, as we learned in Chapter 7, is that low-income students disproportionately are subject to the lowest-order, most rote, and least engaging teaching. In fact, when Eithne Kennedy (2010) reviewed the findings of a broad range of studies on what makes for effective literacy teachers in high-poverty schools in the United States and the United Kingdom, she found that, among other things, they "emphasize higher-order thinking skills" and "teach basic skills in *meaningful* contexts" (p. 384; emphasis added). She concluded, though, that despite consistent evidence of the effectiveness of these instructional commitments, "this kind of approach to instruction is not the norm and is less likely to be encountered by students who . . . attend high-poverty schools" (p. 384). What sorts of expectations are we communicating to low-income students when they disproportionately are subject to the least effective pedagogies?

We can choose a different path. We can express high expectations by choosing to teach in student-centered ways that support higher-order learning. And the research is on our side. For example, based on their study of more than 3,800 students, Valerie Lee and David Burkam (2003) found that students labeled "at-risk" who attended schools that combined rigorous curricula with learner-centered pedagogies achieved at higher levels and were less likely to be early school leavers than their peers who were subject to less engaging instruction. In fact, a decade and a half of scholarship is nearly unanimous on this point: Low-income students, like *all* students, learn best when we teach in student-centered ways that emphasize higher-order learning.

Let's start with higher-order learning. Generally, low-income youth, like all youth, learn best when instruction is driven by high academic expectations (Hoy et al., 2006), when standards aren't lowered based on socioeconomic status or other factors (Ramalho et al., 2010). The job begins with preschool teachers in programs that foster social and cognitive growth with intellectually stimulating curricula (Judge, 2005). Unfortunately, pedagogical segregation begins in preschool, and so even at the earliest ages, if they have access to any formal educational experiences at all, low-income children are subject to those that lack the intellectual stimulation to which children in wealthier communities have access. But each of us, regardless of what subject or grade level we teach, can choose to bolster the learning and engagement of low-income students by adopting cognitively challenging pedagogies over memorization-and-regurgitation methods that encourage only lower-order thinking (Patterson et al., 2008; Poplin & Soto-Hinman, 2006).

In fact, although I hate to encourage pedagogical decisions based solely on their potential to foster test score improvements, which in and of themselves do not guarantee improvements to deeper forms of learning, research has shown that higher-order pedagogies based on high academic expectations are associated positively with test score increases in both reading and math. For example, according to Stanley Pogrow (2006), instituting a higher-order pedagogical approach "yields substantially higher test score gains than remedial or test-prep approaches—approximately three times the growth in reading comprehension—even as it produces gains in overall intellectual and social development" (p. 227). Similarly, after examining data on 13,000 low-income Kindergartners, Annie Georges (2009) discovered that students whose math instruction focused on reasoning and analytic skills rather than on worksheets and other skills-and-drills pedagogies scored higher on standardized math tests than their peers. She concluded that "students in poverty would benefit to be in classrooms that emphasize problem-solving and reasoning skills with greater frequency" (p. 2148).

Recognizing that terms like "higher-order pedagogies" can be somewhat vague, I scoured 2 decades of scholarship on the relationship between teaching and poverty in hopes of identifying some of the specific higher-order instructional strategies that commonly bolster learning and engagement among low-income students. During this process I concluded, not surprisingly, that a good general rule for effectively engaging low-income students is to teach them in ways that their wealthier peers already are being taught. More particularly, though, two themes appeared over and over again: (1) the power of cooperative and collaborative instructional approaches, and (2) the effectiveness of interactive or "dialogic" teaching and learning.

Cooperative pedagogies, in which students work in pairs or small groups in order to support one another's learning, are, as it turns out, virtually universally effective when it comes to increasing student engagement and learning, regardless of socioeconomic status (LaGue & Wilson, 2010; Slavin, Lake, & Groff, 2009). One form of cooperative learning that is especially effective for low-income students is peer tutoring, which has been shown to improve learning for the tutor and the tutored across the curriculum (Maheady, Mallette, & Harper, 2006). Notably, students who participate in peer tutoring become more engaged in school overall (Greenwood & Delquari, 1995), and even the tutors come out of the tutoring relationship with a better grasp of the tutored content (Galbraith & Winterbottom, 2011).

Although it can be difficult to pinpoint why, exactly, these and other cooperative learning strategies work especially well for low-income students, experience tells me that it might have something to do with the fact that in many poor communities, like the one from which my mom's people hail, where affordable childcare, means for transportation, healthcare access, and other basic needs are scarce, people develop cooperative tendencies, a resiliency-tinged effort to survive. It also might reflect the fact that some low-income students have an easier time than many of their teachers relating material to the lives of their poor and working class peers. Whatever the reason for its effectiveness, try to incorporate opportunities for cooperative learning, especially in mixed-ability groups, whenever appropriate.

Similarly, like their wealthier peers, low-income students tend to respond favorably to interactive or "dialogic" pedagogies and to pretty much any instructional strategy that recognizes them as inquirers and excavators rather than empty, stagnant receptacles. According to Robin Alexander (2006), dialogic teaching is characterized by five principles. Dialogic methods are

1. *collective*, so that learning happens interactively among teachers and students;
2. *reciprocal*, so that learning is based on teachers and learners listening to and learning from one another and considering a broad range of viewpoints;
3. *supportive*, so that students feel that they can participate and share their ideas without the fear that they will be shamed and with the goal of striving for shared understandings;

4. *cumulative*, so that students and teachers build on their own and others' thinking over time; and

5. *purposeful*, so that teachers employ dialogic methods in the service of specific learning goals.

Low-income students, and *all* students, learn better and, yes, score higher on those pesky standardized tests when their teachers adopt dialogic methods. This is true across the curriculum. Several studies have demonstrated a link between dialogic teaching and literacy achievement (Barr & Parrett, 2007; Howard, 2007; Wasik, Bond, & Hindman, 2006), even for the youngest learners. For instance, following their evaluation of dialogic teaching in early childhood classrooms in Miami, Judith Bernhard and her colleagues (2008) concluded that literacy interventions that are based on "increasing children's participation in meaningful literacy activities, and that do not overemphasize direct teaching of literacy skills and subcomponents, are effective in increasing the language skills of diverse, urban young children in poverty" (p. 100).

Similarly, participatory, inquiry-driven, dialogic math instruction is, according to a great deal of research, far more effective than lecture, direct instruction, and other lower-order pedagogies (Van de Walle, 2006; Wenglinsky, 2002). The National Council of Teachers of Mathematics (NCTM; 2000) took its stand on this point almost 15 years ago. As Sueanne McKinney and Wendy Frazier (2008) explain based on their analysis of math instruction practices at low-income middle schools, "providing students with participatory and inquiry-driven mathematical opportunities that highlight reasoning and problem-solving skills allows them to develop conceptual understandings of mathematical ideas that are often neglected by traditional instructional approaches" (p. 203).

I doubt any of us are surprised that students in poverty, just like their wealthier peers, prefer engaging pedagogies that validate them as thinkers and learners and doers. Unfortunately, like other higher-order sorts of pedagogies, dialogic teaching remains fairly uncommon, and more rote forms of teaching continue to dominate, in classrooms comprised predominantly of poor and working class youth (McKinney & Frazier, 2008). This, too, is something we can change in our own classrooms and schools.

*Strategy Four: Incorporate Movement and Exercise into Teaching and Learning.* In far too many high-poverty schools, recess and physical education are disappearing as quickly as art and music programs. Obviously, students who are physically fit fare better on average in school than students who do not exercise regularly, as Charles Basch (2011) found in his synthesis of roughly 2 decades of scholarship on the matter. Moreover, childhood physical fitness is a good predictor of students' lifelong health trajectories

(Fahlman, Hall, & Lock, 2006); in other words, youth who are physically fit tend to become adults who are physically fit.

Unfortunately, due to the relative dearth of well-maintained recreational facilities, like ball courts and fields, playgrounds, and recreation centers, in poor communities (Brann-Barrett, 2010; MacLeod, Gee, Crawford, & Wang, 2008), coupled with the growing costs of recreational sports leagues, many low-income youth experience recess or physical education classes as their sole opportunities for organized exercise. This is especially true after middle school, when more poor and working class youth are charged with caring for younger siblings or working to help support their families (Fahlman et al., 2006). Making matters worse, students who are least likely to have access to out-of-school opportunities to exercise also have the most minuscule access to school-based opportunities to exercise, such as physical education courses (Basch, 2011).

The good news is, there are all sorts of easy and applicable ways to incorporate physical movement into classroom instruction, and the list of available resources on how to do so in specific subject areas, or across subject areas, is growing longer every day. Take math, for example. Greg Hatch and Darla Smith (2004) have proposed powerful interdisciplinary ways to integrate physical education into math and physics classes to study, among other things, projectile motion. In her article "Students Hop, Skip, and Jump Their Way to Understanding," Andrea Elkin (2012) shares strategies for using movement to bolster young students' mastery of a broad array of mathematics competencies. When we follow these educators' leads and incorporate movement into our instruction we take advantage of links between physical activity, brain power, and learning while also providing youth who, on average, have fewer opportunities to exercise than their wealthier counterparts with an additional exercise outlet.

*Strategy Five: Make Curricula Relevant to the Lives of Low-Income Students.* Would you recognize "portage" if you saw it? I shared the story earlier about how several years ago one of the Minnesota state standardized math tests contained an entire section of word problems on boating, hiking, and camping in the Northwoods, a rural resort area a several-hour drive north of St. Paul, where I was living at the time. On the face of it, these questions put low-income students from St. Paul and Minneapolis at a considerable disadvantage, as a vast majority of their families could not afford vacations in the Northwoods, much less the equipment necessary for camping, ice fishing, snowmobiling, and other common Northwoods activities. In fact, I spent time in high-poverty schools in St. Paul in which most students had spent little time outside the Twin Cities metro area. And yet they, like their wealthier peers, were expected to relate to these word problems full of words like *portage*, which, by the way, is the act of carrying a boat overland between navigable waterways. Portage is not the kind of thing that low-income urban youth do in their spare time.

All students learn better when the curriculum is made relevant to their lives, when we build teaching and learning experiences around the strengths, cultures, and resources in local communities (Lee, 1995). In his essay "The Pedagogy of Poverty Versus Good Teaching" (1991), Martin Haberman urges us to find ways to connect what students are learning to their daily lives and to the lives of people in their communities. Better yet, he says, put students to work applying what they learn to solve community problems. He explains, "In good schools, problems are not viewed as occasions to impose more rules and tighter management from above. Far from being viewed as obstacles to the 'normal' school routine, difficult events and issues are transformed into the very stuff of the curriculum" (p. 293). Similarly, Neil Duke and his colleagues (2006) have shown how developing what they call "authentic" learning activities that address local community needs can strengthen literacy and school engagement through science education.

Lenny Sánchez (in press), during an ethnographic study of a low-income 3rd-grade class, captured a fantastic example of how this approach can work to engage even elementary-age students and deepen their learning. Their teacher crafted an interdisciplinary project in which they combined math, literacy, and other skills to explore and respond to community problems. One small group of students chose to focus on an issue several of them had bemoaned for months: safety concerns related to the deterioration of the school's playground, which also served as a community park after school hours. Sánchez, also a product of a low-income upbringing, marveled at the students' determination to collaborate with one another and to invite community members into their problem-solving processes. Because they were dealing with issues that were very real to them and their families, they engaged vigorously, always a good thing when it comes to learning.

Barbara Comber and her colleagues (2006) described similar projects led by teachers in a low-income Australian neighborhood that was being disintegrated, literally and figuratively, by a government "urban renewal" initiative. The teachers constructed curricula around the many challenges this disintegration posed to the students, integrating complex architectural and design concepts as well as spatial and visual literacy. The authors explained that

> children were able to become producers of space, re-imagining, rede-signing, and remaking part of their school grounds within a neigh-borhood almost overtaken by urban renewal. Teachers worked with children to build a critically inflected curriculum and pedagogy around the redesign of a barren outdoor space. (p. 229)

In each of these examples, students learned content and skills by applying them to real-world problems that affected them in real-world ways. They were engaged, connected, and appreciative of the opportunity to make visible the issues in their communities often rendered invisible by the curriculum.

*Strategy Six: Teach About Poverty and Class Bias.* On an August day in 1967, 4 years after his "I Have a Dream" speech," Martin Luther King Jr. delivered his presidential address to the Southern Christian Leadership Conference. He titled his talk "Where Do We Go From Here?" You might be interested to know that at the very beginning of his speech he referred to racial and economic inequity in schools, pointing out the "savage inequalities" about which Jonathan Kozol (1992) would later become famous for writing. "In elementary schools," Dr. King lamented, "Negroes lag one to three years behind whites, and their segregated schools receive substantially less money per student than the white schools." Although reframed in the U.S. imagination as a civil rights activist who only fought for equal rights for African Americans, Dr. King's most important contribution to human rights, as illustrated by this short quote, may have been his insistence that race and class are linked inextricably in the United States. Read his speeches from the last few years of his life and you'll see that he bemoaned poverty as he bemoaned racism (as he also bemoaned the Vietnam War because of how poverty and race were pretty good determinants of who was most likely to be sent to the front lines). He was all about intersectionality before intersectionality was cool.

In fact, later in this very speech he said, "And one day we must ask the question, 'Why are there forty million poor people in America?' And when you begin to ask that question, you are raising questions about the economic system, about a broader distribution of wealth. When you ask that question, you begin to question the capitalistic economy." When we teach about Martin Luther King Jr., how often do we discuss how he championed the rights of working class and poor people of every race? How often do we teach that he organized marches against poverty or that when he was assassinated he had traveled to Memphis to help organize African American sanitation workers who were on strike due to unsafe working conditions and unfair pay?

It can be difficult, I know, introducing these difficult issues in class, unsure of how students or parents or administrators might respond. But it's important to remember that despite adults' desire to protect students from controversial topics or difficult issues, youth are more cognizant than we know about economic and other forms of inequity (Chafel, 1997). In fact, Jessi Streib (2011) has documented the ways in which even preschool-age children understand and act out class distinctions and stereotypes, often resulting in the reproduction of inequity. Summarizing her findings for the

*Classism Exposed* blog, Streib (2012) wrote, "The ways that four year olds interacted with each other and with teachers . . . created disadvantages for the already disadvantaged and privileges for those born into privilege. Well meaning people and organizations can produce unintended outcomes" (¶ 6).

One powerful way to make the curriculum relevant to poor and working class students is to teach explicitly about issues associated with poverty, class, and economic justice (Kelley & Darragh, 2011; Mistry, Brown, Chow, & Collins, 2012). Martin Luther King Jr. gives us an "in," as do several other historical figures about whom many of us teach: Helen Keller, César Chávez, Eleanor Roosevelt, Mark Twain, the Black Panthers, and even Albert Einstein. Each spoke or wrote or acted on behalf of poor people and denounced local and federal government agencies—the same agencies that continue to fall short in their support of low-income families—for failing to respond adequately to poverty. Maya Angelou and others continue to do so today, providing us with important opportunities to introduce conversations about poverty in the present tense rather than the past tense.

Of course, we don't have to wait until famous people come up in class to teach about issues related to poverty and class. A math teacher might ask students to calculate what a living wage would be for people in their communities. Judith Chafel and her colleagues (2007) suggest a more direct approach, asking students to draw images of poor people as a way to begin a conversation about biases and poverty. An elementary school teacher might include in a classroom library picture books that introduce concepts related to poverty and class. My personal favorite is Doreen Cronin and Betsy Lewin's (2000) *Click, Clack, Moo,* in which farm animals organize to demand better working conditions from Farmer Brown.

We should be mindful, though, to select books that depict people in poverty and working class people who are standing up to discrimination, contributing to social causes, and pushing through day-to-day challenges with resilience and avoid books that are meant simply to elicit pity or that portray low-income people solely as victims (Kelley & Darragh, 2011). I asked Stephanie Jones, who has studied portrayals of low-income characters in picture books, which books, of those she's reviewed, were her favorites when it comes to positive portrayals of poor and working class families. She responded enthusiastically, ensuring me that there are a lot of fabulous options. Her top recommendations include:

- *Amber Was Brave, Essie Was Smart* by Vera B. Williams (2001, Greenwillow Books, ages 8 and up)
- *¡Sí, Se Puede!/Yes, We Can!: Janitor Strike in L.A.* by Diana Cohn and Francisco Delgado (2005, Cinco Puntos Press, ages 5 and up)
- *Somebody's New Pajamas* by Isaac Jackson and David Soman (1996, Dial, ages 3 and up)

- *Those Shoes* by Maribeth Boetls and Noah Z. Jones (2009, Candlewick, ages 5 and up)
- *Voices in the Park* by Anthony Browne (2001, DK Children, ages 7 and up)

Teaching about poverty and class can serve several purposes. It can be one way to acknowledge the existence of low-income students or to make the curriculum relevant to their lives. It provides opportunities for poor and working class youth to challenge the sorts of biases and stereotypes their wealthier peers might have about them (Dutro, 2009). Best of all, we do not necessarily have to add more content to our curriculum in order to do this. Instead, we can find ways to weave these conversations into existing learning activities just by being a little more determined to find appropriate ways of doing so.

Several well-respected organizations host resource-rich websites chock-full of free ideas, activities, and strategies for teaching about poverty, class, economic justice, and a wide range of other social issues. Figure 8.2 points you to several of my favorites.

*Strategy Seven: Analyze Learning Materials for Class (and Other) Bias.* In that analysis of picture books with themes related to poverty and class, Stephanie Jones (2008) found that poor and working class families regularly were depicted in stereotypical ways. For example, books tended to understate the proportion of White people in poverty while overstating poverty in communities of color. Often these sorts of biases are implicit and difficult to spot if we are not looking for them. Luckily, a variety of useful tools exist to help us uncover class biases, including the National Association for the Teaching of English Working Party on Social Class and English Teaching's (1982) checklist for class bias. Despite being more than 30 years old and focusing primarily on depictions of working class rather than poor characters, the checklist is comprised of contemporarily relevant questions to help us determine the

### Figure 8.2. Online Resources for Teaching about Poverty and Class

Amnesty International Human Rights Education: http://www.amnestyusa.org/resources/educators

Class Action: http://www.classism.org

Make Poverty History: http://www.makepovertyhistory.org/takeaction/

New York Collective of Racial Educators: http://www.nycore.org

Teaching Economics as if People Mattered: http://www.teachingeconomics.org/

Teaching Tolerance: http://www.tolerance.org/

TeachUNICEF's Poverty Curriculum Materials: http://teachunicef.org/explore/topic/poverty

United for a Fair Economy: http://www.faireconomy.org/

extent of bias in children's literature, especially if we modify "working class" to "poor or working class." Some of the questions we might consider when choosing literature and other resources include:

- How are [poor people or] the working class portrayed? As subservient? Brutal? Stupid? Crude? Sexist? . . .
- Are [poor or] working class people portrayed as being in control of their lives?
- Are the middle class or upper class characters shown as being the saviors of [poor people or] the working class? (p. 34)

Better yet, we collaborate with our students to analyze and discuss the biases in their learning materials. Remember that if low-income students are finding bias in learning materials that we, as teachers, are failing to acknowledge, they might interpret our lack of acknowledgment as agreement with the bias. Needless to say, that will not help our efforts to create an equitable learning environment. As equity-literate educators, we must learn how to spot even the most subtle biases.

Remember, too, that class bias pops up not just in language arts materials, but also in social studies textbooks, math workbooks, children's magazines, educational films, and even learning materials made especially for English Language Learners. For instance, Joelle Sano (2009), who analyzed 50 children's books popularly read aloud to English Language Learners in public schools, found alarming rates of class bias (and race bias) in them.

Here, too, is something rather simple we all can commit to doing: Examine all learning materials for class bias. Keep in mind, again, that bias can be very subtle. Consider, for instance, how poor and working class people are depicted with regard to their dispositions toward school and reading, their attitudes about possessions, and their morals (Sano, 2009). If you find class or any other kind of bias in learning materials that you are mandated to use, work with your students to analyze and challenge them.

*Strategy Eight: Promote Literacy Enjoyment.* According to Mary Kellet (2009), "If we . . . acknowledge that literacy proficiency can be a route out of poverty . . . the most powerful strategy is to create cultures that promote reading enjoyment. This is likely to make the biggest impact on literacy proficiency" (p. 399). This means, consistent with the other strategies discussed here, that literacy instruction should not focus solely on reading or writing mechanics. More to the point, though, it means that we ought to find ways to foster in students excitement about reading and writing even when they respond reluctantly at first.

Creative people that we tend to be, educators have used a broad range of strategies to do just that. For example, Debbie Vera (2011) tracked low-income pre-Kindergarten students whose teacher took advantage of their adoration for television characters like Dora the Explorer to engage them in literacy education activities. Compared with a control group, students engaged in this manner showed larger gains in their knowledge of the alphabet and a variety of written language concepts. Vera concluded, "Incorporating the media interests of children within the emergent literacy curriculum can assist high-poverty [students] with early reading skills . . ." (p. 328).

Other creative and effective strategies abound. For example, in order to promote literacy enjoyment you might:

- institute literature circles, in which small groups of students read and discuss a book they choose collaboratively (Whittaker, 2012);
- provide reading material options that align with the stated interests of students (Reis & Fogarty, 2006);
- use a variety of media, such as multimedia software programs and blogs, that engage students actively and interactively (Karemaker, Pitchford, & O'Malley, 2010; Yollis, 2012); and
- incorporate drama into literacy instruction (Baldwin, 2007).

Meanwhile, we should be careful to avoid instructional practices sure to elevate students' reading and writing reluctance. Most definitely avoid forcing them, in Kellet's (2009) words, to publicly "perform" their literacy skills.

## CONCLUSION

Perhaps the most outstanding feature of these strategies, taken together, is that many of them are used as a matter of course in low-poverty schools and classrooms. In those places, we might call this, simply, "good teaching." Perhaps we are not in positions to ensure that all of our students have access to preventive healthcare or shadow education or academic summer camps. But we do all have the power to ensure that we are doing all that we can do so that low-income students, when they are in our classrooms and schools, receive the best possible education.

Whereas in this chapter I focused on describing research-supported instructional strategies for teaching students in poverty, I set aside a separate chapter, Chapter 9, to sketch out what might be considered *relational* strategies. *How*, I ask in Chapter 9, *can I build authentic, collaborative, respectful relationships with students and families in poverty?*

# The Mother of All Strategies

## Committing to Working *With* Rather than *On* Families in Poverty

> Principles of Equity Literacy discussed in this chapter include:
>
> Principle 4: What we believe, including our biases and prejudices, about people in poverty informs how we teach and relate to people in poverty.
>
> Principle 8: Equitable educators adopt a resiliency rather than a deficit view of low-income students and families.

Instructional strategies are important, but they mean nary a whit if we don't build strong, positive relationships with low-income families. Students are smart and intuitive; it's hard to get one over on them. We know this. So every practical strategy in the world (or in the previous chapter) will not work if we treat poor and working class youth or their families, even in the most implicit ways, as though they are broken or some lesser "other." Remember, as we learned earlier, that research has shown that who or what we choose to blame for poverty guides the policies and practices we are willing to implement (Bullock et al., 2003; Williams, 2009). In other words, what we believe about low-income students—how we relate to them—is just as important as how we teach them; in fact, it plays a considerable role in determining how we teach them (Robinson, 2007).

The trouble is that relationship-building, when we pursue it sincerely, is a much more difficult undertaking than incorporating music or cooperative learning into our teaching. It requires, first of all, a tremendous amount of humility and a willingness to ask ourselves awfully hard questions. *What stereotypes do I have about poor and working class people? What assumptions do I have about what shape relationships between teachers and families ought to take? Do I see low-income youth as broken or their families as inferior, even if I believe I don't show it? Do I see myself as their fixer?* These sorts of questions help us take stock of our relational commitments to low-income students by forcing us to reveal to ourselves the biases and dispositions we carry into our interactions with them. They nudge us, as well, toward reflecting on *our* attitudes, *our* behaviors, and *our* roles in improving the educational experiences of youth in poverty when it might be easier to rest on the laurels of our good intentions.

Part of the challenge of relationship-building, though, is that good intentions are of little mitigating consequence against students' perceptions. As a result, sometimes we might create or broaden gulfs between low-income students and ourselves without intending to do so or even realizing we are doing so. For example, one marker of economic privilege in schools is the ability to afford the newest fashions and name-brand clothes. The expectation to dress fashionably in order to fit in at school can be a considerable stressor for low-income students, as Tanya Brann-Barrett (2010) found in the ethnographic study of working class youth I mentioned earlier. Obviously, aside from enforcing a general dress code, I cannot control what students wear unless my school institutes a uniform policy. But I can control what I wear, which is something I never really considered relevant to working with low-income youth before reading Brann-Barrett's study. I can think twice before donning a sweater or carrying a bag with an expensive brand name or logo plastered across it. I can choose, in that way, not to highlight the economic gap between some of my students and me by dressing and accessorizing humbly.

## FOUR RELATIONAL COMMITMENTS

As I pored over a few decades' worth of research on poverty and education looking for the sorts of relational and dispositional educator attributes that are associated with high levels of engagement and academic success for low-income students, four themes kept reappearing. The most successful teachers of low-income students:

1. choose a resilience view, rather than a deficit view, of poor and working class families, focusing on student and family assets;
2. engage in *persistent* family outreach efforts;
3. build trusting relationships with students; and
4. ensure that opportunities for family involvement are accessible to poor and working class families.

*Commitment One: Choose a Resilience View, Rather than a Deficit View.* As we explored in earlier chapters, when we adopt a deficit view of low-income students, we begin with an assumption, however implicit or unintentional, that they are somehow broken, needing to be fixed or rescued from a deficient "culture of poverty." As we fixate on their deficiencies, we might fail to acknowledge the opportunity gaps experienced inside and outside schools by poor and working class families and, as a result, miss opportunities to draw on the resiliencies and community assets low-income students bring to school with them.

Rejecting the deficit view, like having high academic expectations, is not self-esteem fluffiness. No, this is data-driven commitment-making. And it might just be the most essential ingredient in the effective relationship recipe between educators and low-income students.

It is important to remember that low-income youth constantly see deficit reflections of themselves and their communities, whether on television (think *Cops* or *Justified* or *Coal*), in movies, or even, as we learned in Chapter 8, in children's picture books (Jones, 2008; Sano, 2009). Making matters worse, the dominant perception of poor people, particularly in the United States, is drenched in deficit views. Even if they are unwilling to say so in polite company, a majority of U.S. citizens believe that poor people are poor because of their own deficiencies (Carreiro & Kapitulik, 2010), that they are undeserving of any other lot in life. We are flooded with rags-to-riches stories and celebrations of meritocracy despite the fact that upward mobility for poor people is rare and becoming rarer (Mazumder, 2005; Swartz, 2008). As a result, even for the best intentioned of us, a deficit view can feel pretty natural and justified, especially among people who never have experienced prolonged hunger or homelessness or the steady grinding of class bias. It certainly doesn't help, either, that studies (see, for example, Smiley & Helfenbein, 2011) are beginning to show how some of the most popular teacher professional development programs ostensibly meant to help us better understand students in poverty actually leave us with more severely deficit-laden stereotypes than we had to begin with. (Oops!)

When we adopt a deficit view of a low-income student, seeing her poverty itself as evidence of intellectual or moral or spiritual inferiority, her performance and school engagement actually recede. The opposite happens when we focus on student strengths, a reality that holds true whether we're talking about socioeconomic status (Haberman, 1995), gender (Johns, Schmader, & Martens, 2005), or any other student identifier.

Extending the same line of reasoning to families, Kathleen Cooter (2006), who reviewed research on best practices for partnering with low-income, illiterate mothers in order to strengthen the literacy skills of school-age youth, urges us to focus on parent and guardian *strengths*, to celebrate what they bring to the table rather than what they lack. "Build on what the mother can do," Cooter advises. "Value what she knows, how she lives, and the uniqueness of her family." By adopting this sort of "mindset and plan," she explains, "we can respect the mother who can't read as her child's first and best teacher" (p. 701). And we can do so without alienating students or their families.

If it helps to think about this in more selfish terms, J. Gregg Robinson (2007) found, based on a study of more than 400 teachers in low-income urban schools, that the teachers who rejected a deficit view of their students were happier with their jobs than their colleagues who retained a deficit view. Plus, teachers who understood the societal challenges faced by low-income families were more effective at responding to the needs of students whose families were in poverty. Robinson called this phenomenon a "structurally mitigated sense of occupational competence" because it helped teachers in his study understand their work in a larger context of class inequities and, as a result, helped them respond more effectively to the needs of low-income students. So letting go of our deficit views and focusing, instead, on student strengths and resilience is good for teaching, but it's also good for teacher morale, a win-win. This also is why it's such a key component of equity literacy.

So here's the hard part. *Pretending* to have a resiliency view is not enough. Nor is having a deficit view, but believing I can hide it from low-income students and their families. I can't. But more to the point, studies on deficit and resilience perspectives make it clear that the crux of the matter really is about what we *believe*, about our respective ideologies. This is where humility comes in. Certainly, if I have spent my life believing, however quietly, that poor people are poor because of their deficiencies, and if I believe the most common stereotypes about poor people (see Chapter 4) despite contrary evidence, then my task is not to hide these assumptions, but to rid myself of them. There are a variety of ways to do this, but spending time in low-income communities and reading about the sorts of social and educational inequalities faced by poor and working class youth are good places to start.

I was raised, remember, by a father from an urban middle class family and a mother from a poor Appalachian family. Despite this heritage it took a concerted effort on my part to shake the stereotypes the media and school and many of my peers were feeding me *about my own family*. I spent a lot of time with my mother's family growing up and always appreciated the incredible resilience and intelligence and spiritual grit I saw around me. Still, it wasn't until I read Jonathan Kozol's *Savage Inequalities* (1992) and Herbert Gans's *The War Against the Poor* (1995) that I was able to appreciate these attributes in their proper context. It wasn't until I read *Where We Stand: Class Matters* by bell hooks (2000), who grew up in poverty, that I began to understand how remarkable my grandmother was. (I've listed other books that deepened my understanding of poverty and, as a result, strengthened my equity literacy, in Figure 9.1.) But I had to seek out this knowledge; nobody handed it to me or assigned readings on it in my classes. In many ways the resilience view rubbed against almost every other message I received growing up about what it means to be poor. I was conditioned for the deficit

**Figure 9.1. Six Books about Poverty that Grew My Equity Literacy**

*A People's History of Poverty in America* by Stephen Pimpare (2011, The New
     Press)
*Savage Inequalities* by Jonathan Kozol (1992, Harper)
*The Travels of a T-Shirt in the Global Economy* by Pietra Rivoli (2009, Wiley)
*The United States of Appalachia* by Jeff Biggers (2007, Counterpoint)
*The War Against the Poor* by Herbert Gans (1995, Basic Books)
*Where We Stand: Class Matters* by bell hooks (2000, Routledge)

view and *chose* to remake my understanding, a process that continues, and
not without its challenges, today.

   *Commitment Two: Engage in Persistent Family Outreach Efforts.* Keep
in mind that many low-income parents and guardians have experienced
schools and a variety of other public systems as hostile environments (Gorski, 2012), so any hesitance you might experience from them as you begin
outreach efforts is not necessarily about you. It might be a simple reflection
of reasonable distrust for the education system, which, historically, has not
been particularly friendly to poor and working class families. Or it could be
the result of long work hours or a lack of access to a telephone at work. So
we need to be persistent and understanding. We need to establish and build
and sustain trust and, perhaps most importantly, to demonstrate *our* trust
in low-income families (Hoy et al., 2006) by nurturing positive relationships
with them (Machan, Wilson, & Notar, 2005; Patterson et al., 2008).
   How might we build these trusting relationships? We can start by facilitating consistent two-way communication (Barr & Parrett, 2007) rather
than reaching out only when something negative has happened, which, unfortunately, is what many low-income parents and guardians have come to
expect. But equally as important as how often we reach out to parents and
guardians is how we relate to them during our correspondence. Susan B.
Neuman (2009), who has spent a couple of decades studying poverty and
literacy, urges us to recognize parents as partners and to gear our outreach
efforts with that kind of relationship in mind. By doing so, and by being
persistent even during those stretches when parents or guardians might seem
unresponsive, we increase the likelihood that they will feel comfortable
sharing information about students' home lives that might be relevant to
their learning (Howard, 2007). Also, by seeing and treating them as partners, we do our part to make our schools and classrooms welcoming for
low-income families, making it more likely that they will see us as partners,
too (McGee, 2004).
   As with choosing the resilience view, researchers have found a direct,
on-the-ground relationship between parental outreach and student achievement. For example, in a longitudinal study of 71 high-poverty Title I

elementary schools, student achievement grew faster in both reading and math when teachers engaged more actively in parent outreach (U.S. Department of Education, 2001). In fact, "Growth in [reading] test scores between third and fifth grade was 50 percent higher for those students whose teachers and schools reported high levels of parental outreach . . . than students whose teachers and schools reported low levels of parent outreach activities for the third grade" (p. 1).

Of course, as I've stressed throughout this book, test scores are not the be-all and end-all of equity. Coming at the issue of family outreach from a different angle in their report, *Staying in School*, Derek Messacar and Philip Oreopoulus (2012) explained, "When school administrators and educators communicate more regularly with parents regarding their children's performance, they provide a means for parents to take a more active role" (p. 14), increasing the chances that their children will stay in school.

*Commitment Three: Build Trusting Relationships with Students.* Meditate for a moment on this question: Is there some place you've been in your life where you didn't feel completely safe or accepted? All of us have been at social gatherings at which we felt out of place, of course, but try to recall somewhere you *had* to be for sustained periods of time, somewhere from which you could not just walk away when the discomfort set in. Unfortunately, for many low-income students and families, that place—one of them, at least—is school. If you share that experience, you know how difficult it can be. I don't believe this unfortunate reality is the result of rabidly class-biased teachers and administrators doing purposefully class-biased things. I believe, instead, that it is the result of a whole web of implicit, often unintentional, grinding inequities and humilities commonly experienced by poor and working class people in their interactions with schools and a wide range of other public systems. We explored many of these inequities in Chapters 5 and 6.

This, then, is our challenge. Like their parents and guardians, many youth from families in poverty, who are more likely than their wealthier peers to have experienced these inequities and humilities, have no particular reason to trust institutions like schools. Low-income students of color or English Language Learners or Muslim students or others who might have experienced multiple layers of inequities and humilities could be particularly cautious with their trust. Nor do some low-income students have much reason to trust institutional authority figures, whom they might see as representatives of institutions in which they have experienced these inequities and humilities. One of the most troubling components of the popular "culture of poverty" model for understanding poverty is the way in which its proponents actually identify this sort of distrust of authority as a deficiency in the characters of low-income youth. This, of course, is a classic case of a deficit view: Poor and working class people experience bias and other indignities and then are deemed deficient for perfectly reasonable responses to these experiences. It's the double whammy of class bias.

The point here is that as teachers, administrators, and other authority figures, we cannot rely on our positional authority when it comes to gaining the trust of low-income students (Hughes, Newkirk, & Stenhjem, 2010). We do, however, need to find ways to build that trust because it relates directly to student achievement (Kannapel & Clements, 2005; Ramalho et al., 2010), especially in the context of teacher-student relationships. I have listed several specific actions that can help to nurture this kind of trust in Figure 9.2. This can take time because, unfortunately, it might require undoing a lot of damage that has been done to students in the past, often unintentionally, by teachers and counselors who have expressed low expectations of them, assigned books with stereotypical portrayals of people like them, or even treated their parents in subtly condescending ways.

Some of the most important ways to build trusting relationships with low-income students are described in the previous chapter: having high academic expectations of them, naming bias in educational materials, making the curriculum relevant to their lives. But there are other things we can do, or do better, that will help us nurture strong, trusting relationships with low-income students. For example, Lois Weiner (2003) encourages us to pay serious attention to the full range of equity and diversity concerns in our classrooms because it is difficult for students to trust us when we allow any sort of bias or inequity, whether related to class, gender identity or expression, race, sexual orientation, religion, disability, or any other issue, to go unchecked. Of course, in order to eliminate these biases or inequities from our classrooms and schools we need to learn how to see them, even in their most insidious, implicit forms. It's not just about interrupting racist

### Figure 9.2. Actions that Can Help Us Nurture Trust with Students in Poverty

We can:

1. Demonstrate high academic expectations through engaging pedagogies.
2. Avoid learning materials with biased depictions of poor and working class people. When you must use materials with even subtle bias, identify the bias openly.
3. Make curricula relevant to their lives.
4. Address all forms of inequity and bias in the classroom, showing our commitments to creating safe learning spaces for every student.
5. Recognize students in poverty as individuals rather than assuming they belong to a monolithic and stereotyped "culture of poverty."
6. Develop positive relationships with their families.

name-calling. It's also about recognizing ways that Whiteness is subtly presented as "normal," which can be difficult to spot, especially if I haven't been the target of that sort of bias.

Lizette Howard (2007), based on her study of how the most effective teachers teach children from low-income families, argues that we build trusting relationships with poor youth when see them as *whole* students, when we take the time to get to know their hopes and fears and interests. Like all of these relational commitments, this means resisting the temptation to think that all low-income students are alike or share a singular "culture of poverty." It means getting to know students and their families on an individual basis.

Perhaps the most efficient way to lose progress we've made nurturing trust with low-income students is to invalidate or ignore concerns they raise about the biases and inequities they're experiencing (Hamovitch, 1996). It's important, at all costs, to avoid telling a student who is attempting to demonstrate self-advocacy that she is overreacting or seeing things all wrong. This, too, is where humility is important. I must be willing to listen to students' concerns and to consider the possibility that I am the one who is missing something if I don't see the bias they see.

*Commitment Four: Ensure that Opportunities for Family Involvement Are Accessible to Poor and Working Class Families.* As we explored way back in Chapter 4, poor and working class families have the exact same attitudes about the value of school as their wealthier counterparts (Gorski, 2008a). Unfortunately, this doesn't stop a lot of people from assuming that low-income parents and guardians who don't show up for Back to School Night and other on-site opportunities for school involvement simply don't care about education. Shifting our lenses a bit to consider this concern from a different angle, we might assume instead that schools, on average, don't care as much about the involvement of low-income families as they do about the involvement of wealthier families.

Why? Well, let's ask ourselves this: Are most of the opportunities we provide for school-based family involvement as accessible to low-income families as they are to wealthier families? Think, for a moment, about standard approaches for scheduling Back to School events, parent-teacher conferences, and most other school functions. What obstacles might they present for poor and working class parents and guardians?

Time constraints are a challenge, of course (Howard et al., 2009). In her study comparing the lives of low-income and middle class 1st-graders, Annette Lareau (1994) found that the low-income families experienced considerably less time flexibility, making some forms of school involvement, like volunteering during the school day, nearly impossible. Often school events are scheduled at times that do not work well for many low-income people, who are more likely than their wealthier counterparts to work late shifts or to work multiple jobs (Van Galen, 2007).

Affordability is another concern. Family involvement might appear to be free for most of us, but not for a good many poor and working class families. Low-income adults are likely to work wage jobs at which they do not have access to paid leave to take sick kids to the doctor, much less to attend school events. They are more likely than their wealthier counterparts to rely on public transportation to get from place to place, which is another cost, both in terms of money and time. Then there's the issue of childcare if they are unable to bring their children to the school.

When we fall short of responding to, or even acknowledging, these challenges, we send the kinds of messages that a vast majority of us never want to send. We say, however implicitly, that we do not value the involvement of low-income parents or, worse, that we do not expect their involvement. When we fail to respond to or acknowledge these challenges and then, against the clearest of evidence to the contrary, blame educational outcome disparities on the supposed disinterest of low-income parents and guardians, we are, in essence, brewing a perfect recipe for inimical relationships with families in poverty.

So, among the most important relational commitments to low-income families is the commitment to make family involvement as accessible to them as possible (Cooper, 2010; Gorski, 2008b). Schools increasingly are finding ways to mitigate the time and financial challenges associated with on-site school involvement, such as by providing childcare and transportation or by hosting events at community centers in low-income neighborhoods. Howard, in her study, found that many successful teachers of low-income youth relied on phone conferences when parents or guardians couldn't leave work to attend something at the school. The same strategy might be used to defray childcare and transportation costs if your school has not found other ways to defray those costs.

Another strategy people at some schools are using is finding ways to be more flexible when it comes to scheduling events or individual parent-teacher conferences. Some low-income adults will have more availability for early morning, Saturday, or late evening schedule blocks than for late afternoon or early evening blocks (Howard et al., 2009). For those of us who feel we have little influence over the ways our schools schedule events or over how or whether other challenges faced by low-income families are addressed in school event planning, we can, at the very least, apply these principles to our individual communications and relationship-building with parents and guardians.

Finally, I always try to remember, again, that on top of the time and financial constraints, many poor and working class adults experienced school as a hostile environment when they were students (Barr & Parrett, 2007; Graham, 2009). With this in mind, one important step is to ensure that we treat them respectfully, as our collaborators, and as the primary experts about their children and communities. In terms of family involvement, for instance, we must quell our biases and never assume, if a low-income parent or guardian does not show up for a conference or event, that we know why.

## CONCLUSION

Relational strategies might be even more important than practical strategies because they guide the day-to-day decisions we make as educators. They also can be harder than more practical strategies to implement because they require us to honestly examine our biases and predispositions about poverty and people in poverty.

Often I have my students, most of whom are studying to be teachers, keep daily journals in which they record every moment when one of their biases crops up, and they almost always are surprised by how often it happens. There's no shame in the biases, I insist to these teachers-in-training, unless once we identify them we decide not to work them through. It helps, of course, to have a community of colleagues to support you in the process. And it helps to remember that in the end, owning our biases and the harmful aspects of our ideologies, although difficult, also is triumphant. When it comes to Equity Literacy, losing a stereotype might be the biggest possible triumph for those of us who desire, above all else, to give every one of our students the best possible opportunity to thrive. No strategy is so clearly within our individual spheres of influence as that.

In Chapter 10, I nudge us to think about ways we might expand our spheres of influence, lending our energies to more institutional forms of educational equity for families in poverty.

# Expanding Our Spheres of Influence

## Advocating for School, District, Regional, and National Change for the Educational Good

Principles of Equity Literacy discussed in this chapter include:

Principle 1: The right to equitable educational opportunity is universal.
Principle 6: Test scores are inadequate measures of equity.
Principle 7: Class disparities in education are the result of inequities, not the result of cultures.

All the way back in Chapter 1 I explained how, when I began writing this book, I struggled to decide on its focus. Initially I intended to write a book about the big societal conditions we need to change in order to give ourselves a real shot at realizing equitable educational opportunity for all youth, such as greater income equality, more access to living wage work, and universal healthcare. I remain committed to those changes and have written, spoken, and taught about them in a variety of forums. I ultimately decided, though, to write a book about what educators can do *right now* in order to improve the educational experiences of poor and working class students in their classrooms and schools—students who cannot afford to wait for these larger societal changes to occur before gaining access to something more closely resembling educational equity. And so I have focused in this book largely on classroom and school practices, on the attitudes and dispositions we carry or don't carry into classrooms and schools, and on what a few decades' worth of scholarship indicates are key strategies and approaches for creating equitable learning environments for low-income students and their families.

In this spirit I shared in the previous two chapters the relational commitments and instructional strategies that, according to research, are consistently effective when it comes to teaching, engaging, and retaining low-income students. I focused in those chapters on the kinds of strategies and commitments teachers, aides, counselors, and other educators can use at an individual level *right now*, including those who work at schools where they are not necessarily endorsed as part of a central instructional approach. All of these strategies and commitments work better, of course, when a whole school or district full of educators embraces them and when they are endorsed by administrators who build professional development opportunities around them and facilitate collaborative efforts toward incorporating them, and Equity Literacy more generally, into day-to-day practices. Regardless of whether every teacher in a school commits to a resiliency view, incorporates music and art into the curriculum, reaches out to low-income families early and often, and uses student-centered pedagogies, though, it is within our power to find ways, even if they are little ways at first, of doing so in our own teaching. Our instruction and the way we interact with students and families are within our immediate spheres of influence.

This is one of the central tenets of my work and how I make decisions about what sorts of change I will support. I start with my sphere of influence, with what I can control. But another one of my central tenets is to find ways to grow my sphere of influence, both because doing so expands the impact I can have and because thinking a little beyond my current sphere helps me better understand the contextual factors dancing around that sphere, like the inequities that low-income families experience outside of the classroom, the school, and the district.

## ADVOCACY INITIATIVES BEYOND THE CLASSROOM

In this chapter I describe what I believe to be the most critically important and effective strategies for addressing some of those contextual factors. I offer this chapter knowing that many readers will see these strategies and think, "Yeah, that would be great, but it's a little outside my sphere of influence." I get it. Really, I do. There's already a lot to do, and just being a good advocate for low-income students in one's own classroom can be challenging, especially when we're up against high-stakes testing, prescribed curricula, and all matter of other initiatives that we know are bad for youth. My hope, though, is that as more and more of us embrace the relational commitments and instructional strategies described in Chapters 8 and 9, we also will find opportunities to expand our spheres of influence and put our collective advocacy muscle behind bigger policy initiatives that directly affect educational opportunities and outcomes for poor and working class youth.

*Initiative One: Advocate for Universal Preschool and Kindergarten.*
Here's a brief quiz. Name the only industrialized nation in the world not to
have universal early childhood education.

If you guessed the United States, the wealthiest country in the world,
you are correct (Koppelman & Goodhart, 2005). A+ for you, but not so
much for the United States. Preschool and Kindergarten are not universal in
the United States, and that is something we need to change (Freeman, 2010).

Even if poor and working class families can find quality preschool programs in their communities (which is a pretty big "if"), these programs
almost always are far too expensive for them to afford. Add to this the long
list of other challenges we explored in Chapters 5 and 6—lack of access to
everything from preventive healthcare to libraries—and it should come as
no surprise that low-income youth come to school, on average, with lower
levels of the kinds of cognitive development that generally are rewarded in
today's education world. To clarify, this doesn't mean that they are less in-
telligent or have less potential than their wealthier peers. It only means that
they are less privileged.

There is little debate over the fact that early educational intervention is
critical (Neuman, 2009), partly because early cognitive development, and
especially what begins even before a child reaches Kindergarten, is a pretty
good predictor of the developmental path she will take throughout her educational career and beyond. As Alpana Bhattacharya (2010) found in her
extensive review of research on reading development in low-income children, the implications of the inequities in access to resources such as quality
preschool programs in the early lives of youth from families in poverty compound themselves with every school year. Isabel Sawhill (2006), who named
the same concern in her policy brief *Opportunity in America: The Role of
Education*, concluded that intervening "as early as possible" was one of the
key ingredients to addressing socioeconomic disparities in educational access and outcomes.

In fact, speaking more broadly, investments in early intervention, like
enrolling low-income youth in quality preschool programs, have greater
long-term payoffs than any other single school-based strategy for addressing educational outcome disparities (Crosnoe, Wirth, Pianta, Leventhal,
& Pierce, 2010; Fuller, 2007; Heckman, 2006). It comes as no surprise,
I'm sure, that research has uncovered strong links between school performance and preschool participation (Heckman & Masterov, 2007; Kilburn
& Karoly, 2008; Temple & Reynolds, 2007). This is a critical link, because
it demonstrates that early childhood interventions can play a mitigating
role against the higher risk students from poverty have of falling behind
their wealthier peers in some forms of cognitive developmental. For example, Carla Peterson and her colleagues (2010) found that participation
in Early Head Start, a pre-Kindergarten program for low-income families

that focuses on child development starting, quite literally, at the prenatal stage, significantly lowers the likelihood that children will have cognitive or language delays while increasing the likelihood that they will have access to necessary interventions for any challenges that do arise. What's more, quality preschool programs save schools and the larger society resources in the long run. Access to preschool substantially decreases the likelihood that low-income students will need remediation services in the future, such as special education programs or grade retention (Temple et al., 2010). Although debate persists about what constitutes "quality" preschool, there appears to be general agreement that programs that incorporate family support services (again, engaging families early and often) and offer intellectually stimulating curricula (Judge, 2005; Peisner-Feinberg et al., 2001; Reynolds, 2000) are particularly effective at facilitating social and cognitive development in youngsters.

Head Start is, of course, the most well-known early childhood education program for low-income youth in the United States. The Head Start model combines access to a preschool environment with attention to a range of other needs of low-income youth, including nutrition and health services. And to a large extent it works. For instance, in his analysis of the long-term effects of Head Start on students in poverty, Myungkook Joo (2010) found that participation in the program led to lower rates of grade repetition, school suspension, and expulsion throughout the rest of participating youths' educational careers.

Unfortunately, despite its potential to mitigate the effects of economic inequalities in the educational lives of poor and working class youth, the quality of Head Start programs is famously inconsistent (Karoly & Gonzalez, 2011). Even more unfortunately, for a variety of reasons, not least of which is the capacity of Head Start sites themselves and the scarcity of such sites in rural areas, less than half of all children who are eligible for the program actually are in it (Wright, 2011).

But it's a start. It's something upon which to build until every young person has access to high-quality early childhood education.

*Initiative Two: Cultivate Relationships with Community Agencies and Organizations.* Based upon her review of research on the most effective societal initiatives for changing the odds for economically disadvantaged students, Susan Neuman (2009) argues that we ought to coordinate health, education, and social services. Eric Freeman (2010) agrees, urging school and district folks to cultivate relationships with community organizations and agencies that can give students access to some of the services and goods their families cannot afford. In Oregon, for instance, Lane County Schools and the Willamette Farm and Food Coalition are partnering to incorporate fresh, locally grown, organic food into school lunches. The Coalition also provides a series of education programs, from farm field trips to interactive gardening lessons. Oyster School, a high-poverty elementary school in Cincinnati, Ohio, partners with healthcare providers, hosting a health clinic and offering dental checkups on-site (Scott, 2012).

Taking this vision a step further, we even might begin to imagine schools as community organizations that host a wide range of services in low-income communities in a sort of community center role. And by *imagine* I really mean *reimagine*, because it wasn't long ago that public schools did serve as neighborhood resource outlets and public service centers in a lot of low-income communities. There's a proud history of this sort of multipurposing in middle Appalachia (DeYoung, 2002) and other rural areas (Ayalon, 1995; Thurston & Berkeley, 2010), where it is especially important due to geographical isolation and a particular lack of access to a wide range of services. Efforts to sustain a vision of schools as sources of community service started to deteriorate as states began a push to consolidate rural school districts (Peshkin, 1982). Unfortunately, today we appear headed toward greater deterioration of these sorts of efforts, with the most basic services, especially those provided by school nurses, psychologists, and social workers, disappearing. (More on this momentarily.)

Obviously, schools cannot be everything to everybody. But if, at the very least, we can identify some of the core needs of our most economically vulnerable students, then build relationships with community organizations that can help us address some of their needs, we will put them in a better position to learn to their fullest capabilities. And as a result, we will put ourselves in a better position to teach to our fullest capabilities.

*Initiative Three: Advocate for Smaller Class Sizes.* Is it just me, or does it seem as though the most visible people insisting that class size doesn't matter tend to be politicians and other political players who send their kids to private schools? During the 2012 presidential race, Mitt Romney made the mistake of telling a West Philadelphia school full of teachers that class size doesn't matter. Of course, he made that claim knowing that his own children's educational experiences were not at stake. They all attended pricey independent schools, as do President Obama's children. The teachers were not buying what he was selling, and they told him so. They know, as anybody knows who has experienced the difference between teaching 12 or 16 students (the average class sizes, respectively, at Belmont Hill School, where the Romneys sent their sons, and Sidwell Friends School, where the Obamas send their daughters) and, say, 30 or 35 students.

Class size does matter, and despite the illusion of a debate on this point, research consistently has shown this to be the case (Krueger, 1999; Rouse & Barrow, 2006). After analyzing data on more than 11,600 students over a 4-year period, Alan Krueger (1999) found that students in smaller classes performed better than their peers in bigger classes, and that the performance disparity increased each year they were in smaller classes. Notably, based on their review of research on the effects of class size, Cecilia Rouse and Lisa Barrow (2006) found that class size actually matters more for students who are eligible for free and reduced lunch than for their wealthier peers.

And, yes, one positive effect of small class sizes is higher standardized test scores (Shin & Chung, 2009; Smith, Molnar, & Zahorik, 2003). But reduced class sizes also result in more positive student and, of course, *teacher* attitudes (Zahorick, Halbach, Ehrle, & Molnar, 2003) and higher levels of student engagement (Blatchford, Bassett, & Brown, 2011; Dee & West, 2011). And—no big surprise here—smaller class sizes provide teachers with opportunities to teach in more engaging and more *effective* ways (Blatchford, 2003; Zahorik et al., 2003).

*Initiative Four: Attend (and Provide) Ongoing, Nuanced Professional Development Opportunities on Reaching and Teaching Low-Income Youth and Their Families.* All professional development programs are not created equal. In fact, when Addie Smiley and Robert Helfenbein (2011) interviewed well-intentioned student teachers who had been subject to a popular professional development model designed to prepare educators to teach students in poverty, they found that the participants left with deeper prejudices than they had going into it. In essence the professional development model justified their biases, supported their deficit views, and even deepened their softly patronizing savior mentality. These findings highlight the fact that we can't always rely on the popularity of a workshop or framework or consultant when it comes to choosing an effective professional development approach.

So, how do we know good professional development opportunities related to poverty and education when we see them? Scholarship on the matter suggests that we look for three things: (1) a focus on teacher efficacy, (2) a nuanced approach that does not minimize socioeconomic status to simple "cultural" categories, and (3) a customized, context-specific approach rather than a canned "workshop."

Student learning outcomes improve not just when teachers teach well, but when teachers teach with the confidence of *knowing they can teach effectively* (Ramalho et al., 2010). This knowing often is referred to as *teacher efficacy.* And it is particularly important when it comes to a task like teaching low-income youth, particularly for teachers who are not accustomed to doing so. In fact, after studying 12 schools with poverty rates of at least 80%, Joan Richardson (2003) found that one common trait of high-performing high-poverty schools is a high level of efficacy among teachers and principals. They have to believe in their abilities to ensure that all students learn, whatever challenges those students might face.

One consideration for finding the right approach to professional development, then, is that it should be framed positively, based on what educators can do in their spheres of influence. For instance, in my own professional development work with schools I always begin by recognizing teachers' expertise and commitment. You know your students better than I know them, better than any author or researcher knows them. You already have the requisite skills; it's usually only a matter of understanding students and their families more complexly and, with that knowledge, applying those skills in differently informed ways. Any approach that makes educators feel less capable or more shame-ridden is bound to fail, both because it misdirects frustration about big and complex social conditions toward teachers and because it undermines a sense of efficacy.

A second consideration when it comes to choosing a professional development approach is to avoid models that oversimplify class concerns, especially in ways that focus largely on class "cultures." Remember, the popular "culture of poverty" framework was rebuffed close to 50 years ago because, when it comes down to it, there is no such thing as a predictable, consistent culture shared by all, or even most, low-income people. Plus, the culture of poverty approach tends to focus on supposed deficiencies in low-income students and families, many of which—a propensity for alcoholism, a tendency not to value education—fly in the face of decades' worth of research that expose them as false stereotypes.

Bruce Parker and Adam Howard (2009), in their exploration of strategies for engaging high school social studies and language arts teachers in useful conversations about social class, recommend a more nuanced approach to learning about the lives and experiences of low-income people, and one that won't simplify the full diversity of poor and working class families into one singular and fictional "culture." They suggest, for instance, using memoirs and other narrative sources from a diverse spectrum of low-income people, which will help us see them as complex individuals with a variety of experiences, gifts, and needs. Some of my favorite narratives or collections of narratives include:

- bell hooks's (2000) *Where We Stand: Class Matters*, which incorporates an analysis of class conditions (including their intersections with racial conditions) in the United States with bits of memoir-style reflections about the role poverty played in the life of the author;
- Jeff Sapp's (2009) *Teaching Tolerance* essay, "How School Taught Me I Was Poor," available at http://www.tolerance.org/magazine/ number-35-spring-2009/feature/how-school-taught-me-i-was-poor;

- Bobby Starnes's (2008) *Phi Delta Kappan* article, "On Lilacs, Tap-dancing, and Children of Poverty"; and
- D. Stanley Eitzen and Kelly Eitzen Smith's (2009) edited collection, *Experiencing Poverty: Voices from the Bottom*, which is full of honest, reflective essays by people who have intimate experiences with poverty.

Third, avoid canned or prepackaged professional development models that wrongly assume that your context is pretty much the same as any other context in which low-income students attend school. Sure, there is some overlap, but the challenges faced by poor rural Appalachian families whose ancestors settled in their region four generations ago are not going to be the same as the challenges faced by poor Somali refugees who moved to urban Minneapolis 2 years ago. For that matter, two of those Appalachian families might experience totally different sets of challenges (Kennedy, 2010).

It's important to remember, too, that sometimes the best professional development opportunities are not workshops. Sometimes they are ongoing, purposefully scheduled opportunities for teachers, specialists, and other educators to meet, collaboratively plan curricula, share information about students, swap strategies, and support one another. The "purposefully scheduled" part of this is important, because we're all awfully busy with widely varying schedules and growing piles of responsibilities, so if time is not built into the school day schedule, these sorts of collective learning opportunities likely will not work (Chenoweth, 2009).

And, of course, like professional development opportunities on any topic, those related to bolstering the school experiences of low-income families are most effective when they are ongoing rather than being squeezed into a single 1-hour faculty meeting at the end of a school day. They are most effective, as well, when they are engaging and interactive, when participants are treated as experts who together are building an approach for equitable practice. It would seem a little strange, anyway, to be lectured at about how we oughtn't to just be lecturing at low-income students.

*Initiative Five: Extend Health Services and Screenings at Schools.* Due, in large part, to a lack of access to preventive healthcare, low-income students are much more likely than their peers to have undiagnosed health concerns affecting even the most basic functions, like vision (Gould & Gould, 2003). When health services and screenings are available at schools, they tend to be extremely, and in some cases illogically, limited in scope. For instance, the vision screenings offered at many schools—you know, *Cover your right eye and read the third row of letters*—focus solely on nearsightedness, which affects the ability to read at a distance (as from a chalkboard), and not farsightedness, which affects up-close reading (as from a book). Far too often low-income students whose families simply cannot afford regular healthcare are assumed to have a learning disability when, in reality, they just need a pair of glasses, an expense that also might be difficult for a poor or working class family to afford. Marge and Herman Gould (2003) explain, "It is estimated that one out of four school-age children have undiagnosed vision problems" (p. 324), a rate that is even higher for low-income students. Unfortunately, the Goulds continue, the lack of proper care can have implications beyond grades and test scores, including affecting students' self-esteem.

Vision problems are only the tip of the iceberg. As we explored in Chapter 5, low-income youth are more prone than their wealthier peers to a whole host of health concerns that affect them in and out of school, whether or not they are diagnosed. Not the least of these is asthma, a near-chronic problem in urban low-income communities.

One sensible response is to fight to protect school nurse positions (Telljohan, Dake, & Price, 2004), which, as we learned earlier, increasingly are being eliminated, especially at high-poverty schools. But we also might advocate for more and broader healthcare services in high-poverty schools. Obviously schools cannot become full-service hospitals, but increased services and screenings for health risks and other conditions, such as asthma or depression or farsightedness, that are more common or more commonly undiagnosed in people in poverty would go a long way toward mitigating healthcare disparities that impede student engagement and learning (Davis et al., 2011; Karnick et al., 2007).

*Initiative Six: Protect Physical Education and Recess and Encourage Fitness.* Even as we try to incorporate movement and exercise into our individual teaching, a strategy described in Chapter 8, we should defend physical education programs and recess vigorously. Students learn better when they have access to regular exercise opportunities. Unfortunately, low-income youth are less likely than their peers to have these opportunities outside of school (Fahlman et al., 2006), whether because their families cannot afford to sign them up for organized sports, because their neighborhoods lack the sorts of recreational facilities that are common in wealthier communities, or because they are charged with caring for younger siblings while their parents work. It should come as no surprise, then, that the obesity rates of low-income youth exceed those of their wealthier peers (U.S. Department of Health and Human Services, 2005).

Some schools have found creative ways to encourage more exercise among students. For example, several high-poverty elementary schools in Seattle have participated in a "walking school bus" program wherein children and chaperones from the neighborhood walk to school together

(Mendoza, Levinger, & Johnston, 2009). A similar program was instituted in Albuquerque, New Mexico, with an added dimension. The participating school partnered with a physician, who met with participants before and after the program, and a premedical student, who walked with the students and community members, emphasizing the importance of exercise and healthy eating, particularly in the form of fresh fruit. Alberta Kong and her colleagues (2010), who assessed the program, found that participants reported increased levels of physical activity and even increased fruit consumption during the 10-week program.

As cool as they might sound, we certainly should not think of programs like the walking school bus as suitable replacements for physical education or recess. Our first priority, given its benefits to students and to *teachers*— students who are physically active also have been shown to exhibit more positive attitudes and behaviors in class (Grissom, 2005)—should be to protect physical education and recess from the school accountability chopping block.

*Initiative Seven: Protect Arts, Music, and Drama Programs.* In Chapter 8 I made a research-based pitch for why, even as we watch art, music, and drama programs lose funding and disappear from our schools, we should find ways to incorporate the arts into our instruction. The better scenario, though, if you're in a school or district that still places due emphasis on the arts, is to protect them from the chopping block (Catterall, Chapleau, & Iwanaga, 1999; Heath & Roach, 1999; Pogrow, 2006). As I detailed earlier, students who have access to the arts do better academically and are more engaged in school. And, of course, low-income families are significantly less likely than their wealthier counterparts to be able to afford to send their children to music or arts camps, so sustaining these programs is especially important for youth in poverty.

*Initiative Eight: Protect School and Local Libraries in High-Poverty Neighborhoods.* Increased access to books is directly related to higher reading proficiency in youth (Krashen, 2004; Lindsay, 2010). This, you might think, is reason enough to protect *all* school and local libraries from being closed down or from losing funding, which often results in decreased hours or services. And it might be reason enough to advocate for better libraries in high-poverty schools, which, according to a recent study, have significantly fewer resources on average than libraries at wealthier schools (Pribesh, Gavigan, & Dickinson, 2011).

We should feel a particular urgency to protect local and school libraries and their funding in high-poverty and mixed-class communities. Public and school libraries can play mitigating roles in disparities between low-income and wealthier youth when it comes to having access to a wide variety of texts and media as well as computers and the Internet. Demonstrating their mitigating potential, poor and working class people are among the most frequent users of public libraries, both in terms of checking out books and reading newspapers and in terms of using computers and the Internet, as Samantha Becker and her colleagues (2010) learned in their large-scale national analysis of library use. Also, public libraries are among the few public spaces and resources that are available in many poor communities (Ly, 2010), where they can host neighborhood meetings or classes, tutoring services, and other programs.

Unfortunately, socioeconomic disparities in access to books and the Internet are replicated almost exactly in school and public libraries (Neuman & Celano, 2001; Pribesh et al., 2011), meaning that disparities in access to well-stocked libraries in their neighborhoods and their schools is *widening* the literacy gap between low-income and wealthier students. We should do anything we can to disrupt these disparities, from advocating for a more equitable distribution of resources to libraries to lobbying local legislators when library hours are being slashed.

## A FEW OTHER THINGS WE CAN DO

Many of these initiatives are responses to two challenges in the larger education sphere that affect all of us in profound ways. One of these is a general trend toward defunding public schools, in part by privatizing some aspects of public education. The other is the imposition of corporate-style accountability measures like high-stakes testing. Together these challenges seem to have led us collectively down a somewhat illogical path, on which we trade the best of what public education has to offer, like well-rounded and engaging teaching and learning, basic services that bolster the learning environment, and a holistic approach to cultivating lifelong learners, for the worst it has to offer, like rote teaching and learning and a curriculum driven by narrow assessment measures. Of course, the latter we mostly offer at high-poverty schools and in lower academic tracks, where low-income students, as well as students of color and English Language Learners, are disproportionately represented. Even the implications of the defunding are not distributed equally. Parents in wealthier neighborhoods often are able to raise money to hire additional teachers or protect a band program, something that's not so easy to do in neighborhoods where people are struggling to pay the electric bill.

So when we do anything, anything at all, to push back against the defunding of schools or the underfunding of education mandates and to resist the imposition of corporate-style accountability and high-stakes testing, we also are advocating, whether we know it or not, for low-income students. Of course, we also are self-advocating, which is an added bonus.

For those of us ready to take one more step back and broaden our spheres of influence even further, here are a few more possibilities to consider:

1. Schools in many parts of the United States remain racially and economically segregated and, in some cases, are becoming more so (Joyner & Marsh, 2011; Saporito & Sohoni, 2007). We can advocate against redistricting plans that ensure, often purposefully, that this trend continues, leaving low-income students assigned to schools that almost always are less well equipped than schools with wealthier student bodies.

2. Provide supports for English Language Learners and their families, who disproportionately are poor. For example, we should provide translators at school functions and translating services for family members of ELL students who call or visit our schools. Communications, whether on paper or electronic, also should be translated into students' home languages.

3. Many poor and working class parents and caregivers are forced to work multiple jobs because of the lack of living wage full-time jobs in low-income communities. The result is less time to read to their children, to visit their children's schools, and to just *be* with their children. We can support fair wage campaigns so that anybody who works a full-time job makes ample money to support themselves and their families.

4. Healthcare has popped up throughout this book. Anything we can do to increase healthcare access for low-income families, particularly by advocating for universal healthcare for youth, at the very least, would make a tremendous difference in the educational lives of students in poverty.

5. Advocate for affordable housing for low-income families. This can have a direct impact on the educational experiences of youth in poverty, according to Maya Brennan (2011), by minimizing the necessity for families to move, providing low-income families with opportunities to move into areas with strong schools, and reducing homelessness.

6. Despite all the talk about conservation and sustainability these days, we seem to forget that environmental degradation has the most immediate and most violent impact on low-income people. Poor and working class students, especially if they also are People of Color, are much, much more likely than their wealthier peers

and classmates to live near environmental hazard sites, to be exposed to dangerous levels of radon and carbon monoxide, and to be subject to water contamination from mining operations and factory runoffs. We can join local communities in the battle against these environmental injustices.

## CONCLUSION

Sounds like a lot of heavy lifting, right? When it comes to creating schools that are class-equitable, and also creating a society that ensures that every person has an opportunity to take full advantage of those schools, there is much work to be done and many spheres in which to do it. I'm reminded of one of my favorite quotes, by Edward Everett Hale, a late 19th- and early 20th-century U.S. author and Unitarian clergyman: "I am only one; but still I am one. I cannot do everything; but still I can do something; and because I cannot do everything, I will not refuse to do the something that I can do."

Maybe that something, for you, is advocating for a schoolwide commitment to higher-order pedagogy for all students. Maybe it's initiating a working group to look into the possibility of offering more health screenings at your school. Maybe it's simply raising concerns about class equity in faculty meetings or community gatherings.

Maybe, for now, you will choose to focus on your classroom or department, and that's all right, too. The goal, in my view, is that we all begin with our present spheres of influence and then, when we have made good progress there, begin to grow our spheres.

If you do choose to take on any of these bigger concerns, find ways, whenever possible, to do so collaboratively, with colleagues. There is power in numbers, and a support system almost always helps.

# Conclusion

Recently a colleague and I had occasion to take a group of our students, mostly future teachers, to visit 110 6th-graders at a high-poverty school. "If you could give one piece of advice to these future teachers," I asked the 6th-graders, "what would it be?" They were sitting on the floor in the cafeteria, the only space in the building big enough to seat them all simultaneously, fidgety with curiosity about the strangers in their presence.

The couple of requisite responses about eliminating homework and extending recess induced giggles from both groups of students. "What else?" I asked. Then the cafeteria grew quiet. A subtle seriousness fell over many of the youngsters' faces.

"Respect us," a young woman said softly, then repeated forcefully, loudly: "Respect your students!" Several of her classmates nodded. I asked her name. "I'm Tanya," she said.

"How many of you agree with Tanya?" I asked her peers. "How many of you wish your teachers respected you more?" Nearly every student raised her or his hand.

"That would be nice," a young man said, sounding faintly exasperated. His name, he told me, was Tyrique.

It comes down to that in many ways, I thought. It comes down to respect. This sounds simple, I know, but it's not. Respecting our students would be easy, perhaps, if respect were about our intentions. Who among us, after all, doesn't want to respect our students and their families? Who among us doesn't *intend* respect? The challenge, though, is that respect is not about intentions. It's about actions.

Respect and the extent to which we demonstrate it in our teaching is tied up in those things, those sometimes little bitty things, we do or don't do, say or don't say, or even think or don't think. And it's about our willingness to take a stand when one of our students is being shortchanged—not standing *in front of* or standing *in place of,* but standing *next to,* standing *with* low-income students and families. If students know they're being cheated out of the kind of education wealthier or Whiter or more English-proficient students are getting, and if they know we know they're being cheated, and if we're not responding, not just with good intentions, but with equity, then how can we say we're respecting our students? Of course, we all know that students who are being cheated *do* know full well they're being cheated. They might not say so out loud because there's always a price to pay for speaking up. There's the shushing and labeling and ostracizing.

The good news is, we *can* stand up. We can start by standing up to our own biases about families in poverty, even if it means taking the oddly unpopular view that poor people are not poor because of their deficiencies, that something bigger than that is amiss. Then we can do everything humanly possible in our spheres of influence to align our teaching and relationship-building and family outreach efforts with our good intentions.

We can listen.

"What does respect mean," I prodded, "and how do you know when a teacher respects you?"

I glanced at the 6th-graders' teachers. They stood in a small cluster behind their students. *They look a little perplexed,* I remember thinking. Later that day one of them, Ms. Morrison, confided that she was, in fact, a little perplexed, never having seen "the kids" so attentive and respectful of one another in such a large group.

Hands flew up.

"Get to know me, don't treat me based on who you think I am," one student shared. "Get to know my interests."

"Make class fun instead of boring," another student pleaded, "and hands-on like Ms. Greene's science class."

"Believe in us!" and "Don't get mad when I need help!" and "Remember that sometimes when I'm tardy or don't finish my homework it's not my fault!" they exclaimed.

"Be flexible," a young woman said, "but also have rules."

Then a young man, sitting all the way in the back, shouted, "Let me spend time with my friends!" His peers roared with laughter.

It can be easy to read that comment—"Let me spend time with my friends!"—and think, *I knew that was coming eventually. Here is a student who doesn't take school seriously.* I admit that for a moment, a version of that thought popped into my mind. I looked at my teacher education students and noticed several of them laughing. I looked at the 6th-graders' teachers. One half-buried her head in her hands as if she was a little embarrassed.

"What's your name?" I asked the young man.

"Jonathan," he answered, looking a little confused about why so many of his peers were laughing.

"And why would you like your teachers to let you spend more time with your friends?" I probed.

Smiling bemusedly, he threw his hands in the air and replied, as if it was the most obvious thing in the world, "Because we study together. They help me with my math."

I took several important lessons from that visit with 110 6th-graders. First, it cemented for me why cultural competence, cultural proficiency, and especially the culture or mind-set of poverty frameworks are not sufficient guides in our efforts to turn the tide of class inequity in schools. Sure, the students wanted teachers to learn about their cultures, but they saw themselves as individuals, not as one giant cultural group. "Don't treat me based on who you think I am." They wanted equity-literate, not just culturally proficient, teachers.

Secondly, although they didn't use the word *equity*, the young women and men in that high-poverty school demanded it. They demanded the sorts of educational experiences their wealthier peers were getting. Respect, to them, meant high expectations ("Believe in us!") and higher-order, "hands-on," pedagogy.

Thirdly, the most well-meaning of us can communicate low expectations in the most implicit, unintentional ways. Perhaps it's a perplexed look or presumptuous giggle or a throwaway comment that we wouldn't even remember 5 minutes later. Here I am, writing a book about poverty and education, and I catch myself on occasion thinking things, if even for a moment, that ought not to still be in my head. The problem is, those biases are still there, hiding, and making themselves known at the most inopportune times. The other problem is, the students notice, and they don't forget 5 minutes later. This is why we need to have high enough expectations for ourselves to be vigilant about identifying and squashing our biases. It's not enough to *pretend* they're not there or to think we can hide them. Students are way too smart for that.

It is my hope that I, with this book and the Equity Literacy framework, have helped you, as those 6th-graders helped me, think in more complex, holistic ways about students and families in poverty and about what it means to create an equitable learning environment. It is my hope, too, that the strategies in Chapters 8 and 9 and sprinkled throughout the other chapters equip you with ample practical ways to bolster the important, incredible work you're already doing in your classroom, school, or district. Finally, I hope that all of the contextual stuff in those other chapters is useful grounding as you continue to work to understand and support low-income youth.

I end, then, where I began, with the great faith I have in educators, in those underpaid and underappreciated civil servants who care deeply enough about youth to build their lives around educating and mentoring and advocating for them. We are in a unique position in that even if we focus exclusively on creating change within our spheres of influence, we can't help but pay that change forward by a factor of the number of students whose lives we touch. We have no choice in that matter, any more than any of those celebrities who insist they're not role models have a choice in *that* matter.

The only question, I suppose, is, what would we like to pay forward?

# References

Abell, T., & Lyon, L. (1979). Do the differences make a difference? An empirical evaluation of the culture of poverty in the United States. *American Anthropologist, 6*(3), 602–621.

Adeola, F. (2005). Racial and class divergence in public attitudes and perceptions about poverty in USA: An empirical study. *Race, Gender & Class, 12*(2), 53–78.

Alexander, R. J. (2006) *Education as dialogue: Moral and pedagogical choices for a runaway world*. Hong Kong: Hong Kong Institute of Education with Dialogos.

Allard, S. W., & Roth, B. (2010). *Strained suburbs: The social service challenges of rising suburban poverty*. Washington, DC: Brookings Institute.

Almeida, D. M., Neupert, S. D., Banks, S. R., & Serido, J. (2005). Do daily stress processes account for socioeconomic health disparities? *Journal of Gerontology Series B, 60*(2), 34–39.

Almy, S., & Theokas, C. (2010). *Not prepared for class: High-poverty schools continue to have fewer in-field teachers*. Washington, DC: The Education Trust.

Amatea, E. S., & West-Olatunji, C. A. (2007). Joining the conversation about educating our poorest children: Emerging leadership roles for school counselors in high-poverty schools. *Professional School Counseling, 11*(2), 81–89.

American Academy of Pediatrics Council on School Health. (2008). Role of the school nurse in providing school health services. *Journal of School Nursing, 24*, 269–274.

American Library Association. (2010). High-poverty schools hurt by economy. *American Libraries, 41*(11), 13.

Avery, C., Fairbanks, A., & Zeckhauser, R. (2003). *The early admissions game: Joining the elite*. Cambridge, MA: Harvard University Press.

Ayalon, A. (1995). Does multicultural education belong in rural white America? *Rural Educator, 16*(3), 1–6.

Baetan, G. (2004). Inner-city misery. *City, 8*(2), 235–241.

Baisch, M. J., Lundeen, S. P., & Murphy, M. K. (2011). Evidence-based research on the value of school nurses in an urban school system. *Journal of School Health, 81*(2), 74-80.

Baker, B., & Corcoran, S. (2012). *Stealth inequities of school funding*. Washington, DC: Center for American Progress.

Baker, B., Sciarra, D., & Farrie, D. (2010). *Is school funding fair? A national report card*. Newark, NJ: Education Law Center.

Baldwin, P. (2007). In and out of roles, stories and buckets! *English 4-11, 30*, 3–6.

Balfanz, R., & Byrnes, V. (2006). Closing the mathematics achievement gap in high-poverty middle schools: Enablers and constraints. *Journal of Education for Students Placed at Risk, 11*(2), 143–159.

Bancroft, K. (2009). To have and to have not: The socioeconomics of charter schools. *Education and Urban Society, 41*(2), 248–279.

Barnett, W. S., & Yarosz, D. J. (2007, November). *Who goes to preschool and why does it matter?* (NIEER Policy Brief, 15). New Brunswick, NJ: National Institute for Early Education Research.

Barr, R. D., & Parrett, W. H. (2007). *The kids left behind: Catching up the underachieving children of poverty.* Bloomington, IN: Solution Tree Press.

Barton, P. E. (2004). Why does the gap persist? *Educational Leadership, 62*(3), 8–13.

Basch, C. (2011). Physical activity and the achievement gap among urban minority youth. *Journal of School Health, 81*(10), 626–634.

Battle, D., & Gruber, K. (2010). *Principal attribution and mobility: Results from the 2008–09 principal follow-up survey.* Washington, DC: U.S. Department of Education.

Baugh, J. (1983). *Black street speech.* Austin, TX: University of Texas Press.

Becker, S., Crandal, M. D., Fisher, K. E., Kinney, B., Landry, C., & Rocha, A. (2010). Opportunity for all: How the American public benefits from internet access at U.S. libraries. Washington, DC: Institute of Museum and Library Services.

Bergerson, A. A. (2009). *College choice and access to college: Moving policies, research, and practice into the 21st century.* San Francisco, CA: Jossey-Bass.

Bergh, A. (2005). On the counterfactual problem of welfare state research: How can we measure redistribution? *European Sociology Review, 21*, 345–357.

Berliner, D. (2006). Our impoverished view of educational reform. *Teachers College Record, 108*(6), 949–995.

Berliner, D. (2009). *Poverty and potential: Out-of school factors and school success.* Tempe, AZ: Education and the Public Interest Center & Education Policy Research Unit.

Bernhard, J. K., Winsler, A., Bleiker, C., Ginieniewicz, J., & Madigan, A. L. (2008). "Read my story!" Using the early authors program to promote early literacy among diverse, urban, preschool children in poverty. *Journal of Education for Students Placed at Risk, 13*, 76–105.

Bhattacharya, A. (2010). Children and adolescents from poverty and reading development: A research review. *Reading & Writing Quarterly, 26*, 115–139.

Billings, D. (1974). Culture and poverty in Appalachia: A theoretical discussion and empirical analysis. *Social Forces, 53*(2), 315–323.

Bjorklund, A., & Jantti, M. (2009). Intergenerational income mobility and the role of family background. In W. Salverda, B. Nolan, & T. M. Smeeding (Eds.),

*The Oxford handbook of economic inequality* (pp. 491–521). Oxford, UK: Oxford University Press.

Blair, C., & Scott, K. (2002). Proportion of LD placements associated with low socioeconomic status: Evidence for a gradient? *The Journal of Special Education, 36,* 14–22.

Blank, R. M., & Greenberg, M. (2008). *Improving the measurement of poverty.* Washington, DC: The Brookings Institution.

Blatchford, P. (2003). *The class size debate: Is small better?* Maidenhead, UK: Open University Press.

Blatchford, P., Bassett, P., & Brown, P. (2011). Examining the effect of class size on classroom engagement and teacher-pupil interaction: Differences in relation to pupil prior attainment and primary vs. secondary schools. *Learning and Instruction, 21*(6), 715–730.

Bloom, B., Dey, A. N., & Freeman, G. (2006). Summary health statistics for U.S. children: National Health Interview Survey, 2005. *National Center for Health Statistics, Vital & Health Statistics, 10*(231), 1–84.

Bloom, J. (2007). (Mis)reading social class in the journey towards college: Youth development in urban America. *Teachers College Record, 109*(2), 343–368.

Boas, F. (1911). Introduction. In F. Boas (Ed.), *Handbook of American Indian languages* (pp. 1–79). Washington, DC: U.S. Government Printing Office.

Boggs, C. (2007). Corporate power, ecological crisis, and animal rights. *Fast Capitalism, 2*(2). Available at http://www.fastcapitalism.com/

Bomer, R., Dworin, J. E., May, L., & Semingson, P. (2009). What's wrong with a deficit perspective? Available at http://www.tcrecord.org

Books, S. (2004). *Poverty and schooling in the U.S.: Context and consequences.* New York: Lawrence Erlbaum Associates.

Borrego, S. (2008). Class on campus: Breaking the silence surrounding socioeconomics. *Diversity & Democracy, 11*(3), 1–2.

Bourdieu, P. (1982). *Language and symbolic power.* Cambridge, MA: Harvard University Press.

Bower, H., & Griffin, D. (2011). Can the Epstein Model of parental involvement work in a high-minority, high-poverty elementary school? A case study. *Professional School Counseling, 15*(2), 77–87.

Bracey, G. W. (2006). Poverty's infernal mechanism. *Principal Leadership, 6*(6), 60.

Bradshaw, T. K. (2007). Theories of poverty and anti-poverty programs in community development. *Community Development, 38*(1), 7–25.

Brady, D., Fullerton, A. S., & Cross, J. M. (2009). Putting poverty in political context: A multi-level analysis of adult poverty across 18 affluent democracies. *Social Forces, 88*(1), 271–300.

Brann-Barrett, M. T. (2010). Same landscape, different lens: Variations in young people's socio-economic experiences and perceptions in their disadvantaged working-class community. *Journal of Youth Studies, 14*(3), 261–278.

Bray, M. (1999). *The shadow education system: Private tutoring and its implications for planners*. Paris, France: United Nations Educational, Scientific, and Cultural Organization.

Breen, R., & Jonsson, J. O. (2007). Explaining change in social fluidity: Educational equalization and educational expansion in twentieth-century Sweden. *American Journal of Sociology, 112*, 1775–1810.

Brennan, M. (2011). *The impacts of affordable housing on education: A research summary*. Washington, DC: Center for Housing Policy.

Brizuela, M., Andersen, E., & Stallings, L. (1999). Discourse markers as indicators of register. *Hispania, 82*(1), 128–141.

Brown, D. L. (2009, May 18). The high cost of poverty: Why the poor pay more. *The Washington Post*. Available at http://www.washingtonpost.com/wp-dyn/content/article/2009/05/17/AR2009051702053.html?sid=ST2009051801162

Buchmann, C., Condron, D. J., & Roscigno, V. J. (2010). Shadow education, American style: Test preparation, the SAT, and college enrollment. *Social Forces, 89*(2), 435–462.

Bullock, H. E., Williams, W. R., & Limbert, W. M. (2003). Predicting support for policies: The impact of attributions and beliefs about inequality. *Journal of Poverty, 7*, 35–56.

Bullock, H. E., Wyche, K. F., & Williams, W. R. (2001). Media images of the poor. *Journal of Social Issues, 57*, 229–246.

Burchinal, M., Nelson, L., Carlson, M., & Brooks-Gunn, J. (2008). Neighborhood characteristics and child care type and quality. *Early Education and Development, 19*, 702–725.

Burling, R. (1973). *English in black and white*. New York: Holt, Rinehart & Winston.

Byrd-Blake, M., Afolayan, M. O., Hunt, J. W., Fabunmi, M., Pryor, B. W., & Leander, R. (2010). Morale of teachers in high poverty schools: A post-NCLB mixed methods analysis. *Education and Urban Society, 42*(4), 450–472.

Carmon, N. (1985). Poverty and culture. *Sociological Perspectives, 28*(4), 403–418.

Carnoy, M., Jacobsen, R., Mishel, L., & Rothstein, R. (2005). *The charter school dust-up: Examining the evidence on enrollment and achievement*. Washington, DC: Economic Policy Institute.

Carreiro, J. L., & Kapitulik, B. P. (2010). Budgets, board games, and make believe: The challenge of teaching social class inequality with nontraditional students. *The American Sociologist, 41*, 232–248.

Catterall, J., Chapleau, R., & Iwanaga, J. (1999). Involvement in the arts and human development: General involvement and intensive involvement in music and theater arts. In E. B. Fiske (Ed.), *Champions of change: The impact of the arts on learning* (pp. 1–18). Washington, DC: Arts Education Partnership, President's Committee on the Arts and the Humanities.

Ceja, M. (2006). Understanding the role of parents and siblings as information sources in the college choice process of Chicana students. *The Journal of College Student Development, 47*(1), 87–104.

Center for American Progress (CAP). (2007). *From poverty to prosperity: A national strategy to cut poverty in half.* Washington, DC: Author.

Chafel, J. A. (1997). Children's views of poverty: A review of research and implications for teaching. *The Educational Forum, 61,* 360–371.

Chafel, J. A., Flint, A. S., Hammel, J., & Pomeroy, K. H. (2007). Young children, social issues, and critical literacy stories of teachers and researchers. *Young Children, 62*(1), 73–82.

Chambers, J. G., Levin, J. D., & Shambaugh, L. (2010). Exploring weighted student formulas as a policy for improving equity for distributing resources to schools: A case study of two California schools. *Economics of Education Review, 29*(2), 283–300.

Chen, K., Sheth, A., Krejci, J., & Wallace, J. (2003, August). *Understanding differences in alcohol use among high school students in two different communities.* Paper presented at the annual meeting of the American Sociological Association, Atlanta, GA.

Chenoweth, K. (2009). It can be done, it's being done, and here's how. *Phi Delta Kappan, 91*(1), 38–43.

Children's Defense Fund (CDF). (2008). *Child poverty in America.* Available at http://www.childrensdefense.org/child-research-data-publications/data/child-poverty-in-america.pdf

Children's Defense Fund (CDF). (2010). *The state of America's School.* Washington, DC: Author.

Chinni, D. (2005). One more Social Security quibble: Who is middle class? *Christian Science Monitor* [online]. Available at http://www.csmonitor.com/2005/0510/p09s01-codc.html

Chomsky, N. (1965). *The theory of syntax.* Cambridge, MA: MIT Press.

Christensen, L. (2008). Welcoming all languages. *Educational Leadership, 66*(1), 59–62

Clark, C., & Gorski, P. C. (2002). Multicultural education and the digital divide: Focus on socioeconomic class background. *Multicultural Perspectives, 4*(3), 25–36.

Cleaveland, C. (2008). "A black benefit": Racial prejudice among white welfare recipients in a low-income neighborhood. *Journal of Progressive Human Services, 19*(2), 71–91.

Clotfelter, C. T. (2004). *After Brown: The rise and retreat of school desegregation.* Princeton, NJ: Princeton University Press.

Coleman-Jensen, A., Nord, M., Andrews, M., & Carlson, S. (2012). *Household food insecurity in the United States: 2011.* Washington, DC: United States Department of Agriculture.

Coles, G. (2008). Hunger, academic success, and the hard bigotry of indifference. *Rethinking Schools, 23*(2). Available at http://www.rethinkingschools.org/ProdDetails.asp?ID=RTSVOL23N2&d=etoc

Coley, R. (2002). *An uneven start: Indicators of inequality in school readiness.* Princeton, NJ: Educational Testing Service.

Collins, J. (1988). Language and class in minority education. *Anthropology & Education Quarterly, 19*(4), 299–326.

Comber, B., Nixon, H., Ashmore, L., Loo, S., & Cook, J. (2006). Urban renewal from the inside out: Spatial and critical literacies in a low socioeconomic school community. *Mind, Culture, and Activity, 13*(3), 228–246.

Compton-Lilly, C. (2000). Staying on children: Challenging stereotypes about urban parents. *Language Arts, 77,* 420–427.

Constantino, R. (2005). Print environments between high and low socioeconomic status communities. *Teacher Librarian, 32*(3), 22–25.

Cooper, C. E. (2010). Family poverty, school-based parental involvement, and policy-focused protective factors in kindergarten. *Early Childhood Research Quarterly, 25,* 480–492.

Cooper, C. E., Crosnoe, R., Suizzo, M., & Pituch, K. (2010). Poverty, race, and parental involvement during the transition to elementary school. *Journal of Family Issues, 31*(7), 859–883.

Cooter, K. (2006). When mama can't read: Counteracting intergenerational illiteracy. *Reading Teacher, 59,* 698–702.

Crawford, E., Wright, M., & Masten, O. (2006). Resilience and spirituality in youth. In E. Roehlkepartain, P. King, L. Wagener, & P. Benson (Eds.), *The handbook of spiritual development in childhood and adolescence* (pp. 355–370). Thousand Oaks, CA: Sage.

Cronin, D., & Lewin, B. (2000). *Click, clack, moo.* New York: Simon and Schuster.

Crooks, D. (1995). American children at risk: Poverty and its consequences for children's health, growth, and school achievement. *Yearbook of Physical Anthropology, 38,* 57–86.

Crosnoe, R., & Cooper, C. E. (2010). Economically disadvantaged children's transitions into elementary school: Linking family processes, school contexts, and educational policy. *American Education Research Journal, 47*(2), 258–291.

Crosnoe, R., Wirth, R. J., Pianta, R. C., Leventhal, T., & Pierce, K. M. (2010). Family socioeconomic status and consistent environmental stimulation in early childhood. *Child Development, 81*(3), 972–987.

Cunningham, W. G., & Sanzo, T. D. (2002). Is high-stakes testing harming lower socioeconomic status schools? *National Association of Secondary School Principals, 86*(631), 62–75.

Cutler, D. M., & Lleras-Muney, A. (2010). Understanding differences in health behaviors by education. *Journal of Health Economics, 29*(1), 1–28.

Davis, D. W., Gordon, M. K., & Burns, B. M. (2011). Educational interventions for childhood asthma: A review and integrative model for preschoolers from low-income families. *Pediatric Nursing, 37*(1), 31–38.

de Goede, M. (1996). Ideology in the U.S. welfare debate: Neo-liberal representations of poverty. *Discourse and Society, 7,* 317–357.

Dee, T., & West, M. (2011). The non-cognitive returns to class size. *Educational Evaluation and Policy Analysis, 33*(1), 23–46.

Degenhardt, L., Chiu, W.-T., Sampson, N., Kessler, R. C., Anthony, J. C., Angermeyer, M., Bruffaerts, R., de Girolamo, G., Gureje, O., Huang, Y., Karam, A., Kostyuchenko, S., Lepine, J. P., Mora, M. E. M., Neumark, Y., Ormel, J. H., Pinto-Meza, A., Posada-Villa, J., Stein, D. J., Takeshima, T., Wells, J. E. (2008). Toward a global view of alcohol, tobacco, cannabis, and cocaine use: Findings from the WHO world mental health surveys. *Public Library of Science Medicine, 5*(7), 1053–1067.

DeNavas-Walt, C., Proctor, B., & Smith, J. (2011). *Income, poverty, and health coverage in the United States: 2010.* Washington, DC: U.S. Census Bureau.

Denny, S., Clark, T., Fleming, T., & Wall, M. (2004). Emotional resilience: Risk and protective factors for depression among alternative education students in New Zealand. *American Journal of Orthopsychiatry, 74*(2), 137–149.

DeSocio, J., & Hootman, J. (2004). Children's mental health and school success. *Journal of School Nursing, 20*(4), 189–196.

DeYoung, A. (2002). Constructing and staffing the cultural bridge: The school as change agent in rural Appalachia. In P. Obermiller & M. Maloney (Eds.), *Appalachia: Social context past and present* (pp. 166–182). Dubuque, IA: Kendall/Hunt.

Dixon, M. (2012). *Public education finances: 2010.* Washington, DC: U.S. Census Bureau.

Domhoff, G. W. (2012). *Wealth, income, and power: Who rules America?* Available at http://www2.ucsc.edu/whorulesamerica/power/wealth.html

Drewnowski, A. (2004). Obesity and the food environment: Dietary energy density and diet costs. *American Journal of Preventative Medicine, 27,* 154–162.

Drummond, K. V., & Stipek, D. (2004). Low-income parents' beliefs about their role in children's academic learning. *Elementary School Journal, 104,* 197–213.

Dudley-Marling, C., & Lucas, K. (2009). Pathologizing the language and culture of poor children. *Language Arts, 86*(5), 362–370.

Dudley-Marling, C., & Paugh, P. (2005). The rich get richer; the poor get direct instruction. In B. Altwerger (Ed.), *Reading for profit: How the bottom line leaves kids behind* (pp. 156–171). Portsmouth, NH: Heinemann.

Due, P., Holstein, B. E., & Jorgensen, P. S. (1999). Bullying as a health hazard among school children. *Ugeshr Laeger, 161,* 2201–2206.

Due, P., Lynch, J., Holstein, B. E., & Modvig, J. (2003). Socioeconomic health inequalities among a nationally representative sample of Danish adolescents: The role of different types of social relations. *Journal of Epidemiology Community Health, 57,* 692–698.

Due, P., Merlo, J., Harel-Fisch, Y., Damsgaard, M., Holstein, B. E., Hetland, J., Currie, C., Gabhainn, S. N., Gaspar de Matos, M., & Lynch, J. (2009). Socioeconomic inequality in exposure to bullying during adolescence: A comparative, cross-sectional, multilevel study in 35 countries. *American Journal of Public Health, 99*(5), 907–914.

Duke, N. K., Purcell-Gates, V., Hall, L. A., & Tower, C. (2006). Authentic literacy activities for developing comprehension and writing. *Reading Teacher, 60,* 344–355.

Duncan, G. J., Ludwig, J., & Magnuson, K. A. (2007). Reducing poverty through school interventions. *The Future of Children, 17*(2), 143–160.

Duncan, G. J., Magnuson, K., Kalil, A., & Ziol-Guest, K. (2012). The importance of early childhood poverty. *Social Indicators Research, 108*(1), 87–98.

Dupere, V., Leventhal, T., Crosnoe, R., & Dion, E. (2010). Understanding the positive role of neighborhood socioeconomic advantage in achievement: The contribution of home, child care, and school environments. *Developmental Psychology, 46*(5), 1227–1244.

Durso, L., & Gates, G. (2012). *Serving our youth: Findings from a national survey of service providers working with lesbian, gay, bisexual, and transgender youth who are homeless or at risk of becoming homeless.* Los Angeles: The William Institute, True Colors Fund, and The Palette Fund.

Dutro, E. (2009). Children writing "hard times": Lived experiences of poverty and the class-privileged assumptions of a mandated curriculum. *Language Arts, 87*(2), 89–98.

Dye, T. (2002). *Who's running America: The Bush restoration.* Saddle River, NJ: Prentice Hall.

Eberstadt, N. (2006). The mismeasure of poverty. *Policy Review, 138,* 19–51.

Economic Mobility Project. (2012). *Economic mobility of families across generations.* Available at http://www.economicmobility.org/assets/pdfs/EMPAcrossGenerations.pdf

Eitzen, D., & Smith, K. (Eds.) (2009). *Experiencing poverty: Voices from the bottom.* Boston: Pearson.

Elkin, A. (2012). Students hop, skip, and jump their way to understanding. *Teaching Children Mathematics, 18*(9), 524.

Espinoza, O. (2007). Solving the equity-equality conceptual dilemma: A new model for analysis of the educational process. *Educational Research, 49*(4), 343–363.

Evans, G. W. (2004). The environment of childhood poverty. *American Psychologist, 59*(2), 77–92.

Evans, G. W., & English, K. (2002). The environment of poverty: Multiple stressor exposure, psychophysiological stress, and socioemotional adjustment. *Child Development, 73*(4), 1238–1248.

Fahlman, M. M., Hall, H. L., & Lock, R. (2006). Ethnic and socioeconomic comparisons of fitness, activity levels, and barriers to exercise in high school females. *Journal of School Health, 76*(1), 12–17.

Figlio, D. N. (2005). *Names, expectations, and the black-white achievement gap.* Cambridge, MA: National Bureau of Economic Research.

Finders, M., & Lewis, C. (1998). Why some parents don't come to school. *Educational Leadership, 51,* 50–54.

Finley, S., & Diversi, M. (2010). Critical homelessness: Expanding narratives of inclusive democracy. *Cultural Studies–Critical Methodologies, 10*(1), 4–13.

Fleming, R. (2011). Use of school nurse services among poor ethnic minority students in the urban Pacific Northwest. *Public Health Nursing, 28*(4), 308–316.

Flessa, J. J. (2007). *Poverty and education: Toward effective action.* Toronto, Canada: Elementary Teachers Federation of Ontario.

Frankenberg, E. (2009). Splintering school districts: Understanding the link between segregation and fragmentation. *Law & Social Inquiry, 34*(4), 869–909.

Freeman, E. (2010). The shifting geography of urban education. *Education and Urban Society, 42*(6), 674–704.

Frey, W. H. (2005). *Metro America in the new century: Metropolitan and central city demographic shifts since 2000.* Washington, DC: Brookings Institution.

Fulda, K. G., Lykens, K. K., Bae, S., & Singh, K. P. (2009). Unmet health care needs for children with special health care needs stratified by socioeconomic status. *Child and Adolescent Mental Health, 14*(4), 190–199.

Fuller, B. (2007). *Standardized childhood: The political and cultural struggle over early education.* Palo Alto, CA: Stanford University Press.

Futrell, M., & Gomez, J. (2008). How tracking creates a poverty of learning. *Educational Leadership, 65*(8), 74–78.

Gabe, T. (2012). *Poverty in the United States: 2011.* Washington, DC: Congressional Research Service.

Galbraith, J., & Winterbottom, M. (2011). Peer-tutoring: What's in it for the tutor? *Educational Studies, 37*(3), 321–332.

Galea, S., Ahern, J., Tracy, M., & Vlahov, D. (2007). Neighborhood income and income distribution and the use of cigarettes, alcohol, and marijuana. *American Journal of Preventative Medicine, 32*(6), 195–202.

Gándara, P. (2010). Overcoming triple segregation. *Educational Leadership, 68*(3), 60–64.

Gans, H. J. (1995). *The war against the poor.* New York: Basic Books.

García, S. B., & Guerra, P. L. (2004). Deconstructing deficit thinking: Working with educators to create more equitable learning environments. *Education and Urban Society, 36*(2), 150–168.

Garza, R. E., & Garza, E. (2010). Successful white female teachers of Mexican American students of low socioeconomic status. *Journal of Latinos in Education, 9*(3), 189–206.

Gayles, J., & Denerville, D. (2007). Counting language: An exercise in stigmatization. *Multicultural Education, 15*(1), 16–22.

Georges, A. (2009). Relation of instruction and poverty to mathematics achievement gains during kindergarten. *Teachers College Record, 111*(9), 2148–2178.

Glendinning, C., & Baldwin, S. (1988). The costs of disability. In R. Walker & G. Parker (Eds.), *Money matters: Income, wealth and financial welfare* (pp. 63–80). London, UK: Sage.

Gonzalez, N., Moll, L. C., & Amanti, C. (Eds.). (2005). *Funds of knowledge: Theorizing practices in households, communities, and classrooms.* Mahwah, NJ: Lawrence Erlbaum Associates.

Gorman, E. H. (2005). Gender stereotypes, same-gender preferences, and organizational variation in the hiring of women: Evidence from law firms. *American Sociological Review, 70*(4), 702–728.

Gorski, P. C. (2008a). The myth of the "culture of poverty." *Educational Leadership, 65*(7), 32–35.

Gorski, P. C. (2008b). Peddling poverty for profit: Elements of oppression in Ruby Payne's framework. *Equity & Excellence in Education, 41*(1), 130–148.

Gorski, P. C. (2009). Insisting on digital equity: Reframing the dominant discourse on multicultural education and technology. *Urban Education, 44,* 348–364.

Gorski, P. C. (2011). Unlearning deficit ideology and the scornful gaze: Thoughts on authenticating the class discourse in education. In R. Ahlquist, P. Gorski, & T. Montaño (Eds.), *Assault on kids: How hyper-accountability, corporatization, deficit ideologies, and Ruby Payne are destroying our schools* (pp. 152–176). New York: Peter Lang.

Gorski, P. C. (2012). Perceiving the problem of poverty and schooling: Deconstructing the class stereotypes that mis-shape education policy and practice. *Equity & Excellence in Education, 45*(2), 302–319.

Gorski, P. C. (in press). Imagining equity literacy. *Teaching Tolerance.*

Gottfried, A. W., Gottfried, A. E., Bathurst, K., Guerin, D. W., & Parramore, M. M. (2003). Socioeconomic status in children's development and family environment: Infancy through adolescence. In M. H. Bornstein & R. H. Bradley (Eds.), *Socioeconomic status, parenting, and child development* (pp. 260–285). Mahwah, NJ: Lawrence Erlbaum Associates.

Gottlieb, J., & Weinberg, S. (1999). Comparison of students referred and not referred for special education. *The Elementary School Journal, 99,* 188–199.

Gould, M. C., & Gould, H. (2003). A clear vision for equity and opportunity. *Phi Delta Kappan, 85*(4), 324–328.

Grady, S., Bielick, S., & Aud, S. (2010). *Trends in use of school choice: 1993 to 2007.* Washington, DC: U.S. Department of Education.

Graham, M. A. (2009, February). Focus on "culture of poverty" misses the mark. *Counseling Today,* 45–48.

Grant, S. D., Oka, E. R., & Baker, J. A. (2009). The culturally relevant assessment of Ebonics-speaking children. *Journal of Applied School Psychology, 25*(3), 113–127.

Greenwood, C. R., & Delquari, J. (1995). Classwide peer tutoring and the prevention of school failure. *Preventing School Failure, 39*(4), 21–25.

Greve, F. (2009, May 23). America's poor are its most generous. *The Seattle Times*. Available at http://seattletimes.nwsource.com

Grissom, J. (2005). Physical fitness and academic achievement. *Journal of Exercise Physiology*, *8*, 11–25.

Grusky, D. B., & Ryo, E. (2006). Did Katrina recalibrate attitudes toward poverty and inequality? A test of the "dirty little secret" hypothesis. *Du Bois Review*, *3*(1), 59–82.

Guin, K. (2004). Chronic teacher turnover in urban elementary schools. *Education Policy Analysis Archives*, *12*(42). Available at http://epaa.asu.edu/epaa/v12n42/

Gurr, D., & Drysdale, L. (2007), Models of successful school leadership: Victorian case studies. In K. Leithwood & C. Day (Eds.), *Successful school leadership in times of change* (pp. 39–58). Toronto, Canada: Springer.

Haberman, M. (1991). The pedagogy of poverty versus good teaching. *Phi Delta Kappan*, *73*, 290–294.

Haberman, M. (1995). *Start teachers of children in poverty*. Irvine, CA: Kappa Delta Pi.

Hammack, P. L., Robinson, W. L., Crawford, I., & Li, S. T. (2004). Poverty and depressed mood among urban African-American adolescents: A family stress perspective. *Journal of Child and Family Studies*, *13*, 309–323.

Hamovitch, B. (1996). Socialization without voice: An ideology of hope for at-risk students. *Teachers College Record*, *98*(2), 286–306.

Hart, B., & Risley, T. R. (1995). *Meaningful differences in the everyday experiences of young American children*. Baltimore, MD: Brookes.

Hatch, G., & Smith, D. (2004). Integrating physical education, math, and physics. *Journal of Physical Education, Recreation & Dance*, *75*(1), 42–50.

Hattie, J. A. C. (2002). Classroom composition and peer effects. *International Journal of Education Research*, *35*, 449–481.

Hawkins, R. L. (2010). Fickle families and the kindness of strangers: Social capital in the lives of low-income single mothers. *Journal of Human Behavior in the Social Environment*, *20*, 38–55.

Heath, S. B., & Roach, A. (1999). Imaginative actuality: Learning in the arts during the non-school hours. In E. B. Fiske (Ed.), *Champions of change: The impact of the arts on learning* (pp. 19–34). Washington, DC: Arts Education Partnership, President's Committee on the Arts and the Humanities.

Heckman, J. J. (2006). Skill formation and the economics of investing in disadvantaged children. *Science*, *312*, 1900–1902.

Heckman, J. J., & Masterov, D. V. (2007). The productivity argument for investing in young children. *Review of Agricultural Economics*, *29*, 446–493.

Henderson, R., & Kennedy, R. (2004). Educational equity: The concept and its measure. *Research for Educational Reform*, *9*(2), 38–52.

Herbert, M. (2010). Is it segregation or fragmentation? *District Administration, 46*(1), 8.

Hertz, T. (2005). Rags, riches and race: The intergenerational economic mobility of black and white families in the U.S. In S. Bowles, H. Gintis, & M. Osborne (Eds.), *Unequal chances: Family background and economic success* (pp. 165–191). Princeton, NJ: Princeton University Press.

Hill, N. E., & Craft, S. A. (2003). Parent-school involvement and school performance: Mediated pathways among socioeconomically comparable African American and Euro-American families. *Journal of Educational Psychology, 91,* 74–83.

Holme, J. J., & Richards, M. P. (2009). School choice and stratification in a regional context: Examining the role of inter-district choice. *Peabody Journal of Education, 84,* 150–171.

Holme, J. J., & Wells, A. S. (2008). School choice beyond district borders: Lessons for the reauthorization of NCLB from interdistrict desegregation and open enrollment plans. In R. Kahlenberg (Ed.), *Improving on No Child Left Behind* (pp. 139–215). Washington, DC: The Century Foundation Press.

Holtzman, C., & Susholtz, L. (2011). *Object lessons: Teaching math through the visual arts.* Portland, ME: Stenhouse Publishers.

hooks, b. (2000). *Where we stand: Class matters.* New York: Routledge.

Hornsey, M. J. (2008). Social identity and self-categorization theory: A historical review. *Social and Personality Psychology Compass, 2*(1), 204–222.

Horvat, E. M., & Davis, J. E. (2011). Schools as sites for transformation: Exploring the conditions of habitus. *Youth & Society, 43*(1), 142–170.

Hout, M. (2008). How class works: Objective and subjective aspects of class since the 1970s. In A. Lareau & D. Conley (Eds.), *Social class: How does it work?* (pp. 25–64). New York: Sage.

Howard, L. (2007). *How exemplary teachers educate children of poverty, having low school readiness skills, without referrals to special education.* Unpublished doctoral dissertation, George Mason University.

Howard, T., Dresser, S. G., & Dunklee, D. R. (2009). *Poverty is not a learning disability: Equalizing opportunities for low SES students.* Thousand Oaks, CA: Corwin.

Hoy, W. K., Tarter, C. J., & Hoy, A. W. (2006). Academic optimism in schools: A force for student achievement. *American Educational Research Journal, 43,* 425–446.

Huang, M-H. (2009). Classroom homogeneity and the distribution of student math performance: A country-level fixed-effects analysis. *Social Science Research, 38,* 781–791.

Hughes, C., Newkirk, R., & Stenhjem, P. H. (2010). Addressing the challenge of disenfranchisement of youth: Poverty and racism in the schools. *Reclaiming Children and Youth, 19*(1), 22–26.

Hughes, J. (2010). What teacher preparation programs can do to better prepare teachers to meet the challenges of educating students living in poverty. *Action in Teacher Education, 32*(1), 54–64.

Humensky, J. L. (2010). Are adolescents with high socioeconomic status more likely to engage in alcohol and illicit drug use in early adulthood? *Substance Abuse Treatment, Prevention, and Policy, 5*, 1–10.

Isaacs, J., Sawhill, I., & Haskins, R. (2008). *Getting ahead or losing ground: Economic mobility in America*. Washington, DC: The Brookings Institution.

Jackson, S. (2011). Heterosexual hierarchies: A commentary on class and sexuality. *Sexualities, 14*(1), 12–20.

James, R. N., III, & Sharpe, D. L. (2007). The nature and causes of the U-shaped charitable giving profile. *Nonprofit and Voluntary Sector Quarterly, 36*, 218–238.

Jennings, P. K. (2004). What mothers want: Welfare reform and maternal desire. *Journal of Sociology and Social Welfare, 31*(3), 113–130.

Jensen, E. (2009). *Teaching with poverty in mind*. Alexandria, VA: ASCD.

Jervis, R. (2006). Understanding beliefs. *Political Psychology, 27*(5), 641–663.

Jessim, L., & Harber, K. D. (2005). Teacher expectations and self-fulfilling prophecies: Knowns and unknowns, resolved and unresolved controversies. *Personality and Social Psychology Review, 9*(2), 131–155.

Jeynes, W. (2011). *Parent involvement and academic success*. New York: Routledge.

Johns, M., Schmader, T., & Martens, A. (2005). Knowing is half the battle: Teaching stereotype threat as a means of improving women's math performance. *Psychological Science, 16*, 175–179.

Johnston, D. C. (2005, December 19). Study shows the superrich are not the most generous. *The New York Times*. Available at http://www.nytimes.com

Jones, R. K., & Luo, Y. (1999). The culture of poverty and African American culture: An empirical assessment. *Sociological Perspectives, 42*(3), 439–458.

Jones, S. (2008). Grass houses: Representations and reinventions of social class through children's literature. *Journal of Language and Literacy Education, 4*(2), 40–58.

Joo, M. (2010). Long-term effects of Head Start on academic and school outcomes of children in persistent poverty: Girls vs. boys. *Children & Youth Services Review, 32*(6), 807–814.

Joyner, A., & Marsh, B. (2011). Institutionalizing disparities in education: A case study of segregation in Wane County, North Carolina high schools. *InterActions, 7*(1), 1–23.

Joyner, S., & Molina, C. (2012). *Impact of class time on student learning*. Austin, TX: Texas Comprehensive Center.

Judge, S. (2005). Resilient and vulnerable at-risk children: Protective factors affecting early school competence. *Journal of Children & Poverty, 11*(2), 149–168.

Judge, S., Puckett, K., & Bell, S. M. (2006). Closing the digital divide: Update from the early childhood longitudinal study. *Journal of Educational Research*, *100*(1), 52–60.

Judge, S., Puckett, K., & Cabuk, B. (2004). Digital equity: New findings from the early childhood longitudinal study. *Journal of Research on Technology in Education*, *36*(4), 383–396.

Jyoti, D. F., Frongillo, E. A., & Jones, S. J. (2005). Food insecurity affects school children's academic performance, weight gain, and social skills. *Journal of Nutrition*, *135*, 2831–2839.

Kahlenberg, R. (2007). *Rescuing* Brown v. Board of Education: *Profiles of twelve school districts pursuing socioeconomic school integration*. New York: The Century Foundation.

Kannapel, P. J., & Clements, S. K. (2005). *Inside the black box of high-performing, high-poverty schools: A report from the Pritchard Committee for Academic Excellence*. Lexington, KY: Pritchard Commission for Academic Excellence.

Karemaker, A., Pitchford, N., & O'Malley, C. (2010). Enhanced recognition of written words and enjoyment of reading in struggling beginner readers through whole-word multimedia software. *Computers & Education*, *54*(1), 199–208.

Karnick, P., Margellos-Anast, H., Seals, G., Whitman, S., Aljadeff, G., & Johnson, D. (2007). The pediatric asthma intervention: A comprehensive cost-effective approach to asthma management in a disadvantaged inner-city community. *Journal of Asthma*, *44*(1), 39–44.

Karoly, L. A., & Gonzalez, G. C. (2011). Early care and education for children in immigrant families. *Future of Children*, *21*(1), 70–101.

Kaufmann, G. (2011, March 22). U.S. poverty: Past, present, and future. *The Nation*. Available at http://www.thenation.com

Kellett, M. (2009). Children as researchers: What we can learn from them about the impact of poverty on literacy opportunities. *International Journal of Inclusive Education*, *13*(4), 395–408.

Kelley, J. E., & Darragh, J. J. (2011). Depictions and gaps: Portrayal of U.S. poverty in realistic fiction children's picture books. *Reading Horizons*, *50*(4), 263–282.

Kelly, M. (2010). Regulating the reproduction and mothering of poor women: The controlling image of the welfare mother in television news coverage of welfare reform. *Journal of Poverty*, *14*, 76–96.

Kennedy, E. (2010). Improving literacy achievement in a high-poverty school: Empowering classroom teachers through professional development. *Reading Research Quarterly*, *45*(4), 384–387.

Keyes, K. M., & Hasin, D. S. (2008). Socio-economic status and problem alcohol use: The positive relationship between income and the DSM-IV alcohol abuse diagnosis. *Addiction*, *103*(7), 1120–1130.

Kezar, A. (2011). Rethinking postsecondary institutions for low-income student success: The power of post-structural theory. In A. Kezar (Ed.), *Recognizing and serving low-income students in higher education: An examination of institutional policies, practices, and culture* (pp. 3–25). New York: Routledge.

Kieffer, M. J. (2010). Socioeconomic status, English proficiency, and late-emerging reading difficulties. *Educational Researcher, 39*(6), 484–486.

Kilburn, M. R., & Karoly, L. A. (2008). *What does economics tell us about early childhood policy?* Santa Monica, CA: RAND Corporation.

Killeen, K., & Schafft, K. A. (2008). The organizational and fiscal implications of transient student populations in urban and rural areas. In H. F. Ladd *&* E. B. Fiske (Eds.), *Handbook of research in education finance and policy* (pp. 631–650). New York: Routledge.

Kim, M. (1999). Problems facing the working poor. *Proceedings of the Economic Policy Institute Symposium*, Washington, DC. Available at http://www.dol.gov/oasam/programs/history/herman/reports/futurework/conference/workingpoor/workingpoor_toc.htm

Kincheloe, J. L., & Steinberg, S. R. (2007). Cutting class in a dangerous era: A critical pedagogy of class awareness. In J. L. Kincheloe & S.R. Steinberg (Eds.), *Cutting class: Socioeconomic status and education* (pp. 3–69). New York: Rowman & Littlefield.

King, M. L. (1967, August). *Where do we go from here?* Speech presented at the Southern Christian Leadership Conference, Atlanta, Georgia.

Kitchen, R., DePree, J., Celedón-Pattichis, S., & Brinkerhoff, J. (2004). *High achieving schools initiative final report.* Albuquerque, NM: University of New Mexico.

Kivel, P. (2004). *You call this a democracy? Who benefits, who pays and who really decides?* New York: The Apex Press.

Knapp, M. S. (1995). Introduction. In M. S. Knapp (Ed.), *Teaching for meaning in high-poverty classrooms* (pp. 1–10). New York: Teachers College Press.

Kochlar, R., Fry, R., & Taylor, P. (2011). *Wealth gaps rise to record highs between Whites, Blacks and Hispanics.* Washington, DC: Pew Social & Demographic Trends.

Koenig, K. (2007). Pilot study of low-income parents' perspectives of managing asthma in high-risk infants and toddlers. *Pediatric Nursing, 33*, 223–228.

Kong, A., Burks, N., Conklin, C., Roldan, C., Skipper, B., Scott, S., Sussman, A., & Leggot, J. (2010). A pilot walking school bus program to prevent obesity in Hispanic elementary school children: Role of physician involvement in the school community. *Clinical Pediatrics, 49*(1), 989–991.

Koppelman, K. L., & Goodhart, R. L. (2005). *Understanding human difference: Multicultural education for a diverse America.* Boston, MA: Pearson.

Kozol, J. (1992). *Savage inequalities: Children in America's schools.* New York: HarperPerennial.

Kozol, J. (2005). *The shame of a nation: The restoration of apartheid schooling in America.* New York: Crown.

Krashen, S. (2004). *The power of reading.* Portsmouth, NH: Heinemann.

Krashen, S. (2009). Does intensive reading instruction contribute to reading comprehension? *Knowledge Quest, 37*(4), 72–74.

Krashen, S., Lee, S., & McQuillan, J. (2010). An analysis of the PIRLS (2006) data: Can the school library reduce the effect of poverty on reaching achievement? *CSLA Journal, 34*(1), 26–28.

Kraus, M. W., & Keltner, D. (2009). Signs of socioeconomic status: A thin-slicing approach. *Psychological Science, 20,* 99–106.

Krueger, A. B. (1999). Experimental estimates of education production functions. *Quarterly Journal of Economics, 114*(2), 497–531.

Krueger, P. M., & Chang, V. (2008). Being poor and coping with stress: Health behaviors and risk of death. *American Journal of Public Health, 98,* 889–896.

Kumanyika, S., & Grier, S. (2006). Targeting interventions for ethnic minority and low-income populations. *Future Child, 16*(1), 187–207.

Labov, W. (1972). *Sociolinguistic patterns.* Philadelphia, PA: University of Pennsylvania Press.

Ladson-Billings, G. (2006). It's not the culture of poverty, it's the poverty of culture: The problem with teacher education. *Anthropology and Education Quarterly, 37*(2), 104–109.

LaGue, K., & Wilson, K. (2010). Using peer tutors to improve reading comprehension. *Kappa Delta Pi Record, 46*(4), 182–186.

Landsman, J., & Gorski, P. C. (2007). Countering standardization. *Educational Leadership, 64*(8), 40–44.

Lantz, P. M., House, J. S. Mero, R. P., & Williams, D. R. (2005). Stress, life events, and socioeconomic disparities in health: Results from the Americans' Changing Lives study. *Journal of Health and Social Behavior, 46,* 274–288.

Lareau, A. (1994). Parent involvement in schooling: A dissenting view. In C. Fagano & B. Z. Werber (Eds.), *School, family, and community interaction: A view from the firing lines* (pp. 61–73). Boulder, CO: Westview Press.

Lareau, A. (2000). *Home advantage: Social class and parental intervention in elementary education.* Lanham, MD: Rowman and Littlefield.

Lareau, A., & Weininger, E. B. (2008). Class and the transition to adulthood. In A. Lareau & D. Conley (Eds.), *Social class: How does it work?* (pp. 118–151). New York: Sage.

Lee, C. D. (1995). A culturally based cognitive apprenticeship: Teaching African American high school students skills in literary interpretation. *Reading Research Quarterly, 30*(4), 608–630.

Lee, J.-S., & Bowen, N. K. (2006). Parent involvement, cultural capital, and the achievement gap among elementary school children. *American Educational Research Journal, 43*(2), 193–218.

Lee, S. G., & Jeon, S. Y. (2005). The relations of socioeconomic status to health status, health behaviors in the elderly. *Journal of Preventive Medicine and Public Health, 38*(2), 154–162.

Lee, V., & Burkam, D. (2003). Dropping out of high school: The role of school organization and structure. *American Educational Research Journal, 40*(2), 353–393.

Levy, F. (2010). America's 25 richest counties. *Forbes.com.* Available at http://www.forbes.com/2010/03/04/america-richest-counties-lifestyle-real-estate-wealthy-suburbs_print.html

Lewis, O. (1950). An anthropological approach to family studies. *American Journal of Sociology, 55*(5), 468–475.

Lewis, O. (1959). *Five families: Mexican case studies in the culture of poverty.* New York: Basic Books.

Lewis, O. (1961). *The children of Sánchez: Autobiography of a Mexican family.* New York: Vintage.

Li, G. (2010). Race, class, and schooling: Multicultural families doing the hard work of home literacy in America's inner city. *Reading & Writing Quarterly, 26,* 140–165.

Lindsay, J. (2010). *Children's access to print material and education-related outcomes: Findings from a metaanalytic review.* Naperville, IL: Learning Point Associates.

Lindsey, R. B., Karns, M. S., & Myatt, K. (2010). *Culturally proficient education: An asset-based response to conditions of poverty.* Thousand Oaks, CA: Corwin.

Lindsey, R. B., Robins, K. N., & Terrell, R. D. (2009). *Cultural proficiency: A manual for school leaders.* Thousand Oaks, CA: Corwin.

Lipman, P. (2011). Neoliberal education restructuring: Dangers and opportunities of the present crisis. *Monthly Review, 63*(3), 114–127.

Lippi-Green, R. (1994). Accent, standard language ideology, and discriminatory pretext in the courts. *Language in Society, 23,* 163–198.

Liu, G. (2008). Improving Title I funding equity across states, districts, and schools. *Iowa Law Review, 93*(3), 973–1013.

Losen, D. J. (1999). Silent segregation in our nation's schools. *Harvard Civil Rights–Civil Liberties Law Review, 34,* 517–546.

Loughrey, D., & Woods, C. (2010). Sparking the imagination: Creative experts working collaboratively with children, teachers, and parents to enhance educational opportunities. *Support for Learning, 25*(2), 81–90.

Luhby, T. (2012a). American's near poor: 30 million and struggling. *CNNMoney.* Available at http://money.cnn.com/2012/10/24/news/economy/americans-poverty/index.html

Luhby, T. (2012b). Median income falls, but so does poverty. *CNNMoney.* Available at http://money.cnn.com/2012/09/12/news/economy/median-income-poverty/index.html?iid=EL

Luhman, R. (1990). Appalachian English stereotypes: Language attitudes in Kentucky. *Language in Society, 19*(3), 331–348.

Luke, A. (2010). Documenting reproduction and inequality: Revisiting Jean Anyon's "Social Class and School Knowledge." *Curriculum Inquiry, 40*(1), 167–182.

Ly, C. (2010). More than a library?: Urban poverty and an exploratory look at the role of a neighborhood institution. *Perspectives on Urban Education, 7*(2), 22–33.

Machan, S., Wilson, J., & Notar, C. (2005). Parental involvement in the classroom. *Journal of Instructional Psychology, 32*, 13–16.

MacLeod, K. E., Gee, G. C., Crawford, P., & Wang, M. C. (2008). Neighborhood environment as a predictor of television viewing among girls. *Journal of Epidemiology & Community Health, 62*, 288–292.

Macpherson, A. K., Jones, J., Rothman, L., Macarthur, C., & Howard, A. W. (2010). Safety standards and socioeconomic disparities in school playground injuries: A retrospective cohort study. *BMC Public Health, 10*, 542–547.

Maheady, L., Mallette, B., & Harper, G. F. (2006). Four classwide peer tutoring models: Similarities, differences, and implications for research and practice. *Reading & Writing Quarterly, 22*, 65–89.

Marks, G. N., Cresswell, J., & Ainley, J. (2006). Explaining socioeconomic inequalities in student achievement: The role of home and school factors. *Educational Research and Evaluation, 12*(2), 105–128.

Marsh, J. (2011). *Class dismissed: Why we cannot teach or learn our way out of inequality.* New York: Monthly Review Press.

Marotz-Baden, R., Adams, G. R., Bueche, N., Munro, B., & Munro, G. (1979). Family form or family process? Reconsidering the deficit family model approach. *The Family Coordinator, 28*(1), 5–14.

Matthews, H., & Ewen, D. (2006). *Reaching all children? Understanding early care and education participation in immigrant families in the United States.* Washington, DC: Center for Law and Social Policy.

Matthews, H., & Jang, D. (2007). *The challenges of change: Learning from the child care and early education experiences of immigrant families.* Washington, DC: Center for Law and Social Policy.

Mayer, S. E., & Lopoo, L. M. (2008). Government spending and intergenerational mobility. *Journal of Public Economics, 92*, 139–158.

Mazumder, B. (2005). The apple falls even closer to the tree than we thought: New and revised estimates of the intergenerational inheritance of earnings. In S. Bowles, H. Gintis, & M. O. Groves (Eds.), *Unequal chances: Family background and economic success.* New York: Russell Sage Foundation.

McCall, L., & Percheski, C. (2010). Income inequality: New trends and research directions. *Annual Review of Sociology, 16*, 329–347.

McDermott, R., Goldman, S., & Varenne, H. (2006). The cultural work of learning disabilities. *Educational Researcher, 35*, 12–17.

McGee, G. W. (2004). Closing the achievement gap: Lessons from Illinois' Golden Spike high-poverty, high-performing schools. *Journal of Education for Students Placed at Risk, 9*(2), 97–125.

McKinney, S., & Frazier, W. (2008). Embracing the principles and standards for school mathematics: An inquiry into the pedagogical and instructional practices of mathematics teachers in high-poverty middle schools. *The Clearing House, 81*(5), 201–210.

McKown, C., & Weinstein, R. S. (2003). The development and consequences of stereotype consciousness in middle childhood. *Child Development, 74*(2), 498–515.

McLaughlin, H., Uggen, C., & Blackstone, A. (2008). Social class and workplace harassment during transition to adulthood. *New Directions for Child and Adolescent Development, 119,* 85–98.

Meier, D., & Wood, G. (2004). *Many children left behind.* Boston, MA: Beacon.

Meiser, T., & Hewstone, M. (2004). Cognitive processes in stereotype formation: The role of correct contingency learning for biased group judgments. *Journal of Personality and Social Psychology, 875,* 599–614.

Mendoza, J. A., Levinger, D. D., & Johnston, B. D. (2009). Pilot evaluation of a walking school bus program in a low-income urban community. *BMC Public Health, 9,* 122–129.

Messacar, D., & Oreopoulos, P. (2012). *Staying in school: A proposal to raise high school graduation rates.* Washington, DC: The Hamilton Project.

Meyer, B., & Sullivan, J. (2012). Identifying the disadvantaged: Official poverty, consumption poverty, and the new supplemental poverty measure. *Journal of Economic Perspectives, 3,* 111–136.

Michelson, R. A. (2010). Goals, grades, fears, and peers: Introductory essay for special issues on the effects of school and classroom racial and SES composition on educational outcomes. *Teachers College Record, 112*(4), 961–977.

Milbourne, P. (2010). Putting poverty and welfare in place. *Policy & Politics, 38*(1), 153–169.

Miller, P. J., Cho, G. E., & Bracey, J. R. (2005). Working-class children's experience through the prism of personal storytelling. *Human Development, 48,* 115–135.

Miller, R. (2010). *Comparable,* schmomparable: *Evidence of inequity in the allocation of funds for teacher salary within California's public school districts.* Washington, DC: Center for American Progress.

Mistry, R., Brown, C., Chow, K., & Collins, G. (2012). Increasing the complexity of young adolescents' beliefs about poverty and inequality: Results of an 8th grade social studies curriculum intervention. *Journal of Youth and Adolescence, 41,* 704–716.

Mitra, S., Findley, P. A., & Sambamoorthi, U. (2009). Healthcare expenditures of living with a disability: Total expenditures, out of pocket expenses and burden, 1996–2004. *Archives of Physical Medicine and Rehabilitation, 90,* 1532–1540.

Moll, L. C., Amanti, C., Neff, D., & Gonzalez, N. (1992). Funds of knowledge for teaching: Using a qualitative approach to connect homes and classrooms. *Theory into Practice, 31,* 132–141.

Monitoring the Future. (2008). *Monitoring the future: National results on adolescent drug use.* Ann Arbor, MI: Author.

Moynihan, D. (1965). *The Negro family: The case for national action.* Washington, DC: United States Department of Labor.

Muhammad, D. (2009). *Challenges to Native American advancement: The recession and Native America.* Washington, DC: Institute for Policy Studies.

Najman, J. M., Hayatbakhsh, M. R., Claravino, A., Bor, W., O'Callaghan, M. J., & Williams, G. M. (2010). Family poverty over the early life course and recurrent adolescent and young adult anxiety and depression: A longitudinal study. *American Journal of Public Health, 100*(9), 1719–1723.

National Alliance on Mental Illness. (2011). *State mental health cuts: A national crisis.* Arlington, VA: Author.

National Association for the Teaching of English Working Party on Social Class and English Teaching. (1982). Check list for class bias and some recommended books. *English in Education, 16*(2), 34–37.

National Center for Education Statistics (NCES). (2005). *Parent and family involvement in education: 2002–2003.* Washington, DC: U.S. Department of Education.

National Center for Education Statistics (NCES). (2008). *The condition of Education, 2008.* Washington, DC: U.S. Department of Education.

National Coalition for the Homeless (NCH). (2009). *Homeless veterans.* National Coalition for the Homeless website. Available at http://www.nationalhomeless. org/factsheets/veterans.html

National Commission on Teaching and America's Future (NCTAF). (2004). *2004 summit on high quality teacher preparation.* Available at http://www.nctaf.org/ resoruces/events/2004_summit-1

National Council of Teachers of Mathematics. (2000). *Principles and standards for school mathematics.* Reston, VA: Author.

National Employment Law Project. (2011). *A year of unbalanced growth.* New York: Author.

National Institute for Direct Instruction. (2012). *About direct instruction.* Available at http://www.nifdi.org/aboutdi

National Survey on Drug Use and Health. (2004). *Youth substance use and family income.* Rockville, MD: Author.

Nesdale, D., & Flesser, D. (2001). Social identity and the development of children's group attitudes. *Child Development, 72*(2), 506.

Neuman, S. B. (2009). Use the science of what works to change the odds for children at risk. *Phi Delta Kappan, 90*(8), 582–587.

Neuman, S. B., & Celano, D. (2001). Access to print in low-income and middle-income communities: An ecological study of four neighborhoods. *Reading Research Quarterly, 36*(1), 8–26.

Newman, K., & Chin, M. (2003). High stakes, time in poverty, testing, and the children of the working poor. *Qualitative Sociology, 26*, 3–34.

Newmeyer, F. (1985). *Grammatical theory: Its limits and possibilities.* Chicago, IL: University of Chicago Press.

Noguera, P. (2011). A broader and bolder approach uses education to break the cycle of poverty. *Phi Delta Kappan, 93*(3), 8–14.

Noguera, P., & Akom, A. (2000, June 5). Disparities demystified. *The Nation,* 29–31.

Nordhagen, R., Nielsen, A., Stigum, H., & Kohler, L. (2005). Parental reported bullying among Nordic children: A population-based study. *Child Care Health Development, 31*(6), 693–701.

Norton, M. I., & Ariely, D. (2011). Building a better America—one wealth quintile at a time. *Perspectives on Psychological Science, 6*(1), 9–12.

Oakes, J. (2005). *Keeping track: How schools structure inequality.* New Haven, CT: Yale University Press.

Ohmer, M. L., Warner, B. D., & Beck, E. (2010). Preventing violence in low-income communities: Facilitating residents' ability to intervene in neighborhood problems. *Journal of Sociology & Social Welfare, 37*(2), 161–181.

Orfield, G., & Frankenberg, E. (2008). *The last have become the first: Rural and small town America lead the way on desegregation.* Los Angeles, CA: The Civil Rights Project.

Orfield, G., Frankenberg, E., & Siegel-Hawley, G. (2010). Integrated schools: Finding a new path. *Educational Leadership, 68*(3), 22–27.

Ortiz, A. T., & Briggs, L. (2003). The culture of poverty, crack babies, and welfare cheats: The making of the "healthy white baby crisis." *Social Text, 21*(3), 39–57.

Ostrove, J., & Long, S. (2007). Social class and belonging: Implications for college adjustment. *Review of Higher Education, 30*(4), 363–389.

Oyserman, D., Brickman, D., & Rhodes, M. (2007). School success, possible selves, and parent school involvement. *Family Relations, 56*(5), 479–489.

Palardy, G. J. (2008). Differential school effects among low, middle, and high social class composition schools: A multiple group, multilevel latent growth curve analysis. *School Effectiveness and School Improvement, 19*(1), 21–49.

Palmer, M. (2011). Disability and poverty: A conceptual overview. *Journal of Disability Policy Studies, 21*(4), 210–218.

Pampel, F. C., Krueger, P. M., & Denney, J. T. (2010). Socioeconomic disparities in health behaviors. *Annual Review of Sociology, 36*, 349–370.

Paquette, J. (2005). Public funding for "private" education: The equity challenge for enhanced choice. *American Journal of Education, 111*(4), 568–595.

Parker, B., & Howard, A. (2009). Beyond economics: Using social class life-based literary narratives with pre-service and practicing social studies and English teachers. *The High School Journal, 92*(3), 3–13.

Pascale, C. M. (2005). There's no place like home: The discursive creation of homelessness. *Cultural Studies–Critical Methodologies, 5*(2), 250–268.

Patterson, J. A., Hale, D., & Stessman, M. (2008). Cultural contradictions and school leaving: A case study of an urban high school. *The High School Journal, 91*(2), 1–16.

Paulsen, M. B., & St. John, E. P. (2002). Social class and college costs: Examining the financial nexus between college choice and persistence. *Journal of Higher Education, 73*(2), 189–236.

Payne, R. K. (2005). *A framework for understanding poverty*. Highlands, TX: aha! Process.

Payne, R. K. (2006). *Reflections on Katrina and the role of poverty in the Gulf Coast crisis*. Available at http://www.ahaprocess.com/files/Hurricane_Katrina_ reflections.pdf

Peisner-Feinberg, E. S., Burchinal, M. R., Clifford, R. M., Culkin, M. L., Howes, C., Kagan, S. L., & Yazejian, N. (2001). The relation of preschool child-care quality to children's cognitive and social developmental trajectories through second grade. *Child Development 72*(5), 1534–1553.

Perna, L. W., Rowan-Kenyon, H., Bell, A., Li, C., & Thomas, S. L. (2008). Typology of federal and state policies designed to promote college enrollment. *Journal of Higher Education 79*(3), 243–267.

Peshkin, A. (1982). *The imperfect union: School consolidation and community conflict*. Chicago, IL: The University of Chicago Press.

Peterson, C., Mayer, L., Summers, J., & Luze, G. (2010). Meeting needs of young children at high risk for or having a disability. *Early Childhood Education Journal, 37*(6), 509–517.

Piff, P. K., Kraus, M. W., Cote, S., Cheng, B. H., & Keltner, D. (2010). Having less, giving more: The influence of social class on prosocial behavior. *Journal of Personality and Social Psychology, 99*(5), 771–784.

Pogrow, S. (2006). Restructuring high-poverty elementary schools for success: A description of the Hi-Perform school design. *Phi Delta Kappan, 88*(3), 223–229.

Pogrow, S. (2009). Accelerating the learning of 4th and 5th graders born into poverty. *Phi Delta Kappan, 90*(6), 408–412.

Popham, W. J. (2004). A game without winners. *Educational Leadership, 62*(3), 46–50.

Poplin, M., & Soto-Hinman, I. (2006). Taking off ideological blinders: Lessons from the start of a study on effective teachers in high-poverty schools. *The Journal of Education, 186*(3), 41–44.

Prensky, M. (2010). *Teaching digital natives: Partnering for real learning*. Thousand Oaks, CA: Corwin.

Pribesh, S., Gavigan, K., & Dickinson, G. (2011). The access gap: Poverty and characteristics of school library media centers. *The Library Quarterly, 81*(2), 143–160.

Ramalho, E. M., Garza, E., & Merchant, B. (2010). Successful school leadership in socioeconomically challenging contexts: School principals creating and sustaining successful school improvement. *International Studies in Educational Administration, 38*(3), 35–56.

Rampell, C. (2012). Record corporate profits. *Economix.* Available at http://economix.blogs.nytimes.com/2012/11/29/record-corporate-profits/

RAND. (2008). *State and local implementation of the No Child Left Behind Act Volume IV—Title I school choice and supplemental educational services: Interim report.* Santa Monica, CA: Author.

Rank, M. R., Yoon, H., & Hirschl, T. A. (2003). American poverty as a structural failing: Evidence and arguments. *Journal of Sociology and Social Welfare, 30*(4), 3–29.

Ray, N. (2006). *Lesbian, gay, bisexual, and transgender youth: An epidemic of homelessness.* New York: National Gay and Lesbian Task Force Policy Institute and the National Coalition for the Homeless.

Reamer, A., Waldron, T., Hatcher, E., & Hayes, L. (2008). *Still working hard, still falling short: New findings on the challenges confronting America's working families.* Chevy Chase, MD: The Working Poor Families Project.

Reid, J. (2006). *New census data shows 1.3 million children have fallen into poverty since 2000.* Available at http://cdf.childrensdefense.org/site/News2?page=NewsArticle&id=7887

Reis, S., & Fogarty, E. (2006). Savoring reading schoolwide. *Educational Leadership, 64*(2), 32–36.

Reynolds, A. J. (2000). *Success in early intervention: The Chicago child-parent centers.* Lincoln, NE: University of Nebraska Press.

Richardson, J. (2003). *The secrets of "can-do" schools: Louisiana team uncovers traits of high-poverty, high-performing schools.* Available at http://www.learningforward.org/news/results/res2-03rich.cfm

Robinson, J. G. (2007). Presence and persistence: Poverty ideology and inner-city teaching. *Urban Review, 39*, 541–565.

Rodman, R. (1977). Culture of poverty: The rise and fall of a concept. *Sociological Review, 25*(4), 867–876.

Rosemblatt, K. A. (2009). Other Americas: Transnationalism, scholarship, and the culture of poverty in Mexico and the United States. *Hispanic American Historical Review, 89*(4), 603–641.

Rosenthal, S. (2007). *A social definition of class.* Available at http://susanrosenthal.com/articles/a-social-definition-of-class

Rouse, C. E., & Barrow, L. (2006). U.S. elementary and secondary schools: Equalizing opportunity or replacing the status quo? *The Future of Children, 16*(2), 99–123.

Rumberger, R. W., & Palardy, G. J. (2005). Does segregation still matter? The impact of student composition on academic achievement in high school. *Teachers College Record, 107,* 1999–2045.

Rushe, D. (2012, November 1). US has added 1.1m new millionaires under Obama, says study. *The Guardian Online.* Available at http://www.guardian.co.uk/business/2012/nov/01/us-new-millionaires-obama

Rutgers University. (2006). *New Jersey's interdistrict public school choice program.* Newark, NJ: Rutgers Institute on Education Law and Policy.

Ryan, W. (1971). *Blaming the victim.* New York: Vintage Books.

Samoff, J. (1996). Which priorities and strategies for education? *International Journal of Educational Development, 16*(3), 249–271.

Sánchez, L. (in press). Fostering wideawakeness: Third grade children researching their community. In J. Landsman & P. Gorski (Eds.), *The poor are not the problem: Insisting on class equity in schools.* Sterling, VA: Stylus.

Sano, J. (2009). Farmhands and factory workers, honesty and humility: The portrayal of social class and morals in English language learner children's books. *Teachers College Record, 111*(11), 2560–2588.

Saporito, S., & Sohoni, D. (2007). Mapping educational inequality: Concentrations of poverty among poor and minority students in public schools. *Social Forces, 85*(3), 1227–1253.

Sapp, J. (2009). How school taught me I was poor. *Teaching Tolerance, 35,* 52–55.

Sato, M., & Lensmire, T. J. (2009). Poverty and Payne: Supporting teachers to work with children of poverty. *Phi Delta Kappan, 90*(5), 365–370.

Saydah, S., & Lochner, K. (2010). Socioeconomic status and risk of diabetes-related mortality in the U.S. *Public Health Reports, 125,* 377–388.

Sawhill, I. (2006). *Opportunity in America: The role of education.* Princeton, NJ: Brookings Institution.

Saxe, L., Kadushin, C., Tighe, E., Rindskopf, D., & Beveridge, A. (2001). *National evaluation of the fighting back program: General population surveys, 1995–1999.* New York: City University of New York Graduate Center.

Schafft, K. A. (2006). Poverty, residential mobility, and student transiency within a rural New York school district. *Rural Sociology, 71*(2), 212–231.

Scharoun-Lee, M., Kaufman, J. S., Popkin, B. M., & Gordon-Larsen, P. (2009). Obesity, race/ethnicity and life course socioeconomic status across the transition from adolescence to adulthood. *Journal of Epidemiology & Community Health, 63*(2), 133–139.

Scott, A. (2012, May 10). Tackling poverty along with reading and arithmetic. *Marketplace.* Available http://www.marketplace.org/topics/wealth-poverty/one-school-one-year/tackling-poverty-along-reading-and-arithmetic

Seccombe, K. (2002). "Beating the odds" versus "changing the odds": Poverty, resilience, and family policy. *Journal of Marriage and Family, 64*(2), 384–394.

Sen, A. (1992). *Inequality reexamined.* Oxford, UK: Clarendon Press.

Sepe, C., & Roza, M. (2010). *The disproportionate impact of seniority-based layoffs on poor, minority students.* Seattle, WA: Center for Reinventing Public Education.

Shann, M. H. (2001). Students' use of time outside of school: A case for after school programs for urban middle school youth. *Urban Review, 33,* 339–356.

Sheets, R. H. (2009). What is Diversity Pedagogy? *Multicultural Education, 16*(3), 11–17.

Sherman, J. (2006). Coping with rural poverty: Economic survival and moral capital in rural America. *Social Forces, 85*(2), 891–913.

Shier, M., Jones, M., & Graham, J. (2010). Perspectives of employed people experiencing homelessness of self and being homeless: Challenging socially constructed perceptions and stereotypes. *Journal of Sociology & Social Welfare, 37*(4), 13–37.

Shin, I., & Chung, J. (2009). Class size and student achievement in the United States: A meta-analysis. *Journal of Educational Policy, 6*(2), 3–19.

Siapush, M., McNeil, A., Hammond, D., & Fong, G. T. (2006). Socioeconomic and country variations in knowledge of health risks of tobacco smoking and toxic constituents of smoke: Results from the 2002 International Tobacco Control Four Country Survey. *Tobacco Control, 15,* 65–70.

Siefert, K., Heflin, C. M., & Corcoran, M. E. (2004). Food insufficiency and physical and mental health in a longitudinal survey of welfare recipients. *Journal of Health and Social Behavior, 45,* 171–186.

Simoes, E. A. (2003). Environmental and demographic risk factors for respiratory syncytial virus lower respiratory tract disease. *Journal of Pediatrics, 143,* 118–126.

Sirin, S. R. (2005). Socioeconomic status and academic achievement: A meta-analysis review of research. *Review of Educational Research, 75,* 417–453.

Slavin, R. E., Lake, C., & Groff, C. (2009). Effective programs in middle and high school mathematics: A best evidence synthesis. *Review of Educational Research, 79*(2), 839–911.

Sleeter, C. (2004). Context-conscious portraits and context-blind policy. *Anthropology and Education Quarterly, 35*(1), 132–136.

Smiley, A. D., & Helfenbein, R. J. (2011). Becoming teachers: The Payne effect. *Multicultural Perspectives, 13*(1), 5–15.

Smith, A. (2010). *Home broadband 2010.* Washington, DC: Pew Research Center.

Smith, P., Molnar, A., & Zahorik, J. (2003). Class-size reduction: A fresh look at the data. *Educational Leadership, 61,* 72–74.

Sorenson, G., Barbeau, E., Hunt, M. K., & Emmons, K. (2004). Reducing social disparities in tobacco use: A social contextual model for reducing tobacco use among blue-collar workers. *American Journal of Public Health, 94,* 230–239.

Southeast Asia Resource Action Center. (2011). *Southeast Asian Americans at a glance.* Washington, DC: Author.

Spencer, B., & Castano, E. (2007). Social class is dead! Long live social class! Stereotype threat among low socioeconomic status individuals. *Social Justice Research, 20,* 418–432.

Stapleton, D. C., O'Day, B. L., Livermore, G. A., & Imparato, A. J. (2006). Dismantling the poverty trap: Disability policy for the twenty-first century. *Milbank Quarterly, 84,* 701–732.

Starnes, B. (2008). On lilacs, tap-dancing, and children of poverty. *Phi Delta Kappan, 89*(10), 779–780.

Steele, C. M. (2010). *Whistling Vivaldi and other clues to how stereotypes affect us.* New York: W.W. Norton & Company.

Strange, M. (2011). Finding fairness for rural schools. *Phi Delta Kappan, 92*(6), 8–15.

Streib, J. (2011). Class reproduction by four year olds. *Qualitative Sociology, 34,* 337–352.

Streib, J. (2012). Class reproduction by four year olds. *Classism exposed blog.* Available at http://www.classism.org/class-reproduction-year-olds

Stuber, J. M. (2010). Class, culture, and participation in the collegiate extra-curriculum. *Sociological Forum, 24*(4), 877–900.

Sullivan, J., & Lloyd, R. S. (2006). The Forum Theatre of Augusto Boal: A dramatic model for dialogue and community-based environmental science. *The International Journal of Justice and Sustainability, 11*(6), 627–646.

Swalwell, K. (2011). Why our students need "equity literacy." *Teaching Tolerance Blog.* Available at http://www.tolerance.org/blog/why-our-students-need-equity-literacy

Swartz, T. T. (2008). Family capital and the invisible transfer of privilege: Intergenerational support and social class in early adulthood. *New Directions for Child and Adolescent Development, 119,* 11–24.

Taylor, P., Kochhar, R., Dockterman, D., & Motel, S. (2011a). *In two years of economic recovery, women lost jobs, men found them.* Washington, DC: Pew Research Center.

Taylor, P., Kochhar, R., Fry, R., Velasco, G., & Motel, S. (2011b). *Wealth gaps rise to record highs between Whites, Blacks and Hispanics.* Washington, DC: Pew Research Center.

Telljohann, S. K., Dake, J. A., & Price, J .H. (2004). Effect of full-time versus part-time school nurses on attendance of elementary students with asthma. *Journal of School Nursing, 20*(6), 331–334.

Temple, J. A., & Reynolds, A. J. (2007). Benefits and costs of investments in preschool education: Evidence from the child-parent centers and related programs. *Economics of Education Review, 26,* 126–144.

Temple, J. A., Reynolds, A. J., & Arteaga, I. (2010). Low birth weight, preschool education, and school remediation. *Education & Urban Society, 42*(6), 705–729.

Templeton, B. L. (2011). *Understanding poverty in the classroom.* New York: Rowman & Littlefield.

Terry, N. P., Connor, C. M., Thomas-Tate, S., & Love, M. (2010). Examining relationships among dialect variation, literacy skills, and school context in first grade. *Journal of Speech, Language, and Hearing Research, 53*, 126–145.

Thomas, D. (2008). The digital divide: What schools in low socioeconomic areas must teach. *The Delta Kappa Gamma Bulletin, 74*(4), 12–17.

Thrupp, M., Lauder, H., & Robinson, T. (2002). School composition and peer effects. *International Journal of Education Research, 37*, 483–504.

Thurston, L. P., & Berkeley, T. R. (2010). Morality and the ethic of care: Peaceable rural schools, caring rural communities. *Rural Special Education Quarterly, 29*(2), 25–31.

Tivnan, T., & Hemphill, L. (2005). Comparing four literacy reform models in high-poverty schools: Patterns of first-grade achievement. *The Elementary School Journal, 105*(5), 419–441.

Toch, T. (2011). Beyond basic skills. *Phi Delta Kappan, 92*(6), 72–73.

Toutkoushian, R. K., & Curtis, T. (2005). Effects of socioeconomic factors on public high school outcomes and rankings. *Journal of Education Research, 98*(5), 259–271.

Tranter, R., & Palin, N. (2004) Including the excluded: An art in itself. *Support for Learning, 19*(2), 88–95.

Turpin, K. (2009). The cultures of social class and religious educational practice. *Religious Education, 104*(3), 315–331.

U.S. Census Bureau. (2012). *Current population survey: Annual social and economic supplements.* Washington, DC: Author.

U.S. Department of Education. (2001). *The longitudinal evaluation of school change and performance in Title I schools.* Washington, DC: Author.

U.S. Department of Education. (2003). *President's commission on excellence in education.* Washington, DC: Author.

U.S. Department of Health and Human Services. (2005). *Health people 2010: Understanding and improving health.* Washington, DC: U.S. Government Printing Office.

Valadez, J. R., & Duran, R. (2007). Redefining the digital divide: Beyond access to computers and the Internet. *The High School Journal, 90*(3), 31–44.

Valencia, R. R. (2009). A response to Ruby Payne's claim that the deficit thinking model has no scholarly utility. *Teachers College Record.* Available at http://www.tcrecord.org

Valentine, C. (1968). *Culture and poverty: Critique and counter-proposal.* Chicago: University of Chicago Press.

Van De Walle, J. (2006). *Elementary and middle school mathematics.* Boston: Pearson.

Van de Werfhorst, H. G., & Mijs, J. J. B. (2010). Achievement inequality and the institutional structure of educational systems: A comparative perspective. *Annual Review of Sociology, 36*, 407–428.

Van Galen, J. (2007). Late to class: Social class and schooling in the new economy. *Educational Horizon, 85,* 156–167.

Vera, D. (2011). Using popular culture print to increase emergent literary skills in one high-poverty school district. *Journal of Early Childhood Literacy, 11*(3), 307–330.

Vericker, T., Macomber, J., & Golden, O. (2010). *Infants of depressed mothers living in poverty: Opportunities to identify and serve.* Washington, DC: The Urban Institute.

Villenas, S. (2001). Latina mothers and small-town racisms: Creating narratives of dignity and moral education in North Carolina. *Anthropology and Education Quarterly, 32*(1), 3–28.

von Rueden, U., Gosch, A., Rajmil, L., Bisegger, C., & Ravens-Sieberer, U. (2006). Economic determinants of health related quality of life in childhood and adolescence: Results from a European study. *Journal of Epidemiological Community Health, 60*(2), 130–135.

Votruba-Drzal, E. (2003). Income changes and cognitive stimulation in young children's home learning environments. *Journal of Marriage and Family, 65,* 341–355.

Wadsworth, M. E., Raviv, T., Reinhard, C., Wolff, B., Santiago, C. D., & Einhorn, L. (2008). An indirect effects model of the association between poverty and child functioning: The role of children's poverty-related stress. *Journal of Loss and Trauma, 13,* 156–185.

Waldron, T., Roberts, B., & Reamer, A. (2004). *Working hard, falling short: American's working families and the pursuit of economic security.* Chevy Chase, MD: Working Poor Families Project.

Walker, G. P., Mitchell, G., Fairburn, J., & Smith, G. (2005). Industrial pollution and social deprivation: Evidence and complexity in evaluating and responding to environmental inequality. *Local Environment, 10*(4), 361–377.

Wang, W., & Parker, K. (2011). *Women see value and benefits of college; men lag on both fronts.* Washington, DC: Pew Social and Demographic Trends.

Wasik, B. A, Bond, M. A., & Hindman, A. (2006). The effects of a language and literacy intervention on Head Start children and teachers. *Journal of Educational Psychology, 98,* 63–74.

Weber, B., Jensen, L., Miller, K., Mosley, J. M., & Fisher, M. (2005). A critical review of rural poverty literature: Is there truly a rural effect? *International Regional Science Review, 28,* 381–414.

Weinberg, H. (Producer). (1992). *UnEqual education: Failing our children* [Film]. New York: Educational Video Center.

Weiner, L. (2003). Why is classroom management so vexing to urban teachers? *Theory into Practice, 42*(4), 305–312.

Wells, N. M., Evans, G. W., Beavis, A., & Ong, A. O. (2010). Early childhood poverty, cumulative risk exposure, and body mass index trajectories through young adulthood. *American Journal of Public Health, 100*(12), 2507–2512.

Wenglinsky, H. (2002). *How teaching matters: Bringing the classroom back into discussions of teacher quality.* Princeton, NJ: Milken Family Foundation.

West, C., & Fenstermaker, S. (2002). Accountability in action: The accomplishment of gender, race and class in a meeting of the University of California Board of Regents. *Discourse & Society, 13*(4), 537–563.

West-Olatunji, C., Sanders, T., Mehta, S., & Behar-Horenstein, L. (2010). Parenting practices among low-income parents/guardians of academically successful fifth grade African American children. *Multicultural Perspectives, 12*(3), 138–144.

Western Regional Advocacy Project (WRAP). (2010). *Without housing: Decades of federal housing cutbacks, massive homelessness, and policy failures.* San Francisco, CA: Author.

Wetz, J. (2004) Promoting inclusion in school through the arts: A case study. *Support for Learning, 19*(20), 66–70.

Whiteside-Mansell, L., Johnson, D., Aitken, M., Bokony, P., Conners-Burrow, N., & McKelvey, L. (2010). Head Start and unintended injury: The use of the family map interview to document risk. *Early Childhood Education Journal, 38*(1), 33–41.

Whittaker, C. (2012). Integrating literature circles into a cotaught inclusive classroom. *Intervention in School & Clinic, 47*(4), 214–223.

Wider Opportunities for Women. (2010). *The basic economic security tables for the United States 2010.* Washington, DC: Author.

Williams, W. R. (2009). Struggling with poverty: Implications for theory and policy of increasing research on social class-based stigma. *Analyses of Social Issues and Public Policy, 9*(1), 37–56.

Wilson, W. J. (1996). *When work disappears: The world of the new urban poor.* New York: Vintage Books.

Wolff, E. N. (2012). *The asset price meltdown and the wealth of the middle class.* New York: National Bureau of Economic Research.

Women's Legal Defense and Education Fund. (2012). *Women's poverty in the United States, 2011.* New York: Legal Momentum.

Woolard, K. A., & Schieffelin, B. B. (1994). Language ideology. *Annual Review of Anthropology, 23*, 55–82.

Worpole, K. (2000). *In our backyard: The social promise of environmentalism.* London, UK: Green Alliance.

Wright, T. (2007). On Jorge becoming a boy: A counselor's perspective. *Harvard Educational Review, 77*, 164–186.

Wright, T. (2011). Countering the politics of class, race, gender, and geography in early childhood education. *Educational Policy, 25*(1), 240–261.

Yollis, L. (2012). Blogging helps students learn key literacy skills and more. *Curriculum Review, 52*(2), 7.

Yosso, T. J. (2005). Whose culture has capital? A critical race theory discussion of community cultural wealth. *Race, Ethnicity, and Education, 8*(1), 69–91.

Yu, M., Lombe, M., & Nebbitt, V. E. (2010). Food stamp program participation, informal supports, household food security and child food security: A comparison of African American and Caucasian households in poverty. *Children & Youth Services Review, 32*(5), 767–773.

Zahorik, J., Halbach, A., Ehrle, K., & Molnar, A. (2003). Teaching practices for smaller classes. *Educational Leadership, 61*(1), 75–77.

Zhang, H., & Cowen, D. J. (2009). Mapping academic achievement and public school choice under the No Child Left Behind legislation. *Southeastern Geographer, 49*(1), 24–40.

# Index

# About the Author

Paul C. Gorski is the founder of EdChange (http://www.EdChange.org) and an Associate Professor of Integrative Studies in George Mason University's New Century College, where he teaches courses like Equity and Diversity in Education; Poverty, Wealth, and Inequality; Environmental Justice; Social Justice Education; and Animal Rights. He has taught similar courses for a wide range of institutions, including Hamline University, the University of Maryland—College Park, the University of Virginia, and the Humane Society University. He attended the University of Virginia for his B.A., M.Ed., and Ph.D., and is darn near finished with an M.F.A. in creative writing from Hamline University. He has written or co-edited 5 books and has written more than 50 essays on poverty and schooling, educational equity, White privilege, multicultural teacher education, and digital equity. Paul has visited almost every state in the United States and five continents speaking, presenting, and conducting workshops for schools, universities, and other organizations committed to moving beyond celebrating diversity and toward equity. He lives in Washington, DC, with his cats, Unity and Buster.